Explore th

NELLES

CHINA
HONG KONG

Authors:
Engelbert Altenburger, Ulrich Menzel, Peter Hinze,
Claudia Ille, Angelika Lange-Gao, Kai Ullrich Müller,
Gerd Simon, Volker Kienast

An Up-to-date travel guide with 135 color photos
and 37 maps

Second Revised and Extended Edition
1997

Dear Reader,

Being up-to-date is the main goal of the Nelles series. To achieve it, we have a network of far-flung correspondents who keep us abreast of the latest developments in the travel scene, and our cartographers always make sure that maps and texts are adjusted to each other.

Each travel chapter ends with its own list of useful tips, accommodations, restaurants, tourist offices, sights. At the end of the book you will find practical information from A to Z. But the travel world is fast moving, and we cannot guarantee that all the contents are always valid. Should you come across a discrepancy, please write us at: Nelles Verlag GmbH, Schleissheimer Str. 371 b, D-80935 München, Germany, Tel: (089) 3571940, Fax: (089) 35719430.

LEGEND

✴ Place of Interest	⛷ Beach		▬▬▬ National Border
▨ Public or Significant Building	Guanyin Place Mentioned in Text		─── Provincial Border
■ Hotel	✈ International Airport		▭▭▭ Expressway
● Restaurant	✈ National Airport		━━━ Principal Highway
▨ Market	**Emai Shan** 3099 Mountain Summit (Height in Meters)		─── Provincial Road (partly paved)
✝ Church	▬■▬■ Great Wall of China		─── Secondary Road
☾ Mosque			┅┅┅ Railway
		\18/	Distance in Kilometers

CHINA – Hong Kong
© Nelles Verlag GmbH, 80935 Munich
  All rights reserved

Second Revised and
Extended Edition 1997
ISBN 3-88618-117-0
Printed in Slovenia

Publisher:	Günter Nelles	**Cartography:**	Nelles Verlag GmbH
Project Editor:	Gerd Simon	**Photo Editor:**	Heinz Vestner
Editor:	Claudia Magiera		Kirsten Bärmann-Thümmel
Editor-in-Chief:	Berthold Schwarz	**Color:**	ReproLine, Munich
Editor, English Ed.:	Angus McGeoch		Priegnitz, Munich
	Anne Midgette, Marton Radkai	**Printing:**	Gorenjski Tisk

- X05 -

TABLE OF CONTENTS

FEATURES

GUIDELINES

LIST OF MAPS

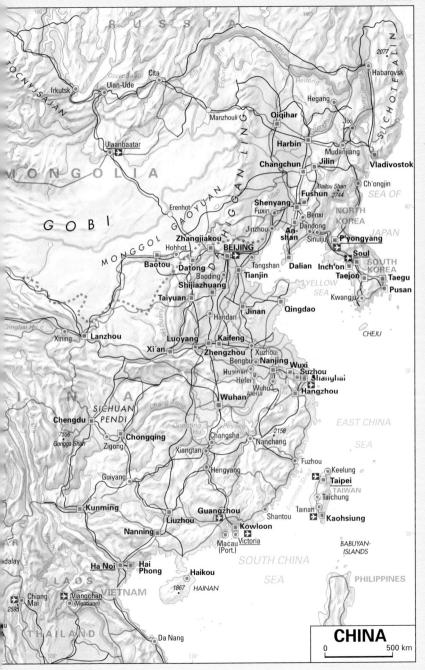

CHINA

0   500 km

A NATURAL SETTING FOR LIFE
Soils, water, growth

The water-based culture of China's agriculture and civilization arose in the heart of the Middle Empire, Zhongguo, where the land was sufficiently supplied in loess and water. Where the Yellow River (*huang he*) swings northward from Lanzhou in a huge meander before heading south again towards Xi'an, there's a layer of loess deposit hundreds of feet thick in places. This Yellow Earth (*huang tu*) was originally borne from Mongolia in the form of dust driven by icy storm winds, and has become extremely fertile because of the river's frequent floods.

China's prosperity has always depended on its rivers. Their primeval force was tamed and controlled by man's ingenuity, with dams, canals, extraction apparatus and irrigated terraces. Three great rivers have shaped China's history: the Huanghe, the Yangtse and the Xijiang, the "Western River" which flows into the South China Sea (*nan hai*) near Macao. Although the Xijiang is considerably shorter than the other two, only 1600 miles (2600 km) in length, the monsoon rains swell its volume to three times that of the Huanghe, and occasionally it carries as much water as the Yangtse.

There are three principal types of land covering China: the forests of the east, the steppes and deserts of the north and northwest, and the high plateaux of Tibet and Qinghai. Because of the adverse prevailing climate in the west and north – dry, cold and windy – agriculture there is mainly limited to pasturing flocks over large areas, except in a few favored spots. The latter include deposits of loess, brought in by winds during the Ice Age,

in the north (Gansu, Shanxi and Shaanxi provinces), and the black earth of Manchuria, rich in lime, which enables vast fields of wheat in the provinces of Heilongjiang ("Black River") and Jilin.

Variations in altitude and climate, as well as human intervention, have created a variety of different soils throughout the forests of southeastern China. In the south, porous red and yellow earths predominate, with laterite soil in the southernmost areas. These soils are generally thin in composition, with a weak mineral structure, a tendency to crumble, and low water-retention. Yet even here favorable local conditions can be found – especially in the fertile Red Basin of Sichuan in the southwest.

The soils of the river plains and deltas are mostly alluvial deposits, slightly acidic and held together by water like a sponge. These are ideal for the high-yielding but labor-intensive cultivation of rice-paddies, which is especially concentrated in eastern central China. In the central northeastern plains south of Beijing, apart from the alluvial floodlands, brown earth plays a decisive role in agriculture. This soil, mainly loess, was carried down from the hinterland; although it's rich in lime and minerals, it is loose in structure and rather dry. Irrigation is necessary to make it fertile enough for rice-paddies for example; when left up to nature, it generally will grow wheat, maize, oilseed and cotton.

CALM AND REVOLT

The repeating pattern of Chinese history

The fact that Chinese history is divided into dynasties allows one to see it as a continuous, scrolling panorama (see p. 36). This might lead one to assume that neither its basic philosophic stance (the Confucian concept of the state) nor its ritualistic representation (Imperial auth-

Previous pages: Curbside idyll in Peking. The Great Wall near Badaling. A procession of ducks near Jinghong (South Yunnan). Right: Terraced rice-fields in the province of Guanxi.

ority) have undergone much change through the millennia. It's a fact thst, despite the overthrow of various dynasties and periods of foreign rule, China's history demonstrates a continuity which is only apparently in contradiction to the numerous rebellions.

The preconditions of the land's geography led to a kind of "Social Contract" between the peasant-farmers who fed the nation and the ruling classes of court aristocrats and the emperor, which Confucianism saw as the apex of society. This ideal system of two socially opposing groups linked by mutual obligation is known as the *"Asiatic manner of produc tion."* The term was coined by Max Weber and Karl Marx while investigating the question of why certain societies lacked what Marx called "that historic energy" which had led, in Europe, to the development of a capitalist economy. The German-American sociologist K.A. Wittfogel took their idea one step further, laying particular weight on China. His recently rediscovered theory of the "hy-

draulic," or water-based, society enables us to explain the inner dynamics, that is the resiliences, of Chinese history on the backdrop of irrigation management. This attempt at explanation is by no means a mere academic diversion; rather, it functions as a kind of X-ray, providing illumination into the often impenetrable, all-too-often stereotyped history of China.

A former Communist who had, as it were, returned to the fold, Wittfogel continued his investigations in an interesting vein, by querying whether it weren't, in fact, true that the "Red Mandarins" had simply stepped into the shoes of the discredited court nobility, taking their place in the social system of the "Asiatic manner of production."

The organization of the "Asiatic manner of production"

China's three great rivers – Huanghe, Yangtse and Xijiang – are at once a curse and a blessing for the country. They make the loess of the semi-desert regions

fertile, and irrigate the high-yielding rice paddies. Yet in times of drought or flood they are the farmers' scourge. They leave the seed to atrophy, the harvests to wither; or they wash away villages, drowning man and beast, fields and gardens, and overpowering huge tracts of land with primeval power by carving out new channels. How can this conflict between blessing and curse resolve itself harmoniously, and the principle of the Middle Way (*zhong*) prevail? Through hydraulic engineering: the construction of dams, canals, retaining basins, hydraulic technology, or – for transportation purposes – locks and towpaths.

Throughout Asia, as well as in Africa and America, there were a wide variety of different manifestations of "the Asiatic manner of production." In Southeast Asia, for example, the apparently unlimited area of fertile flood-plain – un-

Above: Sowing rice near Dali (Yunnan Province). Right: In the tradition of an ancient civilization – a bucket-wheel in Guangxi.

limited, at least when seen in relation to the size of its population – led to very loose bonds of obligation between the state and the largely autonomous village communities. In China, by contrast, it was necessary to carry out huge hydraulic projects which surpassed those of Egypt and Sumeria in technical design as well as their extravagant use of manpower and materials. The dimensions of such tasks necessitated the development of a bureaucratic state, which penetrated more and more deeply into the socio-economic structure of the village communities. The degree of autonomy a village was able to maintain depended on its self-sufficiency.

The family- and village-based agricultural economy centered on the cultivation of one or more staple crops (rice, maize, millet, wheat), supplemented by horticulture, occasional fishing, livestock, and artisan crafts such as basket-weaving. To a modest extent, villagers also cultivated products purely for the commercial purposes, such as mulberry trees for the breeding of silk-worms. In periods of intense production, for instance during rice-planting, they helped each other out; such local projects as canal-digging were also joint undertakings. Surplus produce was sent to the nearest market or was handed over in lieu of taxes. In addition, the villagers were recruited for periodic service on state-organized tasks, which could last for up to three months a year.

For the state, establishing and administrating a water-based civilization both justified its existence and provided a support for its power. Throughout the course of Chinese history, Imperial will was able time and again to prevail against the rebellions of territorial leaders, as a result of the more than 90,000 miles (150,000 km) of navigable waterways, with towpaths, created by the hydraulic projects. This formed an incomparable military infrastructure. At any time, and with comparative speed, the empire could send

soldiers and supplies to the most important cities in the land. At the same time, the farmers' products and tributes were proceeding in the other direction, toward the imperial capital. These facts proved particularly important during the period of dissolution of the eastern Han dynasty (around 200 AD), when the center of Chinese civilization shifted southwards to the provinces of the lower Yangtse (Anhui, Hubei, Jiangsu). Here, water-based agriculture thrived, while the political and military center in the north was busy warding off marauding tribes from the steppes. Linking the two was the massive "Imperial Canal."

In addition to organizing the great hydraulic projects, the state was obliged to maintain central food stores for times of famine. The Imperial Canal proved a useful transport route for gathering in and distributing grain. Figures from the 8th century show that on this canal alone, at least 120,000 tons of rice was shipped north for storage every year – at a time when the population was only about 50 million. Other tasks of the state – or, more accurately, privileges and monopolies – were the organization and exploitation of foreign trade and crafts, something which lasted until relatively modern times. Second only to the organization of water engineering in importance, however, was the state's responsibility for military security. Contributing to the army's defensive mobility was the Great Wall, built by taking advantage of the services the people owed to the state within the framework of the Asiatic manner of production. The wall was at once the most tangible and, because of the human sacrifices it required, most depraved expression of what was originally a sensible way to organize a society.

The origins of the Asiatic manner of production in China go back about three thousand years. As early as the Shang dynasty, the court nobility put the peasants to work on water construction projects. In the declining phase of the Zhou dynasty, Confucianism developed and provided a far-reaching "paradigmal bridge"

15

Thanks to the economic infrastructure of the water-based civilization – whose importance was made manifest by the transfer of the capital to the Guanzhong plain around Xi'an, the imperial heartland on the Yellow River – the Han dynasty which followed was able considerably to expand the empire's territory. In the year 111 BC Wudi, the most eminent of the Han emperors, proclaimed: "Agriculture is the basis of existence. That is why the government has been entrusted with the task of digging canals and side-channels, building dams, and creating reservoirs." With this in mind, other provinces were opened up to hydraulic construction.

Han Wudi enlisted several hundred thousand peasants and soldiers to work on hydraulic projects in the Huanghe provinces of southern Shanxi, northern Henan and western Shandong; even the catchment areas of the Han and Huai rivers were brought under control. When the Han dynasty fell, new areas of water-based civilization developed in the south. This shift in the focus of power led to hydraulic undertakings on a scale which matched the construction of the Great Wall (*chang cheng*).

under which the water projects had their specific purpose. The state had both the authority and the duty to give overall organization to the "hydraulic society." In the ensuing Qin period (221-207 BC), a network of canals brought fertility to the central area of what is today the province of Shaanxi. The brilliantly conceived Zhengguo Canal alone irrigated nearly 400 sq. miles (more than 1000 sq. km) of loess. Shortly after it was put into operation, the fabled emperor Qin Shi Huangdi created the first Chinese empire. Here was a clear demonstration of the authority vested in the central power and the service ethic which it expected of its subjects: Look after our welfare, say the peasants, and we will let you have power; protect us and we will serve you – by building, for example, the Great Wall, which was also begun during the brief Qin dynasty.

The Imperial Canal (actually called the "Great Canal," *da yunhe*) constructed in the years 587-608 AD, remains to this day the longest navigable inland waterway in the world. It ran for over 930 miles (1500 km) from Hangzhou to Beijing, linking various existing canals into one. In order to join up these five old canals, armies of pioneers and enlisted peasants were mobilized. The official government report on the opening of the canal is full of drama and excitement: "Everyone between the ages of 15 and 50 was commanded by imperial decree to gather at an appointed place. Anyone failing to do so faced the death penalty. So it was that the horde which gathered numbered 3.6 million workers. Every family was obliged to send a child for kit-

Above: A backwater of the Imperial Canal near the garden city of Suzhou.
Right: Dragon motif.

chen duty. In addition to the soldiers, 5000 young men were appointed as overseers, to spur the workers on. Including the officials, 5.4 million people were employed on the whole length of the canal (one-tenth of the population of the empire)." The official census for 609 AD revealed that the building of the canal had cost 2.5 million workers' lives, a fantastic number of casualties.

Another hydraulic project, further south still, had already been started in 214 AD, when Chinese troops first reached the shore of the South China Sea near Canton. This was a canal linking the Xiangjiang, which flows northward through Hunan via Lake Poyang to join the Yangtse, with the Lijiang, which flows south through Guilin and into the Xijiang, the southernmost of China's great east-west rivers. Until the north-south railway was completed in 1936, this canal represented the most important military, civilian, and economictransportation route between Canton and the north.

Rebellion in defense of the system

Was Confucianism a revolutionary philosophy? In the sense of being the intellectual principle of harmony between opposing forces, yes it was. Confucianism only wanted the noblest to rule. These most worthy of men were to be virtuous, just, and moderate, respecting the elderly and upholding the rituals. More than anyone, this applied to the emperor, who represented the "Authority of Heaven." Yet even the pre-Confucian *Book of Songs* stated: "The Authority of Heaven does not last forever." It is forfeited when the people justly rebel against a ruler who does not display those virtues expected in a man who has been singled out for power. Mencius (*Mengzi*), who emphasized the Confucian social order, taught that "one becomes a son of Heaven by winning the peasants to one's side." Proceeding thus, from the notion that the Emperor was the "theoretically complete owner" of all land, classical writers called for arable land to be distributed fairly among the peasants, who would then be obliged to pay a tolerable burden of tribute in goods or services. Thus Confucian society was founded unambiguously on the social contract of the "Asiatic manner of production." If the emperor and the court nobles fell short of the ethical service code, rebellion would surely follow. The enormous effort involved in harnessing nature for the "hydraulic" society often exhausted the bonded peasantry both economically and physically. They would then launch a revolt in *defense* of the system. This was quite unlike what happened in Europe, where anti-feudal revolutions seized the property of the Church and the nobility, and utopian revolutions (such as the French) and middle-class liberal revolutions ultimately led to a revolution in economic structure and the development of modern capitalism. In China, rebellions served only to preserve the ethical purity and continuing of the "eternal system."

Even in the Qin period, after the death of the first emperor of all China, Qin Shi Huangdi, revolts broke out among the overburdened peasantry. Discontent grew especially great when their tribute was used not only for water projects and frontier defense, but also for the pomp and display of the ruling class. The Terracotta Army in the side-tomb of Qin Shi Huangdi, which we admire so much today, was built with great suffering on the part of the peasants. They finally overturned the system; in 206 BC, a general of peasant origins founded the Han dynasty. The Han rulers, in turn, rubbed the peasantry the wrong way by extending the Great Wall as far as Dunhuang, resettling about a million peasant families for the purpose (127-107 BC).

Minister Wang Mang, the "Vainglorious," seized the throne and founded

Right: Life at court (Fresco in the tombs of the Tang emperors near Qianling).

the shortlived Xin dynasty (9-23 AD). While he was not, in fact, a "socialist," he did nationalize private property and abolish personal ownership of slaves in his struggle to prevent the collapse of the social contract. Yet Wang, too, was overthrown by a peasant uprising, organized by China's first secret society, the *Red Eyebrows* (whose members had to dye their eyebrows). The construction of the Imperial Canal also unleashed a series of peasant revolts.

The growing political importance of the secret societies, originally religious groups, in times of crisis became evident in the nationwide people's uprising in 1351-1368. This was led by a mixed Buddhist and Taoist sect called the *White Lotus*, which rose against a foreign occupier th Mongolians (Yuan Dynasty). In 1368 a mendicant monk became the first emperor of the Ming dynasty. This overthrow of the Yuan dynasty, though apparently motivated by nationalism, was in fact a reaction against the dire poverty of the peasantry and the Mongolian rulers' neglect of public duties. This was also true of the Manchurian Qing dynasty, which ruled the country from 1644 until 1911. It produced the two important emperors Kangxi and Qianlong.

The fall of the Qing dynasty was only superficially abetted by nationalism. In fact, it can be traced to the state leadership's abandonment of its traditional obligations, which in latter years had also been caused by the weakening of imperial authority through the colonial powers. But droughts and floods resulting from the neglect of the water network were the primary, underlying reason for the withdrawal of the Authority of Heaven. The fact is supported by the theory that when the Manchu emperor Kangxi (1662-1723) ordered the renovation of the water installations which had fallen into disrepair in the late Ming period, he was celebrated as a hero of Chinese history.

The broken-winged Phoenix

The historians of the People's Republic are masters at the presumed Marxist duty of making Chinese history fit the simple formula for development of a modern society from feudalism to capitalism to Communism. The lynch-pin of Chinese history, the *Asiatic manner of production* (a term used by Marx himself and the backbone of Chinese history), is shamefacedly accounted for with the ambiguous term "semi-feudalism." This is a clear demonstration of the predicament of the dogmatist, forced to fit the facts to some predetermined truth. Yet if, like Mao Zedong, we attempt to "seek the truth in the facts," we realize that China in the 19th and 20th centuries did not simply burst from its feudal chains, plunge into capitalism, and then achieve Communism. Rather, the most recent phase of China's long history has seen the evolution of a mosaic-like structure, shaped partly by external forces. Such a structure is characteristic of the underde-velopment of many southern countries: Persisting elements of the Asiatic manner of production both compete and combine with the foreign factor of colonial capitalism. The reason that China did not see a development from feudalism to dynamic capitalism lay in the persistence of an unusual tradition of social and economic organization.

Certainly, the Asiatic manner of production was far from unchallenged as a social model. Time and again, the system had to defend against the private appropriation of land and water. In contradiction to the emperor's "theoretically complete ownership" of all land, a class of landowning gentry (*shenshi*) developed wherever "the emperor was distant." These resisted the court nobility, even taking upon themselves official duties such as the apportioning of water. The peasant rebellions, therefore, never aimed at a revolutionary future, but rather at restoring the *status quo ante*, a system which bound the peasants to pay tribute in return for services from the state, but

19

left them free, rather than serfs bound to the soil.

Another peculiarity of the Asiatic manner of production was that the state controlled and exploited trade and higher forms of craftsmanship, which prevented the development of a pre-industrial economy. Nor were there any free cities, which might have provided a focus for intellectual, social and economic development. The state-administered system of trade (both internal and foreign) had evolved gradually since the Sung period, and was handled by authorized mercantile organizations (*tong*). This didn't lead to fundamental change, since these merchants invested their capital in real estate instead of turning it into industrial assets.

Towards the end of the Ming period (1644), Dutch and Spanish traders landed on the coast of China as early agents of

Above: Grinding maize near Qufu (Shandong). Right: Factories established by the European powers in Canton about 1800 (Chinese glass-painting).

colonial penetration. They brought new ideas that influenced the country's formal structure even in the interior. The farmers learned to grow rice on irrigated terraces, and cotton-planting gave birth to a textile industry. Porcelain manufacturing blossomed in Jingdezhen. The growth of internal trade promoted a cash economy. But the state's hand still lay heavily upon everything. One example of this was its embargo on maritime trade with foreign countries. Earlier, in a period of adventurous trade and naval policy from 1405 to 1435, seven heavily armed Chinese fleets, led by the palace eunuch Zheng He, had reached the coasts of Africa. But this one and only expansionist phase of Chinese history was brought to an end by an Imperial decision, made for what reasons we cannot know. Not until the late Qing period, through the 19th century to 1911, did the arrival of colonialists bring with it such overwhelming changes that the Asiatic manner of production began to rot like a fish, from the head downwards.

CHINESE CARICATURES AND FOREIGN DEVILS

The western image of China

Since Marco Polo, the image of China entertained in the West has swung between the extremes of mythical conjecture and benighted fear, between Chinoiserie and caricature. These paradoxes persist to the present day. It was not so long ago, in 1969 to be exact, that Chancellor Kiesinger of Germany was raising the vague specter of the "Yellow Peril" by declaring: "I just say to you, China, China, China..." At the same time, young people in the west began to get enthused by the radical Maoist ideas, as if they were like Alexander's cut through the Gordian Knot of history, and could serve, for example, as a solution to the problems of developing countries. Meanwhile, the old fascination with China (*ex oriente lux*: "The sun rises in the East, whence comes our salvation") had developed a new variant: the search for the esoteric.

The Venetian Marco Polo was the first European to bring back eyewitness reports from China. He spent 17 years (1275-1292) travelling through the Chinese empire on missions for the Yuan emperor. Imprisoned in Genoa on his return, he wrote his memoirs; these only provoked anger in Roman Christendom, which, exactly like China, imagined itself to be the center of the world.

This displeasure was transformed into missionary zeal. In 1307 the Pope appointed the Franciscan Monte-Corvino "Archbishop" of Khanbalik, the name for Beijing in those days. The Mongolian Yuan dynasty was open to foreigners, but after this dynasty was overthrown in 1368 by a nationalist and religious rebellion led by the Buddhist monk Zhu Yuanzhang, whose purpose was to further the interests of the peasantry, the Roman mission also met with opposition.

After Ming rulers abruptly reversed the country's maritime policy, China lapsed into "splendid isolation." Its economy was self-sufficient, and its self-confidence so secure that the emperor Jiaqing, (1522 -1566) sent word to the English king, Henry VIII, that he saw no need for his goods, unless they were sent as tribute; however, he was generously prepared to sell King Henry some silk and porcelain, as a kind of civilizing aid to England's development. This arrogance with regards to the cultural and military superiority of the empire of the "Middle Empire" was later unable to survive the onslaught of colonial gunboat diplomacy. The devastating religious, cultural and economic impact of the West ultimately brought about a traumatic and long-drawn-out crisis of confidence in the ancient empire.

Oil for the lamps of China, opium for its people

Before the Industrial Revolution in Britain – which meant exploiting colonial territories as a source of raw materials and a market for manufactured products – began to give a new face to colonialism in the 19th century, colonial powers in China, bearing a predominantly Latin stamp, tended to be rather naive and primitive. The Spanish and Portuguese arrived with the simple purpose of procuring gold, tea, porcelain, and other luxuries – a greed which they endeavored to justify through bigoted missionary activity. In 1517, the Portuguese landed in Canton, where they were regarded as bringers of tribute from barbarian lands. They were followed by the Dutch and the Spanish, and only much later by the British, who followed the lure of the rapidly developing tea trade.

In the wake of the armed merchant vessels came the missionaries, especially the Jesuits, who proved themselves ingenious at adapting. The Italian Matteo Ricci, who arrived in Macao in 1582, laid the foundations of a missionary policy which was distinguished by knowledge of the Chinese language and culture as well as scientific qualifications in mathematics, astronomy and technology. From Cologne came the Jesuit Adam Schall von Bell (1592-1666), who rose to become head of the Chinese Emperor's Office of Astronomy. In Europe, the reports of the Jesuits gave rise to an enthusiasm for China both in the fashionable and intellectual worlds. "Chinese" rooms or garden pavilions were decorated with silk, wallpapers, porcelain and lacquer-work. Philosophers such as Voltaire and Leibniz made studies of Chinese doctrines of morality and social organization. What developed was an idealized image of a country which was administered and guided by a wise bureaucracy on the model of the "Asiatic manner of production."

When, in 1715, the Pope forbade Catholics to take part in those Chinese state rituals which served as a tangible confirmation of the system's moral underpinnings, this period of friendly and mutual interest came to an abrupt end. After the missionaries were driven out of the country, the image of China in the West was suddenly transformed into a caricature. Crude cartoons of slit-eyed, subhuman creatures served one purpose only: justification of the brutal colonial onslaught. The age of gunboat politics and the cynical opium mafia had dawned. Its gangsters and ruffians had an open door to the Foreign Office, or even took on the "God-blessed" title of Emperor, as did Kaiser Wilhelm II. In the infamous speech for the send off of a German punitive expedition after the Boxer Rebellion, he delivered a prime example of cheap oratory calculated to stir up racial hatred.

The late Qing dynasty, which in the 19th century continued the myopic introspection and arrogance of the Confucian imperial court, sensed danger only from the peoples in the north, and was there-

Right: Chinese opium-smokers in 1843 (copper engraving by T. Allom).

fore completely at the mercy of the colonial powers' military might and tactical finesse. The British East India Company, which had had sole control of trade with Asia since 1600, extended its sphere of influence in the second half of the 18th century to the east – from India to China. The China tea trade, which was later to lead to the building of fast "tea-clippers" like the *Cutty Sark,* grew rapidly, and had already reached £30 million by 1823. This impressive sum far surpassed all the East India Company's revenue from sales *to* China. The colonialist strategists of the Company therefore decided to present the Chinese with a poisoned chalice. Through private traders, they organized massive and illegal imports of opium into China from plantations which they controlled in Bengal (over 2300 tons in 1839). Their purpose was twofold: the sale of opium for silver coin would fill the company coffers; and the drug would undermine public health and the military morale of the Chinese to such a point that this huge country could become a colo-

nial prize with the minimum use of force. It was a strategy that betrayed total contempt for humanity and that only crassly racist minds, armed with Christian proselytizing zeal, could have dreamed up.

In 1839 the Emperor's special commissioner Lin Zexu ordered the destruction, near Canton, of 1400 tons of opium which the British had previously declared the property of the Crown. This appeared to lend legitimacy to the act of aggression which the British had long been planning. A British fleet bombarded the fortifications at the mouth of the Pearl River near Canton and sailed into Shanghai. Later, in 1842, the British imposed a penal treaty in Nanking, which, though it ended the First Opium War, left China powerless and shattered its traditional economy. China had to pay high war reparations; Hong Kong was ceded to the British; the ports of Canton, Shanghai, Amoy (Xiamen) Ningbo and Fuzhou became "Treaty Ports," gateways for colonial interests, from which railroads later ran into the interior; Britain continued to

be granted Most Favored Nation status in commerce; and British consuls supervised the customs service. In the second half of the 19th century, European colonial powers competed to divide up the vast territory of China between them.

In 1856 Chinese frontier troops broke into a British ship caught smuggling opium. This time France also joined in the reprisals. In 1860 a force of 20,000 British troops landed at Tianjin (Tientsin) and began escalating the colonial war. The Qing emperor Wenzong fled to his palace at Chengde. The Anglo-French force captured Beijing and burned down the Summer Palace. In the same year the *Unequal Treaties* were extended. Britain gained Kowloon, on the mainland opposite Hong Kong; access to other ports; unrestricted navigation on the Yangtse; the right to acquire land and extraterritoriality in judicial matters – in effect, Euro-

Above: Boxer Rebellion in Peking, 1900.
Right: Aattack by the Taiping Rebels on Nanjing in 1864 (woodcut).

pean jurisdiction on Chinese soil. These legal privileges were later extended to Christian Chinese, which led to a rash of conversions among crooks and prostitutes. Around the colonial adventurers gathered a glittering European *demi-monde*. The sign on the gates of the international compound in Shanghai baldly illustrated the complete subjugation of the Chinese in their own country: "No dogs or Chinese allowed."

The decrepit Qing government was forced to accept further humiliations: among them the loss of Annam (North Vietnam) to the French, Russia's occupation of Manchuria, and the establishment of a German settlement at Qingdao in 1899. At the same time, the Manchu Qing rulers were overthrown by internal opposition in the form of secret societies and the Taiping Rebellion. The Qing dynasty became a scapegoat for all the wrongs which the Chinese people were suffering. Thus, when the secret society of the *Boxers* (*yihe tuan*) rebelled in 1900-01, they were as much against the dowager empress Cixi, who was banished to Xi'an, as against the Europeans, whose embassy quarter in Beijing they occupied. This 55-day-long uprising provoked a concerted reaction on the part of the European and Japanese powers, who dispatched a combined army to advance on Beijing. The Germans, being late arrivals on the colonial scene, were given the dubious honor of leading the advance ("Germans to the front!").

The Boxer Rebellion ended with the Chinese state's being forced to pledge all its customs and tax revenues to the colonial powers for many years to come. This meant that it lost not only its political authority but also its financial footing. From 1900 onward, the construction of railroads from colonial ports into the hinterlands meant that colonial capitalism made even stronger inroads into the country. This time, the Chinese themselves began to participate in the econ-

omic boom. Some of them acted as local agents for foreign business concerns intent on buying up Chinese assets, and were therefore dependent on the colonial rulers; but there was also a class of Chinese entrepreneurs who attempted to instigate the development of an independent industrial economy. This is how the textile industry, for example, grew up in Shanghai – but it also led to the growth of an industrial proletariat, which consisted of impoverished peasants and artisans.

From the Taiping Rebellion to the Republic

Seeing their powerful state humiliated by Europeans and their technical superiority drove the Han people, for thousands of years a proud, self-confident nation, into a profound identity crisis. At the same time, however, ideas of recovery, reform and revolution began to mature, manifest in everything from the republican revolution of 1911 to the founding of the People's Republic in 1949.

The most extreme reaction to the consequences of colonialism was the rebellion of *Taiping* ("Great Peace") in 1850-64. Its leader, Hong Xiuqian, who had failed the entrance examination for imperial service, was converted to Christianity by American evangelists. He made use of the fundamental ideas of Christian love and concern for one's fellow-men in his struggle to restore the traditional social order of the Asiatic manner of production. The rebels of Taiping distributed the property of rich landowners among poor and landless peasants. They tried to make the bureaucracy accept the obligations of the old social contract. They banned the decadent and inhuman practice of binding women's feet into tiny "lily-feet", and stood up for equal rights for the "barefoot" country women. Their idealistic, if backward-looking, campaign against private property and private trade was, after some impressive successes, crushed by an alliance between the Qing regime and the colonial troops.

25

the *Guomindang* (Nationalist Party), was founded in Tokyo. Its intellectual leader was Sun Yatsen (Sun Zhongshan, 1866-1925), a doctor trained in Western medicine, republican reformer, and nationalist from Canton, whom all Chinese revere as the father of modern China. He drew up a radical political program for the modernization of China, entitled *The Three Basic Doctrines of the People* (*san min zhuyi*), which served as a manifesto for the revolution of 1911. This revolution was triggered by a proposal that foreign investors should build a railroad across the fertile Red Basin of Sichuan, even though substantial government funds had already been set aside for this purpose. Strikes and uprisings flared up in Sichuan in May 1911, followed by an army rebellion in Wuhan. The fate of the imperial dynasties that had ruled China for thousands of years was sealed.

Chinese intellectuals, trapped in old philosophical traditions, struggled to find their own new path forward under the motto: "Learn from the foreigners' vast superiority how to remedy our own weaknesses." Adopting the West's technological civilization was a process that was to proceed selectively, in the Chinese spirit. Students returned from the USA and Europe with the realization that the West's economic development was not born solely of ruthless barbarity, but rather from humane and civilized principles. As their numbers grew, their demands for changes in the constitution and power-structure increased, articulated chiefly by Kang Youwei, Tan Sitong and Liang Qichao. But their desire to reform the system from within foundered upon the autocratic power of the court.

In 1905 the *League of Allies* (*tong-meng hui*), an organizational precursor of

FROM THE REPUBLIC TO THE PEOPLE'S REPUBLIC

On December 29th, 1911, Sun Yatsen was provisionally named president of the new republic. By January 1st, 1912, a period of republican turmoil had already set in. Thus a progressive intellectual came to be leader of a people torn between tradition and revolution, which recalled the many-limbed creatures of Chinese mythology. As early as February, Sun handed over his office to Yuan Shikai, the most powerful of all the military commanders, in an attempt to prevent a civil war. That traditionalist forces were still strongly at work in the republic was demonstrated by Yuan's attempt to re-establish the monarchy in 1915; his attempt, however, failed, both as a result of internal and foreign pressure and of Yuan's death. On the other hand, student circles were forming societies for a *Renewal Movement*, out of which grew the *Fourth of May Movement* (*wusi yundong*). On May 4th, 1919, a pa-

Above: Dr. Sun Yatsen, the father of modern China. Right: The Long March – an ordeal that lasted for years.

triotic demonstration was held in Beijing to protest the proposal of the Versailles Powers to hand the former German "protectorates" over to Japan. This protest movement eventually spread to the entire population.

The Fourth of May Movement reflected the contradictions of the reformist republicans. On the one hand, they were fascinated by the ideals of the French and American revolutions, with such enlightened concepts as freedom, equality, fraternity, the supremacy of science and equal rights for all nations; on the other, the avarice and racism of the colonial powers' army officers, merchants and missionaries left Chinese patriots with no choice but to adopt a xenophobic stance.

In 1919, Sun Yatsen founded the Guomindang (National People's Party); but factional quarrels broke out within this party after his death in 1925. In 1921, in Shanghai, the Communist Party came into being, led by Li Dazhao and Chen Duxiu. Mao Zedong was also present, but this second phase of the republic (1928-

1936) was dominated by another powerful personality, Chiang Kaishek. Formerly an ordinary soldier, Chiang had a meteoric rise to power, bringing an end to the terrible years of the warlords with two campaigns in 1926 and 1928. Nanking (Nanjing) was promoted to the rank of capital city, and Chiang to that of president with full dictatorial powers.

In 1931 the Japanese invaded Manchuria and eventually occupied the whole of eastern China as far south as Shanghai. In addition they imposed a naval blockade, preventing trade through every port from Wenzhou to Hainan. This Japanese Reign of Terror cost millions of Chinese lives.

Yet Chiang did not challenge the external enemy, turning instead against the Communists. The latter paid a high price for their indecision in the question of where to fight their revolution – in the cities or in the countryside? They finally opted for the cities, a strategic blunder that claimed many victims. In Chiang's campaigns of annihilation, over 30,000

workers and trade unionists were killed in Shanghai in the single month of April, 1927. Mao Zedong's concept of a revolution of the impoverished peasants did prove successful in the long run, but it demanded great sacrifices along the way. In 1933-34 Chiang, with German military advisers, sent out an army of 800,000 men to encircle the heartland of Communist support in Hunan. The Red Army broke out and set off with 100,000 soldiers on a terrible route of suffering. This Long March led some 7,500 miles (12,000 km) to the border of Tibet, and continued in October, 1936, to Yan'an in northern Shaanxi, where the 10,000 who had survived hid out in caves in the loess.

In Yan'an, the Communists developed organizational structures for rural areas. These activities were protected by the

Above: Mao Zedong proclaims the People's Republic of China on 1 October 1949.
Right: Mao inspects the Red Guards during the Cultural Revolution (Peking, 1966).

fact that in December, 1936, the armies of Xi'an temporarily arrested Chiang, thereby forcing the formation of a united front against Japan; its headquarters were in Chongqing, where Zhou Enlai represented the Communists. After Japan surrendered in 1945, the civil war flickered on for another four years, until Chiang Kaishek and his staff fled to Taiwan at the end of 1949. Even before this, on October 1st, 1949, Mao Zedong had already proclaimed the People's Republic of China from Beijing's Gate of Heavenly Peace.

THE EAST TURNS (BLOOD) RED
Communist campaigns

"Every revolutionary spirit evaporates. All that is left is the scum of a new bureaucracy." This observation by Franz Kafka also holds true of the Communist revolution in China. Yet how boldly these revolutionaries burst upon the scene, filled with the certainty of their historic task, declaring the millennia of China's history to be no more than a pile of shards. In a poem based on Mao Zedong's *Thoughts during a flight over the Great Wall*, Bertolt Brecht wrote: "All the miserable/ kings of Ch'in and Han/ They knew but little./The Tang and Sung with their irresponsible excess!/ And the arrogant/only son of a dynasty, Jinghis Khan,/ not even he could do more/ than draw the bow./ All turned to dust."

Mao Zedong saw China as "a clean slate;" upon which it was now time to paint the most beautiful calligraphic characters. This revealing image expresses the historic aspiration of the peasant revolutionaries, who were swept to power by a turn in the tide of history, and explained this as a historic inevitability in the Marxist sense – a new variation on the old idea of the "Authority of Heaven." The revolutionaries saw themselves as moral rebels, both in the Confucian sense and in that of the social con-

tract of the "Asiatic manner of production," against the degeneration of power. Even today, sixty years after the Long March, the gerontocrats, Deng Xiaoping and the Methuselahs around him, still use the sufferings of these early revolutionaries in their struggle, and the initial enthusiasm of the Chinese people at being liberated from the foreign yoke, as a way to justify their own disciplinary action against the Chinese people. The events of June, 1989, in the sadly misnamed Square of Heavenly Peace demonstrate the unquestioning and by now senile and self-righteous obsession with authority on the part of the leaders. This has led to repeated attempts to accelerate China's development with alternating campaigns of encouragement and punishment.

Some examples: in June, 1950, the law on land reform was introduced; the Korean War broke out in the same month. Both events ushered in the age of mass campaigns in China. With ferocious zeal, the Chinese Communists attempted to create an artificial "New Man" in their own image. There followed a series of attempts at the "ideological education of the masses:" the *Hundred Flowers Movement* of 1956, an alleged cultural liberalization after bureaucratic paralysis; followed by the Anti-Law Movement; 1958 saw the start of the *Great Leap Forward*, which aimed at overtaking the United States in five years, and the formation of people's communes.

The failure of the "Blast-furnace Policy" (when every village had to produce a quota of steel) led to a merciless tug-of-war between the "right" and the "left," which Mao settled in his own favor by unleashing the *Great Proletarian Cultural Revolution*. The "Gang of Four" (Jiang Qing, Zhang Chunqiao, Yao Wenyuan, Wang Hongwen) formed the nucleus of power. The great Zhou Enlai was only partly able to moderate the politically sanctioned excesses of the young generation. Millions of people lost their lives, and the country's economy withered.

In 1976, however, the foremost personalities of the revolution – Zhu De,

Mao and Zhou Enlai – all died, each after a natural disaster. The "Authority of Heaven" suddenly no longer held sway. In 1978, Deng Xiaoping's "dynasty" began with its rehabilitation. In 1979, the Cultural Revolution was officially criticized. Democracy and liberalization seem at last to be on the horizon. Yet all these apparent achievements were no more than garlands ornamenting the "Four Pillars of Power:" party, bureaucracy, army, secret service. Deng proved to be a specifically Chinese kind of Communist: pragmatic, with regards to the economy; strict in his Confucianism, if it served the power of the ruling elite. The massacre in June 1989 was the real symbol of this policy. Before this event the young poet Gu Cheng had written: "On the coast of the sea of dreams / stand my companions / silent / in the premonition of danger."

Above: Bride and groom in Peking.
Right: Even two are too many! China encourages the one-child family.

The stubborn old men who still rule Cuba, North Korea and China are guarding the cemetery where the dreams of mankind are buried. What will happen when they die? Where is the coast of the dream-sea of the Chinese youth? Or will dreams in China degenerate into mere selfish consumerism?

China is part of the dynamic western Pacific region of rapid economic development, led by Japan, Taiwan, South Korea, Hong Kong and Singapore – all countries under sway of the Confucian ethos of duty. Will China, like all these countries (with the exception of Japan) go through a phase of dictatorship and only later achieve the goal of democracy? Or will it, like Thailand, seek to combine modernization with democratization? Can China learn from the kind of economic breakdown that has taken place in other formerly socialist countries, and prevent its economy from declining into a vicious form of early capitalism, if it does, in fact, aim at the fundamental restructuring necessary to transform itself into a free market economy?

The future is, in fact, looking a little dreary, especially after the sentencing of the dissident Wei Jingsheng to 14 years in prison in December 1995. He was a Nobel Peace Prize candidate The court's arguments were interesting: Wei is alleged to have attempted to overthrow the "democratic dictatorship of the people" in "counterrevolutionary manner." The old Communist patriarch Deng Xiaoping, who died on February 19th, 1997, is said to have brought his influence to bear upon this show trial.

The calligraphy of the future has yet to be written on the unfolding scroll of Chinese history, but the inks have been prepared and the brush lies ready. The scribes are the new men of China, such as Deng's Crown Prince, government chief and Party chairman Jiang Zemin, Prime Minister Li Peng (a genuine *apparatchik*), the reformist Chairman of the Na-

tional People's Congress Qiao Shi and the economic reformer Zhu Rongji.

CHINA'S LITTLE EMPERORS

Population growth

China's population now numbers 1.2 billion; in 1953, it was scarcely 600 million. In spite of the country's enormous size, productive land is scarce: only two-fifths of the land area has any value for farming, grazing or forestry, and only one-tenth is worth cultivating. Desert, steppe and barren mountainside take up three-fifths of the country. 90 percent of the area has only scattered and unevenly distributed settlements; 90 per cent of the population lives on 20 per cent of the nation's territory (eastern and southeastern China). The population density on the lower Yangtse is about 5200 per square mile (2000 per sq. km). The proportion of city dwellers has increased due to a flight from the land and the movement of migratory workers, and is today around 30 per cent – conurbations are at once expanding and becoming more densely populated, while the number of cities with populations of 1 million or more is steadily increasing. Could the pressure be taken off these centers by settling the empty regions? It could only be done by creating industrial employment there, resolving the political and cultural problems with the indigenous racial minorities, and, not least, creating an attractive cultural and consumer-friendly environment that's not light-years away from Shanghai's. But China is still a socialist developing country, whose future economic and political direction is still uncertain. It may well be that the skyscrapers piercing the skyline of Shenzhen and other cities are pointing the way to a development that will match that of Singapore or Thailand.

Birth control

At present, however, the most urgent task facing the nation is that of birth con-

Above: Taoist ceremony in the Baiyunguan temple (Peking). Right: Pilgrims in the Buddhist temple of Gangu (Gansu province).

trol.When the People's Republic was proclaimed in 1949, a new day for socialism seemed to be dawning. Plans for the future began to resemble the announcement of a new Messiah. The larger the population, the greater its productivity, and the better everyone's living conditions – thus ran the calculations. Family planning and birth control were seen as the concoctions of hostile imperialists anxious to slow the development of poor countries.

This was the view represented by China in international forums as well as at home. As it became clear, however, that the size of the population, rather than the economy, was making the "Great Leap Foward," family planning suddenly became necessary for the country's very survival. According to economic studies, China would reach saturation with 1.4 billion inhabitants – beyond that lay the abyss. In 1971, the birth rate increased by 2.3 per cent, but by 1979 this growth had been reduced to 1.2 per cent. This made China, along with Thailand, one of the developing countries that was most successful in the field of birth control. Since then, however, the birth rate has begun creeping up again (to 1.24 per cent). Even at the lower rate of 1.2 per cent, the population of China would almost double by the year 2050 – from a current base of over 1.1 billion. Planners want to limit population growth to 1.25 billion by the year 2000 – a figure which has recently been revised upward several times. After this point, a determined campaign of birth control is to bring about a decline in population, down to an "ideal" population figure of 700 million.

Giant posters show a naive vision of the future, of the kind which prevailed in the West in the late 1950s: a beaming, squeaky-clean couple with their little daughter pose in high-tech surroundings, where the earth is made up of freeways and the sky is full of airplanes. The rosy-cheeked little girl is a key figure in the future of China. She symbolizes both hope and danger. She represents – for the planners at least – the desired one-child family so necessary for negative population growth; as a girl she stands for the victory over traditional prejudices. For the one-child family comes up against particular resistance when the child is a daughter, and her father is a peasant. Farming, especially in the private sector, has scarcely been mechanized and needs many toiling hands – this means sons who do not leave home when they marry. Furthermore, Confucian beliefs are still very much alive, which hold, for example, that only sons can assure the family line and the well-being of their ancestors by honoring them in ritual. It is not much use that peasant families with one child receive a double allocation of private land, if their one child is not a boy. In the district of Anhui alone, according to official evidence, 195 baby girls were deliberately drowned in a single year; the true figure could well be much higher. The Chinese press coined the phrase " childbearing guerillas," referring to pregnant women who, at the second or multiple birth, hide out with relatives in the country, in order to avoid registering the birth or to kill a female offspring.

The Chinese model of family planning relies on material incentives to achieve compliance, and punishes non-cooperation. But whether it can be made to work in the countryside remains uncertain as does the economic future of China.

PHILOSOPHY OR RELIGION

Confucianism – Taoism – Buddhism

The Chinese are certainly not religious dogmatists, still less fanatics. It would be truer to say that they are pragmatists, eclectic in the best sense of the word.

This means that they use the building-blocks of Confucianism, Taoism, Buddhism and simple spirit-worship to construct a multi-faceted ecumenical temple, oriented toward practical life and able to survive a variety of eventualities.

The afterlife in the here and now: There is no word in the Chinese language which corresponds precisely to "religion." Belief-systems which could be described as religions all came into China from outside: Buddhism arrived from India, Islam came from Arabia, and Christianity – less important in China than either of these – was brought from Europe and America. The indigenous Chinese doctrines of Taoism and Confucianism did not take on religious characteristics until later, in order to defend against the spiritual and emotional attractions of Buddhism. Although a Confucian cult evolved for state and ceremonial purposes, Master Kong was never elevated to divine status. Spiritually, the Chinese are truly rooted in the soil. They seek the principle of salvation in the here

33

and now. They experience the natural and spiritual worlds as a harmonious unity of meaningful conflicts, as the living dynamic of that which will ultimately fall into a logical pattern: night and day, winter and summer, male and female, life and death, creation and dissolution. Associated with the ordering, energizing principle (*dao/tao*: way), are the directional poles of *yin* and *yang*; everything in the world is infused with the power of these elements to create harmony from opposites. Seeking to be at one with this principle of harmony is the leading tenet of Chinese thought.

The Chinese "heaven on earth:" The Chinese don't conceive of a punishing or a forgiving God, who reveals himself through stories of creation and apocalypse. In the eternal course of cyclical events, they strive for individual perfection, peace and well-being in the here and now (although Buddhism, admittedly, has the ultimate goal of liberation from this cycle). Right into the present century, the Chinese people's abstract idea of heaven took on concrete form through the Emperor, the "Son of Heaven," who exercised celestial authority. This Son of Heaven, however, did not possess divine infallibility; if he forsook his duty, he lost the Authority of Heaven. As recently as 1976, millions of Chinese saw this belief confirmed when natural disasters were followed by the deaths of their leaders Mao, Zhu De and Zhou Enlai: heavenly authority was therewith revoked.

A religion of the senses: Behind the abstract doctrines and symbols of all sophisticated systems of belief, you can usually see the development of tangible, colorful folk traditions and religious practices. Chinese folk religion made free with the sensory manifestations of other religious persuasions, using them to form a pantheon of their own – indeed, more of a pandemonium, full of gods, spirits and demons. Mountains, trees, earth, stones, rivers and rain were given life as spirits and honored with sacrifices. Scholars and heroes (e.g. the war-god Guandi, a 3rd-century figure) were taken into the pantheon. Just as in the Roman Catholic worship of saints, a network of close relationships grew up between the faithful and specific "auxiliaries."

Ancestor-worship – the familiar life after death: Ancestor-worship was the earliest form of faith concerned with the hereafter, and Confucius elevated it to a moral and philosophical plane. The Confucian moral system, based on the respect and obedience of youth towards the aged, transcended through ancestor-worship into "life after death." Tending graves and house altars to ancestors are not just outward expressions of the required filial piety, but also a lasting *memento mori,* philosophical awareness of death within daily life. Ancestor-worship is based on the idea that when people die, they split into two entities, the bodily soul (*po*), which is wafted away by death, and the immortal spirit-soul (*hun*). Only the eldest son of a family may offer sacrifices to the ancestor-spirits, who grant blessings in return. Neglect of these duties incurs malediction. This is why, in many families, it is still considered extremely important to have male offspring.

Taoism – harmony with nature: Understanding nature, adapting yourself to its wisely ordered creation – this is what it means to follow the *dao* (*tao*), the "proper way." It also involves merging into oneness with eternal nature, overcoming adversities and obstacles along the way, and personal liberation even to the extent of withdrawing from the world and practicing a hermit's life of self-denial; at least, so Laozi or Laotse, who is traditionally held to have taught in the 6th century BC, believed. One characteristic of Taoism is the renunciation of worldly power; in this, it differs from the morally

Right: In the Taoist Daimiao temple of Tai'an on Mount Taishan.

justified striving for power that is a feature of Confucianism.

The Taoist desire to conserve one's physical powers and achieve an eternal existence led to some great medical discoveries, as well as the development of breathing and exercise techniques and special dietary regimens designed to intensify physical self-awareness.

Chinese Buddhism – the Promised Land on Earth: In the 1st century AD, Buddhism arrived in China along the Silk Road from India and began its spread throughout the country, competing with Taoism for adherents. Taoists promptly began to create figures of saints and gods, similar to those of Buddhism, in order to make their faith more comprehensible. At the same time, Mahayana Buddhism, in its peculiarly Chinese form, took on the influence of Taoism's magical elements. In the foreground of Buddhism's Chinese incarnation stood a tangible hope of salvation, which was available to anyone who turned to Guanyin (a Bodhisattva) and the Amitabha-Buddha.

Confucianism – the philosophical morality of earthly existence: Confucius probably lived from 551 to 479 BC. In contrast to Taoism's concentration on the self, Confucianism strove for the happiness and well-being of the community. Except for ancestor-worship and the *Authority of Heaven*, Confucian philosophy was very much concerned with *this* world; its strict prescriptions for education, social order and morality have formed a state doctrine for Chinese civilization, and molded it accordingly, for over 2000 years. Confucius' study of the early Zhou period led him to see that epoch as a model for the ideal society of the future. The devotion to and respect for the past which his philosophy involved was to characterize the historic conception and vision of the Chinese for thousands of years. Until the fall of the Qing dynasty in 1911, the Emperor and his officials acted as guardians of this state ideology. Many people see the regime of the "Red Mandarins" as merely a continuation of this tradition.

PANORAMA OF
CHINESE HISTORY

PREHISTORIC TWIGHLIGHT
(Over 4000 years ago.)
A legendary period in which the foundations of Chinese culture were laid. Mythical rulers as idealized moral and political figures. Cradle of civilization in cultivated plain of the Yellow River. Cultural achievements: installations for controlling water, breeding of silk-worms, calendar, spinning-wheel, magnet.

XIA DYNASTY (2200–1700 BC)
Historically this cannot be identified with precision: probably a small state in southern Shanxi around the beginning of the Bronze Age.

SHANG DYNASTY (1600–1100 BC)
The king stands at the head of an aristocratic elite, whose task is to perform military and ritual services. Emergence of ancestor-worship. The latter makes use of the highly ornamented bronze vessels which can be admired in museums today.

ZHOU DYNASTY
Western Zhou Dynasty (1100–771 BC),
Eastern Zhou Dynasty (770–221 BC)
China's Classical Age. Nomadic herdsmen conquer the kingdom of the Shang. For administrative purposes a system of fiefdoms is developed.
Spring and Autumn periods (770–476 BC), **Age of the Quarrelling Kingdoms** (475–221 BC).
In the second phase of the Zhou period the kings lose their political power, but continue to officiate at state rituals. The fiefdoms become independent principalities. The political chaos gives birth to the principles of Chinese philosophy: Confucius (*kongzi*), Laozi and Zhuangzi develop their doctrines, which have shaped Chinese though to this day.

QIN DYNASTY (221–207 BC)
The Prince of Qin succeeds in subjugating all other rulers and creates the first empire in Chinese history. He is proclaimed Emperor Qin Shi Huangdi and many legends grow up around him. Achievements: centralized system of government, standardization of the written language and of technical measurement, start of construction of the Great Wall.

HAN DYNASTY
Western Han Dynasty (206–24 BC),
Eastern Han Dynasty (25 BC–220 AD)
Under the Han Emperors the empire is greatly enlarged ("Roman Empire of the East"). The Silk Road facilitates the exchange of goods and ideas.

Buddhism reaches China. Confucianism has been elevated to a state doctrine and is embodied by a scholarly bureaucracy which is subordinated to the emperor. Paper-making is invented.

AGE OF THE THREE KINGDOMS
Wei (220–265AD), **Shu Han** (221–263 AD), **Wu** (222–280 AD)
The collapse of the Han Dynasty is followed by four centuries of shortlived periods of domination (see below). In the midst of these troubles comes the Age of the Three Kingdoms, in which adversity produces a kind of *fin de siècle* blossoming in literature.

JIN DYNASTY
Western Jin Dynasty (265–316 AD), **Eastern Jin Dynasty** (317–420 AD)
After only a brief period of unification under the (Western) Jin Dynasty, the northern half of the empire is lost to foreign nomadic peoples. It is split up into a mosaic of small chieftainships, and a mass emigration to the south takes place.

SOUTHERN AND NORTHERN
DYNASTIES
Until the reunification of the empire by the newly-founded Sui Dynasty in 581 AD the country is governed by feudal barons and warlords in a series of shortlived dynasties:
Southern dynasties
Song Dynasty (420–479), **Qi Dynasty** (479–502), **Liang Dynasty** (502–557), **Chen Dynasty** (557–589)
Northern dynasties
Northern Wei Dynasty (386–534), **Eastern Wei Dynasty** (534–550), **Western Wei Dynasty** (535–556), **Northern Qi Dynasty** (550–577), **Northern Zhou Dynasty** (557–581)

SUI DYNASTY (581–618)
In the few years of its existence the newly founded dynasty succeeds in reuniting the empire and secures a permanent place in history with the construction of the Imperial Canal (at 930 miles / 1500 km the longest artificial waterway in the world).

TANG DYNASTY (618–907)
High period of Chinese culture and development of foreign policy. Conquest of Central Asia, Korea and North Vietnam. The capital Chang'an (with two million inhabitants) numbers among the great cities of the world both in cultural and civic as well as economic terms. However, in time the real military power shifts away to the frontier garrisons. Rebellions which originate there eventually lead to the fall of the dynasty.

PERIOD OF THE FIVE DYNASTIES

The fall of the Tang Dynasty is followed by half a century during which the empire is broken up and briefly dominated by different rulers.

Later Liang Dynasty ( )07–923), **LaterTang Dynasty** (923–936), **Later Jin Dynasty** (936–946), **Later Han Dynasty** (947–950), **Later Zhou Dynasty** (951–960)

LIAO DYNASTY (916–1125)

In the north-east the military might of the Kitan, a nation of Manchurian horsemen, leads to the founding of the Liao Dynasty, which attempts to emulate the imperial prestige of China.

SONG DYNASTY

Northern Song Dynasty (960–1127), **Southern Song Dynasty** (1127–1279)

Before the turn of the millennium a warlord establishes the Song Dynasty, which once again produces a flowering of Chinese culture. In the arts, painting and ceramics develop. Confucianism undergoes a transformation into Neo-Confucianism.

WESTERN XIA DYNASTY (1038–1227)
JIN DYNASTY (1115–1234)

The non-Chinese dynasties of the Western Xia (Tanguten) and Jin (Jurchen), who had only left a southern portion of the empire for the Song dynasty, themselves fall victim in the 13th century to the "Mongol storm" under Jinghis Khan.

YUAN DYNASTY (1280–1368)

Kublai Khan conquers the whole of China and founds the Mongolian Yuan dynasty. China becomes part of a vast empire, which embraces almost the entire Eurasian land-mass. The religious tolerance of the Mongols allows Buddhism and Taoism scope to develop. Under the *pax mongolica* there is active commerce over the land route to Europe. European "guest-workers " like Marco Polo broaden the horizons, and also bring back descriptions of their experiences to an astonished medieval Europe. The dynasty is toppled in a rebellion by a secret society of Han Chinese.

MING DYNASTY (1368–1644)

The son of an itinerant farm-worker founds the mighty Ming dynasty. He mistrusts the educated bureaucrats and reforms the military – putting all the levers of power in his own hands. His successors extend the Great Wall. Ambitious maritime expeditions, led by the court eunuch Zheng He, take the Chinese as far as Africa.

QING DYNASTY (1644–1911)

Manchurian tribes conquer the empire. By adopting Chinese culture (Sinification) the Qing dynasty is able to rule for nearly three hundred years. Peace and prosperity result in a doubling of the population. At the end of the 18the century the ruling elite neglects its duties (esp. in water supply and canals), and the Europeans set about opening up the country to trade ("gunboat diplomacy"). Porcelain and tea becomes China's most important export commodity. In order to finance the exporting of tea the British force China to import Opium (Opium War). The loss of their authority to the colonial powers, and xenophobic rebellions (Taiping Rebellion), lead in 1911 to the fall of the Qing Dynasty.

REPUBLICAN CHINA (1911–1949)

Sun Yatsen, "Father of modern China," is both the intellectual and political leader of the republican movement. On 29th Dec. 1911 he is named provisional President of the Republic, though loses this office in February 1912 to the military commander Yuan Shikai.

There now begins a politically troubled period, which lasts until the founding of the People's Republic in 1949. In 1919 Sun founds the Guomindang ("Nationalist People's Party"), but after his death in 1925, factional quarrels break out within it. In 1921 the Communist Party comes into being in Shanghai.

The second phase of the Republic (1928–36) is dominated by Chiang Kaishek . In two campaigns (1926 and 1928) Chiang brings to an end the period of the warlords. Nanking becomes the capital, and Chiang is president with dictatorial powers. In 1931 the Japanese occupy Manchuria and the eastern flank of China. Chiang turns against the Communists: 1927, massacre in Shanghai; 1933-34, the Red Army is encircled by 800, 000 troops, but manages to break out (the Long March). Following the surrender of the Japanese in 1945, civil war rages on for four more years. In 1949 the peasant army and its leaders Zhu De, Mao Zedong and Zhou Enlai enter Peking, and Chiang Kaishek flees to Taiwan.

PEOPLE'S REPUBLIC (from 1949)

On 1st October 1949 Mao Zedong proclaims the People's Republic. Start of decade-long political campaigns, proclamation of people's communes and the proletarian cultural revolution, nationalization of private property. Reformers take over after Mao's death in September 1976. Deg Xiaoping opens the country to the West in 1978, gradually ends the planned economy, introduces a socialist free-market economy, and surrounds himself with hand-picked successors to guarantee the continued modernization of China after his death (February 19, 1997).

HEAVENLY PEACE, EARTHLY POWER

PEKING / BEIJING

TRADITION AND CHANGE

The Yellow Emperor, rickshaws drawn by coolies, camel caravans setting out for the Silk Road – such nostalgic dreams quickly fade once you really get to know Peking, or Beijing, as we must learn to call it.

It was a painful experience for China's vast and ancient capital to be thrust into the modern world. Images of the city have flashed around the globe – the most unforgettable in recent times being those of tanks drawn up in the **Square of Heavenly Peace**. Beijing pulls the strings of imperial power. Just as the imperial palace, at its hub, determines Beijing's layout and construction in concentric circles as far as the city limits, so also does central power spread downwards and outwards into the most distant parts of the country. The people of Beijing live under the watchful eye of those in power.

A historical flashback

Even in antiquity, there were settlements in the northern tip of the north Chinese plain, which includes the Beijing area.

Previous pages: View of the Forbidden City in Peking. Cycles parked in Peking. Left: Pipe-smoker near the Imperial Palace.

Situated close to the steppe region that ultimately runs into the Gobi Desert, this dusty place was long a garrison town on the Great Wall with which the Han Chinese sought to keep at bay the nomadic peoples of the north. These tribes nonetheless seized power several times during the Han dynasty. After the Kitan, who had ruled from the north (Liao dynasty 947-1125) and given it the name Yanjing, the Jürchen (Jin dynasty, 1126-1234) ruled the whole of northern China. Beijing's subsequent history was directed by Jinghis Khan. In 1215 the Mongol hordes overran the Great Wall. They razed the city to the ground, and then – after some years spent in consolidating their power – employed the best Chinese architects to build that splendid city which Marco Polo described so enthusiastically: Khanbalyk. When the Mongols were driven out by the Chinese in the 14th century, they left a country in economic ruins behind them, turning it over to the Ming dynasty, which ruled until 1644 from within the walls of the new palace-city of Beijing. Thereafter, a barbarian people once again seized the imperial throne: the Manchu, Tungusic Jürchen tribes from the northeast. These Manchu rulers of the Qing dynasty governed in the city from 1644 to 1911, leaving its main physical features virtually intact. After

43

the 1911 revolution, Beijing (the "north-ern capital") lost its status as capital and bore the unassuming name of Beiping ("northern peace"); the Taiwanese, be-cause of their political convictions, still call the city by this name today. In Oc-tober 1949, when Mao Zedong stood on the Gate of Heavenly Peace to proclaim the People's Republic of China, Beijing once again witnessed emotionally charged, often violent events: demonstra-tions, the struggle for political orthodoxy, the Cultural Revolution, the violent sup-pression of democratic aspirations.

The people of Beijing

In its capital, China puts on its Sunday best. To the visitor the vast country only reveals its true face – one of rural poverty – grudgingly and in carefully measured doses. Beijing sees itself as the political benchmark of the nation and aims to

Above: Entrance to a typical tenement in Peking.

demonstrate the potential for develop-ment in the last great Communist empire. Yet if you talk to people in the streets of Beijing they prove to be the greatest cynics in China. They know all about events behind the political bamboo cur-tain and weave around them a tissue of rumor and speculation. They seem proud and taciturn, as if the vastness of the steppe still lay deep in their nature. To foreigners they are condescending, just as they are to the hundreds of thousands of peasants from poorer provinces who come here looking for work.

Today, small businesses are thriving in Beijing. Cobblers, tailors and bicycle re-pairers are mostly self-employed. On major streets, take-away food vendors are busy till late at night selling specialities from all over the country. In 1991, they were finally officially permitted to serve food outdoors on the sidewalks.

To restrain the worst excesses of growth, the city allocates makeshift stalls to these entrepreneurs. Some of the state-owned department stores lease part of their floor space to traders – putting re-formed Socialism into practice.

Packed shelves and displays of gourmet foods can give a misleading impression of the generally Spartan lifestyle of Beij-ing's inhabitants. Even couples in which both partners work have to watch every *fen*; many of them hold down a second job. For years, wages have not kept pace with inflation. The self-employed take home considerably more money than aca-demics, which keeps people's desire for higher education in check. People would rather learn a foreign language. It's not uncommon to find a promising young surgeon working in a fast-food chain or a woman with a degree in chemistry in charge of the sauna in a Holiday Inn.

Three faces of Beijing

Three architectural and chronological periods have left their mark on the face of

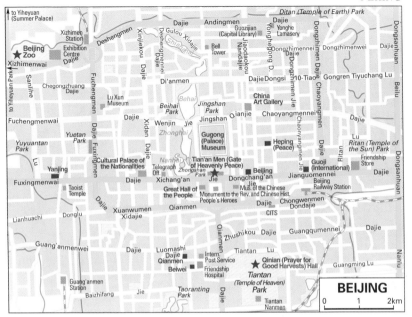

Beijing. Its early history as the imperial city of the Ming and Qing dynasties is reflected in palaces, temples and altars, and attracts tourists from all over the world. The legacy of the period from the 1950s to the 1970s – years that saw the growth of Chinese Socialism – are unadorned, utilitarian, predominantly four-storey buildings. The reforming zeal of the 1980s brought about a building boom which swept away the typical *hudong* (alleys) and old courtyard dwellings. Multi-level overpasses, banks and hotels, owing an unmistakable debt to Hong Kong in their concrete, steel and glass architecture, tower above the shabby apartment blocks of less affluent days. They symbolize the period following the Cultural Revolution and the ambitious goals of the economic reformers. In 1980, hardly a building was more than five storeys high; today, 14- to 16-storey towers are rowed up like dominos through the city. Six-lane urban motorways encompass the city in four rings; a fifth is under construction. The city is swallowing up the surrounding villages.

"Matchboxes" is how the people of Beijing derisively refer to the high-rises. It was with mixed feelings that they bade farewell to their idyllic courtyard houses (*siheyuan*). To be sure, the privacy of lockable doors, central heating and one's own toilet seemed tempting when compared to the cramped, coal-heated dwellings shared by several families and often far from the communal neighborhood toilets. But even in the new high-rises, space is at a premium; most families share one room.

The changing image of the city

A glance at a map of the city reveals not just the rationale behind much of this building but also the outlines of the old city itself. The tidy, grid-like pattern of streets is reminiscent of drawing-board cities like Manhattan or Mannheim. Yet this plan was laid out centuries ago, back in the days of Jinghis Khan. The Ming period has been preserved in the rectangle of the walled **Forbidden City**, built on a north-south alignment and surrounded on all four sides by the **Palace City**, also walled; beyond that, on the south side, is the so-called "Chinese City."

The **Front Gate** (*qian men*) was the middle portal of the three that led into the Palace City. The impressive 14th-century city wall was sacrificed in the 1960s to make way for the urban motorway (Ringway II) and for the new subway. The fundamentalist faction would have liked to use the opportunity to demolish all the city's historic buildings. The map of the city shows how, instead of this, "the old was made to serve the new," in Mao's words. Two of the eleven gates into the Manchu city, the Andingmen and the **Deshengmen**, were situated on the northern East-West boundary. The latter has been restored and gives some idea of the strength of the 9.5 mile (15 km) long wall, whose foundations are about 65 ft (20 m) thick. The new building of the Academy of Social Sciences was also built on historic ground: that of the halls where examinations were held for the imperial civil service. The favorite palaces of Cixi, the last empress, were once located around the **Middle** and **South Lakes** (*zhongnan hai*), to the west of the imperial palace. Today, members of government live in this area, including, once, Mao Zedong. The walled area extending to the **North Lake** (*bei hai*) is off-limits; this is the new Forbidden City. The **Temple of the Imperial Ancestors** (*tai miao*) now has the equally resonant name of People's Palace of Culture. Beijing is increasingly losing its old familiar character. Even officials now regret the radical break with the past, and are protecting, at least, the Old City in the immediate vicinity of the Imperial Palace from the demolition squads. But it's precisely Beijing's contrasts and contradictions that hold visitors in its spell.

Right: View from the Square to the Gate of Heavenly Peace.

GETTING AROUND

The best way to get to know Beijing is to stroll through the narrow alleys of the Old City, which can be reached from every hotel.

Cycling gives you mobility, and also gives you a sense of sharing the Chinese way of life. Long cycle rides through the city are not, however, recommended because the air is so heavily polluted. Moreover, the most important sites are generally a long way apart – the distance from one side of Beijing to the other is about 25 miles (40 km).

The bus network is extensive. Timetables are available in hotels and bookshops. Don't, however, get caught up in the rush-hour struggles. The days are long gone, alas, when the Chinese eagerly gave up their seats to "long-nose" Europeans. As recently as 1979, the citizens of Beijing were officially exhorted to show courtesy to foreigners, yet at the same time one sensed that they were discouragement from making any real contact with overseas visitors. This author once asked a bus driver the way to the White Pagoda, only to see him lose his temper, slam the door in her face and stubbornly look the other way. These days, curiosity gets the better of reserve; it's easier to make contact, and you can get by perfectly well with English. Many taxi drivers are learning different languages: taxis are still fairly cheap and can be hired by the day.

If you are travelling alone rather than in a group, it makes sense to use the map and visit sights that are conveniently grouped together. There are plenty of outdoor snack bars and modest eating-houses, so you're not forced to return to your hotel for lunch. Because there are so many sites located so close together, the following sites are presented in historical or thematic groupings, with an indication of other places nearby that are also worth visiting.

The Square and Gate
of Heavenly Peace

The central **Square Of Heavenly Peace** – Tiananmen Square, vast enough for a million people to gather – is where sightseeing tours usually begin. It lies on the busy **Chang'an Street** (*chang'an jie*), which runs east-west, on the south side of the Imperial Palace. This square made international headlines on June 4, 1989, when a students' revolt was turned into a bloody massacre. **The Great Hall of the People** (*renmin dahui tang*, or Congress Hall), stands on its west side and the **Museum of History** (*lishi bowuguan*) to the east. These two massive buildings, erected in 1959, show unmistakable Soviet influence. The obelisk of the **Memorial to the Heroes of the People** (*renmin yingxiong jinian bei*) rises in front of the **Mausoleum of Chairman Mao** (*mao zhuxi jinian tang*), constructed in 1966-67 on the south side of the square. Lined with government buildings and hotels, Chang'an Street has

little to tempt the stroller. But the **Beijing Hotel**, an oasis for footsore tourists, is an easy walk from the square.

The **Gate of Heavenly Peace** (*tianan men*), which gave the square its name, today forms the approach to the Imperial Palace. For parades and demonstrations during anniversary celebrations in the 1950s, spectator tribunes and boxes were built here, painted imperial red to match the palace walls. During the Republic, a portrait of Sun Yatsen adorned the gate; a gigantic image of Mao has since taken its place. In 1989, this was pelted with paint-bombs during the student demonstrations. A new picture was quickly brought in, hoisted into place with a crane while a crowd of onlookers stared up at the visage swaying above them. A murmur went through the crowd. "Sshh," said a warning voice, "don't go waking him up!"

The Imperial Palace

China's most sublime complex, the **Imperial Palace** (*gu gong*) is a creation

47

other men who were willing to do without "the little difference," and thus qualify for high office and distinction in the service of the imperial household. Many did not survive the operation.

Of the three huge gatehouses, each with three arched entrances, the **Meridian Gate** (*wu men*) provides the main entrance to the **Forbidden City** (*zijin cheng*) and a view of the central courtyard. The Golden Water Canal flows past in a graceful bend. Five marble bridges, symbols of the Confucian virtues, lead to the **Gate of Supreme Harmony** (*taihe men*), guarded by two bronze lions. It was here that petitions to the emperor were deposited and the imperial seals kept. Hidden behind it lies the very heart of the palace, the **three great Ceremonial Halls** (*san da dian*) raised up on a three-tiered marble terrace. The first of these, the **Hall of Supreme Harmony** (*taihe dian*), was the setting for the dragon throne, from which the emperor, on the most important ceremonial occasions, would receive the homage of the court. This largest hall in China, supported by 24 columns, was once Beijing's tallest building, as well; it was forbidden to build anything taller than its 115-ft (35 m) height. The 18 bronze vessels on the south side symbolize the country's 18 provinces. Cranes, delicately fashioned in bronze, adorn the terrace as symbols of happiness, while the tortoise (*haoheng*) with a dragon's head promises long life. In the smaller **Hall of Middle Harmony** (*zhonghe dian*) the Son of Heaven prepared for the ceremonies. In the third one, the **Hall of Preserved Harmony** (*baohe dian*), he received successful candidates for the civil service examination or princes from client states.

On the north side, the adjoining complex of three buildings is a smaller version of the three ceremonial halls. Through the Gate of Heavenly Purity (*taihe men*) you reach the palace of the same name, which even in the Ming

of the Ming period and was built between 1406 and 1420. The splendor of its red walls and sea of yellow roofs is especially impressive in the sunshine. Its overwhelming size sends out a clear message. This palace was not just a seat of terrestrial power and government; it was also the holy spot where the cosmos was conjoined with its earthly representatives. According to traditional belief, the harmony of *yin* and *yang*, and thereby the well-being of the entire empire, was guaranteed by the emperor's virtue and his unfailing observance of the rituals demanded by Heaven. A massively fortified wall enclosed the Forbidden City, which stretched for over a thousand yards (nearly 1 km) from north to south. In this palace ruled the emperor (*huangdi*), surrounded by countless women, serving girls and eunuchs. Outside the gates, surgeons stood in wait for

Above: A lion guarding the Imperial Palace. Right: Square in front of the Hall of Supreme Harmony in the Imperial Palace.

period provided both living and working accommodation. The central building served as the empress's smaller throne-room. Beyond it, in the **Palace of Earthly Peace** (*kunning gong*), daily sacrificial rituals were conducted by shamans in accordance with Manchu practice. In the east wing you can visit the **Imperial Bridal Chamber,** decorated completely in red. The Kunning Gate leads to a jewel of Chinese horticultural art, the **Palace Garden**. To the east and west, residential palaces still convey something of the ambiance of the imperial life-style.

Within the isolation of these walls, human dramas were played out. Intrigues, assassinations, courting the favor of the powerful: all were traditional power-plays performed with a high degree of theatrical artistry. Usually the leading roles were taken by women, among them the empress Cixi. Her most vigorous adversary, the empress-mother Zi An, with whom she had to share the regency during the lifetime of the child

emperor Tongzhi, met her death in the **Palace of Peaceful Repose**, probably by eating poisoned cakes. The emperor kept a set of jade tablets in his chambers, each bearing the name of one of his many concubines. If he laid out a tablet in the evening, the eunuch on duty had to hurry off to fetch the chosen one and bring her, naked (to prove she was unarmed) and wrapped in a blanket, to lay at the emperor's feet. For in the palace mistrust poisoned all human relations.

Turn eastwards from the last great ceremonial hall and you come to the famous **Nine Dragon Wall** (*jiulong bi*) made of glazed ceramic tiles, decorated in various colors with the figures of nine five-toed – and therefore imperial – dragons. Immediately to the north are the marvellous palace buildings which the emperor Qianlong built in 1723, when he was 62, as a retreat for his old age and a place of repose, after conferring the regency upon his son, a rare event in China even in those days. This **Palace of Quietude and Longevity** today forms

part of the Treasure Chambers which occupy the entire north-eastern section of the palace. Those who wish to visit it separately can reach it via the north gate.

Treasure Chambers

The Treasure Chambers exhibit priceless collections of Chinese art and foreign gifts to the imperial court, arranged thematically and displayed in the palace's northeastern pavilions. In 1933, to save the palace treasures from the Japanese, the government had most of them packed up in thousands of boxes and transported to Nanjing (Nanking). From there, they were later shipped over to Taiwan by the fleeing Guomindang (Kuomintang) in 1949. Nevertheless, what remains is enough to constitute an exquisite exhibition. Pride of place goes to the valuable jade carvings, but amuse-

Above: White bottle-pagoda on Jade Island in Beihai Park. Right: Arched bridge in the grounds of the Summer Palace.

ment is provided by 19th-century pinball machines. Notable are the resplendent jewelry and jewel-encrusted cloisonné work in the Treasure Chamber. The visitor leaves the Palace Museum through the north exit, the **Gate of the Divine Warrior** (*shenwu men*).

The view from Coal Hill

Cross Jingshan Street and you soon reach the park of the same name (*jingshan gongyuan*), with its *jing shan*, which translates as **Coal Hill**. There in 1644, after his defeat by the Manchu, the last Ming emperor took his own life. The climb up to the airy **Pavilion of Perpetual Spring** on the summit of the hill is rewarded by the unique view across the yellow roofs of the palace and the rest of the city. About 500 yards (meters) east of here you reach the **Hall of Chinese Art** (*meishu guan*).

Beihai Park

From Jingshan Park you can walk in a westerly direction to Beihai Park (*beihai gongyuan*: North Lake Park). The middle and south lakes to the south of the bridge are closed to the public and reserved for government personnel. The park used to belong to the Mongolian Palace of the Khan. In this leisure park, popular because it is so central, thousands of visitors from every province throng daily across the bridge towards the **White Dagoba,** a bottle-shaped pagoda on **Jade Island**, which can be seen from a long way off. Boat rentals are ever popular with visitors; in the winter, the frozen lake is crowded with skaters. The 118 ft (36 m) high Tibetan-style **Dagoba** (*bai ta*), and the temple that is attached to it, were erected in 1651 to commemorate the first visit of a Dalai Lama to Beijing. On the north shore of the island, within ancient walls, beckons the **Fangshan**, one of the best traditional restaurants in Beijing,

serving Manchu specialities. On the far side of the park, there's a second **Nine Dragon Wall**; and the marvellous **Five Dragon Pagoda** lures in visitors. To the west of the south entrance, in the **Round Fort** (*tuan cheng*) you can admire valuable objects dating from 1417, including a white Burmese jade Buddha and the fascinating wine-goblet of Kublai Khan, carved from a huge piece of dark green jade.

The complex of water stretches northwards in three smaller lakes, named **Shichahai**. The middle lake, **Houhai**, is said to have long ago formed a harbor fed by the Imperial Canal. Here in the heart of the city, yet untouched by its bustle, you can feel the heartbeat of old Beijing. Through old decorated gateways you can glimpse courtyards ablaze with flowers.

The Drum and Bell Towers

Turn away from the Middle Lake towards the west and you will suddenly come upon these two towers, dating from 1420. They stand guard over the city, at the top of its north-south axis. The northern **Bell Tower** (*zhong lou*), rebuilt in 1747 after a fire, stands on raised foundations. During the day a huge bell used to strike the hour, while at night 24 drums were beaten in the Drum Tower.

The Summer Palace

As early as the 12th century, there were summer palaces adorning the northwest part of Beijing. The artistic emperor Qianlong had them extended to form a unified complex, designed as a residence for his mother and influenced by South Chinese landscape gardening.

In 1860 and again in 1900, the palaces were destroyed by western colonial troops. On both occasions Cixi, the dowager-empress and power behind the throne, spent huge sums of money on restoration. In 1888 she misappropriated funds from the naval budget and used them to realize her dreams of luxury and power in the **Garden of Cultivated Har-**

mony (*yihe yuan*). Here Chinese architecture foregoes its usual severity in favor of the playfulness of a dynasty that traced its origins back to nomadic princelings.

One of the few remaining **Arches of Honor** (*pai lou*) sweeps elegantly over the road leading to the east gate of the Summer Palace. The place's former dignity is reflected in the lofty names of its buildings, such as the **Hall of Mercy and Long Life** (*renshou dian*); today, these buildings have been turned into museums. Going north past the **Hall of the Jade Waves**, where the hapless emperor Guanxu had to pay for his reforming zeal with years of imprisonment, you reach the **Garden of Virtuous Harmony** (*dehe yuan*). It is dominated by the three-storey theater of the self-centered Cixi, who loved to watch her own works being performed there. Chinese women in court dress received visitors here. In the **Hall of the Joys of Longevity** Cixi had her private apartments. A portrait here immortalizes the old lady, complete with her impressively long fingernail shields. Beyond, you can walk along the half-mile-long (700 m) **Promenade** (*chang lang*) parallel to the lake shore. The path to the quieter southern shore takes you past the famous **Marble Boat** (*qingyan fang*), decorated with mosaic and paid for with money purloined from the navy. Crossing the **Hill of Longevity** (*wanshou shan*) you arrive, on the north side, at temples built in the Tibetan style (since many of the Manchu emperors were attracted to Lamaism). Here you can relax and work out what you want to see next.

The Old Summer Palace

The emperor Qianlong, fascinated by European culture, commissioned the Jesuit Fr. Giuseppe Castiglione to design

Right: The Altar of Heaven is considered to be the most beautiful building in China.

a little rococo palace, the ruins of which lie among clusters of pine trees and lotus ponds east of the Summer Palace. The **Garden of Perfect Purity** (*yuanming yuan*) was once the setting for the most splendid buildings in the entire complex. In 1860 the buildings were completely destroyed by colonial troops; but today parts are being reconstructed.

The Altar of Heaven and Imperial Altars

To demonstrate their humility and appeal with sacrifices for the mercy of heaven, the emperors of the Ming and Qing dynasties observed the strict rites, following the rhythms of the seasons, at six altars around the palace city.

The **Altar of Heaven** (*tian tan*) also called the Temple of Heaven, stands out by virtue of its architecture and its spacious grounds. The emperor, attended by over 2000 dignitaries, was carried to the sacrificial ceremonies on the back of an elephant, and would pass the night of the winter solstice in fasting and meditation. The north-south alignment both of the site and the ritual ceremonies that were performed there, make the **South Gate** (*nan men*), in the eastern part of Yongdingmen Street, the best approach to the altar; you can leave the park through the **North Gate** (*bei men*) in Tiantan Street. The number of the stone slabs on the three-tiered altar terrace, which are laid out in a circular pattern, can be divided by three and nine, the numbers symbolizing the heavenly *yang*. The three levels of the altar represent Heaven, Earth and Man. Genealogical tables were preserved in the Imperial Vault of Heaven, the adjoining rotunda on the north side, which is roofed with blue-glazed tiles. The courtyard is enclosed by an **Echo Wall**, but if you want to hear the echo of spoken words rebounding from one wall to the other, you'll have to visit on a very quiet day.

A raised marble pavement runs north-ward towards the **Hall of Harvest Prayers** (*qinian dian*), perhaps the most beautiful building in China. The round hall, with its triple-tiered, blue-glazed roof surmounted by a gilded sphere, rises from a terrace of white marble. It was re-built as recently as 1889, after a devastating fire. Often mistakenly referred to as the "Temple of Heaven," it was not ac-tually used in the sacrificial ceremonies of the Altar of Heaven. In point of fact it was here, at the beginning of spring, that the emperor prayed for the crops to ripen. The roof of the hall is supported by 28 wooden pillars. The four inner columns symbolize the seasons, the two surround-ing circles, each with twelve pillars, stand for the twelve months and the twelve double hours of the day.

Outside the park of the Altar of Heaven, you are plunged into the bus-tling life of the old **South City** with its shops and little markets. The streets here are laid out less formally than in the more elegant northwest. In the narrow alley-ways between rickety houses a different dialect is spoken from that in the north of the city. If you have the time and leisure to do so, walk from the North Gate west-ward to **Qianmen Street** in the Tianqiao quarter and then north towards the **Qian-men Gate** – detouring briefly along, say, **Dashalan Street,** with its old department store façades, or **Liulichang Lane**, lined with antique shops. East of the park's north gate, the big **Yuanlong store** is a temptation to shoppers, and collectors can sometimes pick up bargains at the many little stalls in the antiques market across the street. If you have a taxi wait-ing for you or are cycling, you can take a circuitous route from the Altar of Heaven westward past the Fayuan Temple to the Baiyunguan Temple.

Today, the five other altars are less at-tractive than the Altar of Heaven. On the west side, facing the Altar of Heaven, all you will find on the site of the former Altar of Agriculture is a sports ground and an architectural museum. The **Altar of the Moon** (*yue tan*) in the west of the

palace city is also a disappointment, but in the eastern park of the **Altar of the Sun** (*ri tan*) there is at least a good open-air restaurant. In **Ritan Park** (*ritan gongyuan*), elderly Beijing residents practise *qigong* and shadow-boxing, or even seek rejuvenation in disco dancing. The **Altar of Harvests** (*shenji tan*) is to be found in what is now **Sun-Yatsen Park** (*zhongshan gongyuan*) next to the Imperial Palace. To the northeast, small exhibitions by modern artists are occasionally held in the park of the **Altar of the Earth** (*di tan*); the altar's rectangular terrace is lined with tiles the color of yellow earth.

Temples and monasteries of the Lamas

Beijing's most beautiful temple is in a **Lama monastery** (*yonghe gong*), which is today again occupied by monks, situ-

Above: Sutra drum in the Tibetan Lama Temple. Right: In the Temple of the Sleeping Buddha.

ated on the northeast quadrant of the second Ring Road. In 1745, the Emperor Qianlong, who was a devotee of the *Yellow Bonnet* sect (*gelugpa*), had the Palace of the Princes converted to a Tibetan-Mongolian monastery in order to emphasize the close ties between the Chinese imperial court and its "vassals." To make the same point, the inscriptions on the plaques in the monastery are in four languages: Chinese, Manchurian, Tibetan and Mongolian. The idea was that the Panchen and Dalai Lamas should be accommodated here during their stays in Beijing.

A side gate in Yonghegong Street leads across a courtyard to the front gardens with a bell-tower and drum-tower. Five temple halls devoted to the illustration and practice of Buddhist doctrine are arranged one behind the other in a straight line, surrounded by secondary buildings. This is the basic layout of all Chinese temples. The merry, pot-bellied Buddha named Milefo welcomes visitors to the **first hall**; he is flanked by fierce Chinese gatekeepers trampling on evil demons. Weituo, the custodian of Buddhist doctrine, watches over the inner recess of the temple. In the next courtyard there is a representation of the Buddhist **Mountain of Paradise** (*xumi sham*) and in the **Yonghe Hall** (*yonghe dian*) you can see the *Buddhas of the Three Ages* sitting on lotus flowers, and the 18 *luohan* or proto-Buddhas. The immense incense-bowl is presumably there to keep them in a benevolent frame of mind. In the outer buildings you can admire the valuable *tangka* (Tantric banners). In the **Hall of Eternal Protection** you find three gilded statues of Buddhas: standing beside the *Buddha of Long Life* are the *Buddha of Medicine* and the *Proclaimer of the Law*.

The *Wheel of Law* gives its name to the **fourth hall**. A bronze figure of Tsongkhapa, the founder of the Yellow Sect, is framed by murals showing scenes from his life. Buddhist scriptures are preserved

here. The three-storey **Hall of Ten Thousandfold Happiness** (*wanfu ge*) contains something rather unexpected. As your eyes gradually become accustomed to the dim interior light, you begin to make out the outlines of a remarkable sight: the huge **statue** of the Tibetan Maitreya Bodhisattva, 60 ft (18 m) high. Carved from the trunk of a single sandalwood tree, the statue was an appreciative gift from the eighth Dalai Lama Buddha to the emperor Qianlong. The Lama Temple is lavishly decorated with images of the Buddha. In the front outer buildings you can see Tantric deities, modestly draped but joined in an ecstatic embrace, thereby revealing a spiritual break with indigenous Chinese culture.

Afterwards you can cross the road to walk through the beautiful **Triumphal Arches** (*pai lou*) and visit the **Temple of Confucius** (*kong miao*). It was here that officials and emperors made sacrifices to the supreme state idol. The hierarchical ordinances laid down by Confucius have not entirely lost their force even today.

The adjacent building to the south is the former **Imperial Academy** (*guozi jian*). To the north, not far from the Lama Temple and beyond the ring road, lies the Park of the Altar of the Earth mentioned above.

The Temple of the Source of the Law

This attractive temple (*fayuan si*), situated in the South City, houses the Buddhist Academy as well as a comprehensive library. Jinghis Khan established the monastery in honor of the Taoist sage Qi Changchun, founder of the northern school of Taoism, to whom the third of the five temple halls is also dedicated.

The Temple of the Five Pagodas

This temple (*wuta si*) is hidden between the tower-blocks north of the stadium and the zoo, in the Northwest City. The complex was destroyed in 1900; all that remains today is the (restored) five-pointed **Indian Diamond Throne Pa-**

goda, which stands on a high, square podium decorated with reliefs.

From here, it's not far to the **zoo** (*dongwu yuan*), worth a visit for the pandas alone. These beloved animals romp or doze near the entrance. Only a few stops away on the bus is Beijing's university and college district, as well as **Haidian Street**, which has been declared a special zone for high-tech businesses. Here you can check the Chinese computer scene, talk shop (in English), and buy software cheaply.

Back on the bus, with one change, you reach the **Temple of the Great Bell** (*dazhong si*). Today, this is a bell museum, with the 15th-century bell of the Huayuan sect as its showpiece. More than 200,000 Buddhist *sutra* symbols are cast on the surface of this great bell, which, at nearly 23 ft (7 m) high and weighing 46 tons, is the largest in China.

Above: Statue of a watchman in the Temple of the Sleeping Buddha.

Museums

Special exhibitions are listed in the English-language newspaper *China Daily*.

Regularly changing art exhibitions are held in such galleries as the **Hall of Chinese Art** (*meishu guan*) and the **Yanhuang Hall of Art.** The **Cultural Palace of Nationalities** often puts on excellent shows offering insight into the art of China's ethnic minorities. The **Museum of Chinese History** is also worthwhile, even though virtually all the exhibits are labelled in Chinese only. In the **Xu Beihong Museum** (*xu beihong bowuguan*), named after the famous painter, you can admire his portrayal of horses, as well as pen-and-ink drawings by other notable masters of this genre. The **Mao Mausoleum** opens only irregularly: getting in is a matter of luck. There are countless rumors circulating as to the authenticity of the embalmed occupant of the glass coffin, which is aligned, in imperial fashion, on a north-south axis.

EXCURSIONS

Temple of the Sleeping Buddha and Monastery of the Azure Clouds

An eminently worthwhile day-trip is a visit to these two monastic sites in the **Western Hills**, perhaps taking in the Summer Palace at the same time.

The popularity of the **Temple of the Sleeping Buddha** (*wofo si*) with day-trippers is demonstrated by the amount of litter; environmental awareness is not a Chinese virtue. Ancient cypresses border the broad flight of steps leading to the temple. A bronze Buddha reclines in the third hall, smiling benignly. The immense feet of the statue, which is over 16 ft (5 m) long, are bare. Pilgrims therefore bring him shoes as offerings, and a pair is always there ready for him to put on. He is guarded by a 14th-century group of

PEKING AND SURROUNDINGS

0   10   20   30   40   50   60 km

twelve disciples. The small **Hotel Wo-fosi**, north of the entrance, provides a rare opportunity to spend a night in a building that was once part of the imperial Chinese court.

The **Monastery of the Azure Clouds** (*biyun si*) is hidden away in a large walled park with old trees, on the eastern slope of the **Fragrant Hills** (*xiang shan*). The white, Indian-style **Pagoda of the Diamond Throne** towers above it on its richly decorated plinth. The five hundred gilded wooden statues of *luohan* (Buddhist sages) in a side hall were carved by gifted artists, and each one is quite distinctive.

A path leading to the crest of the hills behind the Sleeping Budddha gives you the option of a longer walk to the sights of the Western Hills. After climbing for about two hours in a southwesterly direction, you reach the summit of the Park of the Fragrant Hill (*xiangshan gongyuan*). An overloaded chairlift also goes to the top. Once an imperial hunting-ground, the park contains an octagonal pagoda

seven storeys high, as well as a weathered Lama temple; both are beguiling. Outside the temple there is an impressive decorative gateway.

Beijing's oldest monasteries

The most venerable monasteries lie some 25 miles (40 km) away in an unspoilt woodland in the Mentougou district very popular for day trips. These are the **Tanzhe** and **Jietai monasteries** (*tanzhe si, jietai si*), set among ancient pine trees. The first dates back to the 3rd century. The 12th- to 14th-century burial pagodas at the foot of the temple convey a keener sense of Buddhist seclusion than city temples do.

This trip is an opportunity for a short cross-country drive through rural villages; but returning from the Jietai monastery one is struck by the ugly reverse side of the industrialization coin. The steelworks may employ 200,000 workers, but its belching chimneys dominate the city from this angle.

Above: Processional avenue to the thirteen Ming Tombs near Changping.

The Great Wall

It is really called the "Long Wall" (*chang cheng*). Dissident Chinese artists sometimes depict it as an imprisoning chain or a Gulag wall. But most Chinese regard it simply as their country's most famous landmark. For more than 3700 miles (6000 km) this stone dragon winds its way across steep-sided mountain ridges to the edge of the Gobi Desert in western Gansu. Qin Shi Huang, who unified China and reigned as its first emperor from 221 to 210 BC, compelled hundreds of thousands of workers to construct this bulwark against the Huns from the north. Existing stretches of wall were linked and fortified with a wooden superstructure. In the early Ming period the ramparts were faced with brick and extended to form the defensive system we see today. It was wide enough for six horsemen to ride abreast. Smoke signals, visible from afar, rose from the fortified towers.

The wall at the **Badaling Pass**, 50 miles (80 km) north of Beijing, attracts most tourists. You can walk along other stretches of wall, as well, but it is at this point, strategically the most important, that the gigantic feat of construction is most impressive. You can glimpse large, renovated remains of the older wall as you drive up through a narrow valley, where you can also see the foundations of a 14th-century Mongolian gate, the **Terrace of Clouds**, rich with ornamental reliefs.

On both sides of the double gate of the Badaling fortress there are flights of steps, quite steep in places, leading up to the high tops and marvellous views of the massive **Watchtower** and **Beacon Tower**. Because of the crowds, especially on public holidays, it's wise to set out early.

The sections of wall at Jinshaling, Simatai and **Mutianyu**, restored but not quite such a tourist attraction, are no less astounding. A cable-car takes you to the highest bend. On clear days the view of treeless mountain ranges, rolling towards the distant horizon, is truly awe-inspiring.

The Ming Tombs

An excursion to the Great Wall is easily combined with a visit to the **thirteen Ming Tombs** (*shisan ling*) situated in the Changjing district, 30 miles (50 km) northwest of Beijing. Chinese travel agencies offer this combination.

The entire tomb precinct was once protected by a fortified wall and was strictly guarded. The emperors were laid to rest in red, walled burial mounds. Passing through temple precincts and sacrificial halls with red lacquer work you reach the Stela Gate, the entrance to the subterranean palace.

From the **Great Palace Gate** (*dagong men*), the **Avenue of Stone Figures** (*shen dao* or "Street of the Spirits") leads to the central **Changling** tomb. This processional avenue through China's Valley of the Kings is guarded by pairs of animals and Confucian officials carved in stone. At the Changling Tomb, resting-place of the emperor Yongle (1403-1424), there's usually a throng of tourists. The only surviving sacrificial hall is supported by 32 pillars, 40 ft (12 m) high, fashioned from massive teak tree-trunks, with a tiered marble terrace. This reconstructed tomb, though the largest, is empty.

In the restored **Dingling Tomb**, that of the emperor Wanli (1573-1610), only the subterranean palace is accessible. The burial-chambers and the museum halls that form part of the complex illustrate the burial practices of the Chinese imperial court. Tourists tend to ignore the 11 tombs of the other Ming emperors, on either side of the approach to the Changling Tomb. Among the crumbling, overgrown walls of these tombs, persimmon groves add a happy note of color.

PEKING / BEIJING
Arrival and onward travel
Most visitors arrive by air. The **airport** lies 19 miles (30 km) north-east of the city center, which can best be reached by taxi or airconditioned busses. Beijing is the transportation hub of China; from here (and often only from here) there are connections to all provincial cities. Most international airlines fly into Beijing, many of them several times a week.

Air China flights can be booked at travel agencies and in most big hotels. Other sales-points for Air China tickets: CAAC, 155, Dongsi Xidajie; Air China Beijing Booking Office, 15, Xichang'an Jie; Air China Office, China International Trade Center, 1 Jianguomenwai Lu The offices of most international airlines are located in the China World Trade Center or in the SCITE-Tower (1, Jianguomenwai Dajie).

The **train station** is situated in the south-east part of the inner city. You will find the special ticket service for foreigners in the east wing of the underground mall. Advance reservation is advisable.

Organising of trips and arranging of all tickets: China International Travel Agency, 103, Fuxingmennei Lu, Tel. 6601 1122, und China Travel Service, Tel. 661 2569.

Accommodation
The hotels are concentrated in the East City, along Chang'an Street and in northwestern district of Haidian.

Because of the considerable distances, no single area of the city can be particularly recommended as a base for sightseeing. Close to the pulse of city life are the hotels of the East City, between Wangfujing Street and Ritan Park.

LUXURY: East City: **Palace Hotel**, Wangfujing Jinyuhudong, Tel. 6512 8899. **China World Shangri-La**, 1 Jianguomenwai Lu, Tel. 6505 2266. **Holiday Inn Crown Plaza**, 48 Wangfujing, Tel. 6513 3388. **Great Wall Sheraton**, Donghuan Beilu, Tel. 6500 5566. **New Otani**, 26 Jianguomenwai Lu, Tel. 6512 5555. **Kempinsky Hotel**, 50 Liangmaqiao Lu, Tel. 6465 3388 **Grand Hotel** (Annex of Peijing Hotel), 35 Dongchang'an Lu, Tel. 6513 7788. **Beijing Hotel** (colonial origins, cent. location nr. Wangfujing Lu and Imperial Palace, good food), 33 Dongchang'an Lu, Tel. 6513 7766. **Jingguang New World Hotel**, Hujialou Lu, Tel. 6501 8888. *Near the airport:* **Mövenpick**, **Capital's Resort**, South Xiaotianzhu Lu, Tel. 6456 5588. **Holiday Inn Lido** (combined appartment complex and office building for foreign subsidiary companies; if you want to keep China at arm's length, this is for you: you will

find European restaurants, good pizzas, Thai food, snacks, bar, disco, delicatessen shops selling European specialities, and a gymnasium), Jiangtai Lu, Tel. 6437 9988. (Continued overleaf).
Shangrila (Northwest City; stylish good French and Chin. food), 29 Zizhuyuan Lu, Tel. 6841 2211.
MID-PRICE: **Beijing Minzu Hotel** (Nr Xidan shopping street), 51 Fuxingmennei Lu, Tel. 6601 4466. **Qianmen Hotel** (South City), 175 Yong'an Lu, Tel. 6301 6688. **Beijing Bamboo Garden Hotel** (in the walls of an old princely palace in the heart of the Old City), 24 Xiaoshiqiao Lane (or Hudong), Tel. 4032229. *Northwest City:* **Friendship Hotel** (Russian hotel complex of the 1950s, renovated, restaurants, lovely garden), 3 Baishiqiao Lu, Tel. 6849 8888. **Xiangshan Hotel** (at the lower end of Xiangshan Park, designed by the brilliant Chinese-American architect, Pei), Fragrant Hill Park, Tel. 6259 1166. **Olympic Hotel** (opp. the Beijing Library, French and Chin. restaurant), 52 Baishiqiao Lu, Tel. 6831 6688. **Xiyuan**, Erligou, Tel. 6831 3388.
BUDGET: **Guanghua Hotel** (East City), 38 North Dongsanhuan Lu, Tel. 6501 8866. **Beijing Mandarin Hotel** (formerly Dadu Hotel, Northwest City), 21 Chegongzhuang Lu, Tel. 6831 0988. **Beiwei Hotel**, 11 Xixing Lu, Tel. 6301 2266. **Wofosi Hotel** (near the Reclining Buddha in the Botanical Garden), Tel. 6259 1459.

Sightseeing

Beihai Park, open till 8pm, south entrance: Wenjin Lu, north entrance: West Di'anmen Lu **Summer Palace**, terminus of bus-route 332 from Zoo, many halls are only open till 4.30pm. **Garden of Perfect Purity**, bus 331 from Pinganli (or bus 332 and change in Zhongguancun). **Ritan Park**, entrance from Guanghua Lu, entrance to restaurant from Ritan Lu
Altar of Heaven, south entrance: East Yongdingmen Lu, north entrance: Tiantan Lu (opp. Yuanlong department store). **Liulichang Lane of antique shops**, crosses Xinhua Lu east-west. **Dashalan Street**, south of the Qianmen Gate, west of Qianmen Lu
Temples and monasteries: **Lama Temple**, entrance from Yonghegong Lu, open daily, 9am–4.30pm, subway station Yonghegong. **Temple of the Source of the Law**, far end of Fayuansi Lane. **Baiyunguan monastery**, Xibianmenwai Lu **Wutasi Temple**, in the little lane east of Baishiqiao Lu (beyond the zoo). **Dazhongsi Temple**, West Beisanhuan Lu **Computer district**, Haidian Lu (Bus 332, get out at Huangzhuang). **Temple of the Sleeping Buddha**, bus 333 from Summer Palace. **Biyunsi Temple** and **Fragrant Hills**, bus

360 from zoo. **Fahaisi Temple**, bus 336 from Zhanlan Lu, open till 4pm.
Great Wall and Ming Tombs: Chinese tourist buses leave every morning from Chongwenmen Lu or from the square south of the Qianmen Gate, where you will also find ticket-booths (book the day before and enquire about the place and time of departure). Hotels will arrange or sell you tickets for trips to all the more distant tourist destinations. *Museums:* **Hall of Art** (*meishu guan*), 1 Wusi Dajie (North end of Wangfujing Lu). **Yanhuang Hall of Art**, in the Asian Games Village (*yayun cun*). **Palace of Nationalities**, 49 Funei Dajie. **Museum of History**, Tiananmen Square. **Xu Beihong Museum**, 53 Xinjiekou Beidajie.

Food

Of all the highly praised duck-roasteries, none makes such a delcious Peking Duck as the **Restaurant Quanjude**. The cuisine of Beijing is simpler than the sweet-and-sour or hot, spicy cooking of the south; its most common ingredients are garlic, soya sauce and ginger. But Beijing's truly numberless eating-houses also serve the specialities of Cantonese, Sichuan and Shandong cuisines (and that covers the three most famous). And what an extraordinary choice there is: Mongolian camel's hump, snake and dog-meat (tastes repulsive!)... or why not try the quail (delicious!)?
The Chinese equivalent of ravioli are *jiaozi*, which make a satisfying snack; the crispy, fried variant is called *guotie*. Early in the morning the locals fortify themselves with doughnuts and soya-milk from a take-away shop, and late at night with a highly nutritious soup of *doufu* (soya-bean curd). The thought of a Mongolian lamb stew with sweet garlic leads you unhesitatingly to East Baitasi Street, where several tiny establishments divide up the trade between them.
Delights for the eye and the taste-buds are offered by "food alleys", which are reviving an old tradition. The stalls are not set up until the evening, but in no time at all a crowd has gathered, shouting for boiled prawns, doughnuts, kebabs, *Hundun* soup or sweet-and-sour spare-ribs.

Restaurants:

Peking duck: **Quanjude – Beijing Roast Duck Restaurant** ("Super duck"), Hepingmen, Tel. 6301 8833. **Beijing Kaoyadian** ("The Peking Duck"), Tuanjiehu-Beikou. **Pianyifang Roast Duck Restaurant**, 2 Chongwenmenwai Lu, Tel. 6705 0505 and 73 Tiantan Donglu, Tel. 6705 6904.
Shandong Cuisine: **Beijing Fengzeyuan Restaurant**, Xingfu Sancun, Chaoyang District, Tel. 6421 7508.

Lamb stew: Many small private restaurants in East Baitasi Street stay open until late at night; you will also find this speciality at: **Donglaishun Restaurant** (Mongolian), 16 Jinyu Hutong (only till 7.30 pm), Tel. 6505 0069. **Kaorou Ji** (Muslim cuisine, stews and roast lamb), 14 Qianhai Dongyan, Tel. 6404 5921. **Duyichushao Restaurant**, 36 Qianmen Dajie, Tel. 6511 2093.

Vegetarian: **Gongdelin Vegetarian Restaurant**, 158 Qianmen Lu, Tel. 6511 2542. **Beijing Vegetarian Restaurant** (Zhengsuzhai), 74 Xuanwumennei Lu, Tel. 6605 3181.

Exquisite specialities: **Fangshan Restaurant** (in Beihai Park), 1 Wenjin Jie, Tel. 6401 1879. **Tingliguan Restaurant** (imperial cuisine in the old walls of the Summer Palace), Tel. 6258 1955.

Speciality alleys, night markets: **Donganmen Street** (leading off Wangfujing Lu). Other markets outside Great Wall Hotel; along the street from the Jianguo to the Jinglun Hotel; outside the Grand Hotel; outside the Minzu Hotel; in the Shichahai quarter, north of Beihai Park; around the Bell and Drum Towers.

Sichuan cuisine: **Sichuan Restaurant** (in the former Prince's Palace; good smoked duck and *mapo doufu*, highly spiced beancurd), 51 Rongxian Hutong, Tel. 6605 6348. **Ritan Restaurant** in Ritan Park, Tel. 6500 5939. **Yuan Tai Restaurant** in the Great Wall Hotel (rotating restaurant on the roof; expensive but excellent).

Cantonese cuisine: **Dasanyuan Restaurant** (very unusual menu: even snake and tortoise are served), 50 Jingshan Xijie, Tel. 6401 3920. Good Cantonese cooking is offered by the restaurants in most international hotels.

Recommended private restaurants: **Mamacai Restaurant** (Beijing cuisine), 134 Xijiaominxiang Lu, Tel. 6601 1138. **Deli-Restaurant** (Cantonese cusine), 37 Beixiaojie, Tel. 6401 4044. **Sichuan Restaurant**, 18 North Dongsanhuan Lu, Tel. 6502 2074.

Evenings out

A list of events can be found in the English-language newspaper *China Daily*. The simplest way to get tickets for the **Peking Opera** is to ask your hotel to do it for you. You can be sure of some eccentric entertainment at a *Karaoke* evening of Chinese revolutionary songs – the call for the reintroduction of "folk tradition" gave birth to this peculiar art-form. The Beijing Acrobatic Troupe usually performs at the **Chaoyang Theater**.

Night bars: Among the hotel bars we recommend the one where resident foreigners like to meet: **Charly's Bar** in the Jianguo Hotel. Even Beijing's *jeunesse dorée* foregathers in hotel bars.

Private bars: Privately run night bars offer an international selection of drinks and a revealing insight into the Peking scene. **AQ Bar**, 30 Xinzhong-Lu, Tel. 65015992. **Mexican Wave Bar**, Guanghua Lu, Tel. 6506 3961. **Frank's Place**, 7 West Building, Sanlitun Lu, Tel. 6507 2617.

Discothèques: **Rumours** in the Palace Hotel (*New-wave* music, mixed young clientele). **Xanadu** in the Shangrila Hotel. **Glass House Discotheque** in the Kunlun Hotel, 2 Xinyuan Nanlu.

Shopping suggestions

Friendship Store, 17 Jianguomenwai Dajie and on Kempinski Hotel. **Yuanlong department store**, 55 Tiantan Street, **Huaxia Arts and Crafts Store**, 12 Chongwenmennei Dajie. **Beijing Antique Store**, 64 East Liulichang. **China Arts and Crafts**, 200 Wangfujing Dajie. **Beijing Foreign Language Bookstore**, 235 Wangfujing Dajie. **Beijing Hongshen Musical Instruments**, 225 Wangfujing Dajie. **Beijing Marco Polo Carpet Store**, 1 Jianguomenwai Dajie. **Sales department of the Beijing Theatrical Costume Factory**, 130 Qianmen Dajie. **Bichun Tea Shop**, 142 Wangfujing Dajie. **New World Silk Shop**, 118 Wangfujing Dajie. **Rong Bao Zhai Studio** (Artists' materials and woodblock prints), 19 Liulichang Xijie. **Wangfujing Bookshop**, 214 Wangfujing Dajie. **Chaowai Antiques Market**, south of Chaoyanmenwai Lu **Jingsong Market**, Dongsanhuan Nanlu. **Carpet Factory No 1** (has a large sales department): Xiaoguan, Andingmenwai, Tel. 6422 4331.

Taxi

Peking Taxi Co., Tel. 6832 2301 and 6831 2288.

Theater and cinema

Beijing People's Theater (Renyi), 22 Wangfujing Dajie, Tel. 6513 5801. **Beijing International Club**, Jianguomenwai Dajie, Tel. 6532 2188. **Chaoyang Theater**, Dong Sanhuan Beilu 36, Tel. 6507 2421.

Beijing Operahouse and Ballet, 2 Nanhua Dongjie, **Haidian Theater and Cinema**, 84 Haidian Lu., Tel. 6255 5898.

Beijing Concert Hall, 1 Xianhua Jie, Liubukou, Tel. 6655 812.

Medical care

Emergency number for foreigners: (24 hours a day), Tel. 6513 0828.

Hospitals: **Beijing Emergency Medical Center**, 103 Qianmen Xidajie, Tel. 6601 3877. **International SOS Emergency**, Kunlun Hotel, Tel. 6600 3419.

THE FULCRUM OF CHINESE HISTORY

MANCHURIA (*DONGBEI*)
LIAONING
JILIN
HEILONGJIANG

MANCHURIA (*DONGBEI*)

Manchuria is in the northeastern part of China (dongbei); its heartland is the immense Manchurian plain, which continues the lowland plain of north China. Only a low watershed separates the southern part of the plain in the **Liaohe** catchment area, with its intensively cultivated farmland (chiefly producing soya, millet and wheat), from the northern part. The latter is densely forested with larch, pine, maple, birch and willow, and is drained by the **Nen** and **Sungari** rivers.

In the clefts of the mountains which border the plain to the south is a layer of coal deposits from the Carbon Age, a vast resource which is partially utilized through open-cast mining. The center of mining for hard coal lies in northeast Shenyang, close to the town of **Fushun**. Because the seams of coal are buried under a deep layer of oil-shale, oil extraction plants take their place alongside the coal excavators and massive slag-heaps in the local landscape. Of even greater importance are the deposits of ore in southwest Shenyang, which have made the town of **Anshan** the center of the Chinese iron and steel industry. The

Left: The Festival of Ice-lanterns in Qiqihar (Heilongjiang).

neighboring province of **Liaoning** has significant deposits of gold, zinc, lead, magnetite and bauxite, which have contributed to southern Manchuria's development into China's largest industrial region. The natural wealth of Manchuria – forests in the north, agricultural land in the center and minerals in the south – makes it easy to understand why in recent history both Russia and Japan have coveted this territory.

In prehistoric times, the harsh climate of the area kept the population sparse; the first settlers were nomadic Manchu tribes belonging to the Jürchen (Alguqu) group. In the 16th century, the nomadic tribes were politically unified under the leadership of the tribal chieftain Nurhaci; in 1616, this leader proclaimed an independent Manchurian empire. Following the precedent set by the Kitan and the Mongols, he announced his claim to the Chinese imperial throne and invaded China. In 1664 he succeeded in establishing Manchu rule there under the name of the Qing dynasty, which was China's last imperial dynasty, surviving until the republic was founded in 1911.

Manchuria did not begin to open up to Chinese settlement on a large scale until the 19th century, in response to the expansionist incursions of tsarist Russia. Initially, Manchuria was occupied for the

purpose of building a railroad link with the ice-free port of Lüshun, formerly Port Arthur, at the southern tip of the Liaodong peninsula. This project attracted the attention of neighboring Japan, which was rapidly industrializing and largely without its own natural resources. Japan's designs on Manchuria came to a head in the Russo-Japanese War of 1904-1905, which led to the region's being partitioned into Northern and Southern Manchuria. After the collapse of the Manchu (Qing) dynasty in 1911, Manchuria became independent under military rule. The policy of the military governor, aimed at resisting Japanese claims, provoked that ambitious and power-hungry nation. Japan occupied Manchuria in 1931, and established the puppet state of Manchukuo in 1937. Japanese sovereignty, which was given spurious legitimacy by the installation of Pu Yi, the "last Emperor of China," as

Above: The Manchurian imperial palace in Shenyang (Liaoning).

puppet ruler, lasted until the end of the Second World War in 1945. During this period, and entirely for the benefit of Japan, the Manchurian economy boomed as never before.

LIAONING
China's smokestack region

The province of **Liaoning** (meaning "pacified Liao territory") is the smallest of the three northeastern provinces, with an area of 58,000 sq. miles (151,000 sq. km), but it has the highest population density. It stretches in a horseshoe shape around the Bay of Laodong and the Yellow Sea. Roughly a quarter of the province consists of the fertile, heavily cultivated central plain beside the Liao River. Because of its southerly situation and maritime aspect (it has over 1000 miles / 1650 km of coastline), it enjoys the best climate in Manchuria.

The most beautiful place in Liaoning, and indeed the whole of Manchuria, is **Shenyang** (once known as Mukden and

Fengtian), the home of the Manchu emperors. With their arrival in the 17th century, the city, which had been a market center for cattle-breeders since the Middle Ages, entered a period of true historic significance. In 1625, the Manchu proclaimed Shenyang as their royal capital and began to enlarge it according to Chinese principles of city planning and fortress-building. In 1632, the city walls and fortifications were built, followed by the royal palace in 1636. Apart from the Forbidden City in Peking, the Manchurian **Imperial Palace** (*gu gong*) is China's only remaining imperial residence, and reflects the formal organization of the Manchu army. The Imperial City stood in the center of the rectangular residential city of Mukden. It is divided into two main sections: the palace area with its exquisite throne room and accommodation for Nurhaci's elite army units, and then the ruler's own residence with a spacious front courtyard, state reception rooms and private apartments. The unmistakable cultural influences of China, Mongolia and the nomadic Manchu are clearly evident in the different architectural styles and the decor and furnishings of the buildings, today a museum. In the **Dazheng state hall**, business was transacted and harvest rituals performed. Bright red pillars support the double roof with its yellow ceramic tiles. The hall stands at the head of a marble staircase and is surrounded by an artistically carved stone balustrade. The **Chongzheng hall**, where the military were quartered, also has a roof of ceramic tiles. Two pillars are decorated with dragons.

The only tangible reminder of the former rectangular residential city, which is just over half a square mile in area (1.5 sq.km) and forms the core of the inner city, is the checkerboard layout of the streets. Prominent among numerous former religious and official buildings were the **Drum Tower** and the **Bell Tower**,

which still stand today as historic monuments at the two northern intersections on the main thoroughfare.

As the Manchu had adopted the entire administrative system of the Chinese, Shenyang developed into a sophisticated military and government center. The newer settlements on the outskirts of the city were enclosed in 1681 by a circular earth rampart, within which lay the rectangular fortress of the inner city. According to the rules of Chinese geomancy (*feng shui*), Shenyang was laid out on a plain sloping slightly southwards, protected to the north by mountains and bordered to the south by the waters of the Hunhe.

The two imposing **tomb complexes** in the northeast and northwest of the city, which now form attractive parks in the outer residential area of the modern city, had a special significance. The **East Tomb** (*dong ling* or *fu ling*) is the resting place of Nurhaci, founder of the Qing Dynasty. The **North Tomb** (*bei ling* or *zhao ling*) holds the remains of his son

65

Abahai, father of the first Manchu emperor of China (1627-1643). This extensive burial complex, built in the style of the Chinese Ming tombs, is adorned with wooded parkland, lakes and pavilions; it was a place of pilgrimage for the Manchu emperors and a center of Confucian ancestor-worship until it fell into decay in the 19th century with the decline of the Qing dynasty.

Intent on creating a new and greater Chinese empire, Abahai had already forged close links with Tibet in 1640 and introduced Tibetan Buddhism to China. The emissaries from Lhasa stayed in the **Lama monastery**, near the North Tomb.

Zhongshan Street, which runs from east to west, is now the main traffic artery. It connects the historic inner city with the main railroad station, opened in 1903. This massive brick building is

Above: Steam locomotive Zhu De in Harbin (Heilongjiang). Right: Bridge over to North Korea near Dandong (Liaoning).

reminiscent of northern European architecture. Around the turn of the century Shenyang developed into one of the most modern cities in China, and was even linked to Europe through the Russian rail network. With Japanese intervention Shenyang became the center of the south Manchurian industrial belt, with a rail connection to the enlarged and modernized port of **Dairen** (today: **Dalian**). As the railroad had such a profound influence on the city's history, the Steam Locomotive Museum is worth a visit. In 1950, postwar reconstruction brought a fresh phase of development, though in the characterless, utilitarian style of Chinese socialism. Thirty miles (50 km) east of Shenyang lies the modern industrial city of **Fushun**, China's coalmining center. Its attractions include the prison in which Pu Yi, the deposed "last Emperor," was incarcerated by the People's Republic. On the **Gao'ershan**, north of the Hunhe, are the ruins of a 7th-century stronghold against the Koguryo empire of Korea.

From Shenyang, a road runs through the steel town of **Benxi** southeast, past impressive landscapes of limestone and chalk, to **Dandong** and the Korean border. From the hilltops of the town, situated above the estuary of the **Yalu River** (*yalu jiang*), there are stunning views across into North Korea. Northwest of Dandong, further up the Yalu, are a number of frontier towns which once played a key role in commerce between China and Korea. An important ruined city, dating from the time of the Koguryo empire, can be seen at **Fengchen** on the **Phoenix Hill** (*feng-huang shan*). It is surrounded by a stone wall 10 miles (16 km) in circumference.

To the south, the road leads from Shenyang to Liaoyang, 45 miles (73 km) away, where the impressive 12th-century **White Pagoda** (*bai ta*) recalls the age of Jürchen sovereignty (the Jin empire). About 17 miles (27 km) further south are the belching smokestacks of **Anshan**, home to China's largest steelworks and one million inhabitants. A guided tour of

the vast plant with its antiquated blast-furnaces and steam locomotives gives a vivid impression of what the Industrial Revolution must have been like.

After the heavily polluted environment of Anshan, you can breathe clean air in the **Park of a Thousand Hills**, 12 miles (20 km) to the east. This is an enchanting granite landscape of rocky gorges, springs, pine woods and paths leading to temples, pavilions and scenic overlooks.

At the southern end of the Liaodong peninsula lies **Lüda/Dalian** (formerly Dairen) and the naval base of **Lüshun**, China's third largest port, which was in Soviet possession until 1954. Dalian is well known these days not only for its industry (locomotive building and petrochemicals) but also for its fine sandy beaches and as the gateway to Shandong. Bangchui Island, Tiger Beach, Xinghai Park and Xiuyue Park are some of Dalian's most popular recreation spots.

From Dalian you can catch a bus to the **Valley of Bingyu** (a tributary of the Zhuanghe). Lying 124 miles (200 km) to

67

the northeast, it is famous for its peaceful, unspoilt forests.

JILIN
The heart of Manchuria

With an area of 72,000 sq. miles (187,000 sq. km), **Jilin** (called Kirin by the Japanese) forms the central region of Manchuria. The provincial capital of **Changchun** ("Eternal Spring") lies deep in Jilin's broad fertile plain, close to the watershed between the Sungari and Liao rivers in the Manchurian heartland. Changchun's land was originally pasture owned by a Mongolian chieftain who in 1791 was allowed by the imperial court to establish a settlement of Chinese emigrants. Until the turn of the century, Changchun was no more than a local market town. But in 1906 it was chosen to be the northern frontier town of Japanese-controlled Manchuria, and the construction of a "railroad town" began.

With the Japanese takeover of the whole of Manchuria in 1931, the town grew into the *xinjing* ("New Capital City") and the seat of the Chinese quisling government of Manchukuo. Xinjing (Changchun) was laid out in grandiose style as a modern city, with Japanese colonial-style public buildings predominating. Xinjing was to be elevated to the status of political and cultural center of Manchukuo, while industry was to be promoted in other large cities.

After the devastation brought by the invading Soviet troops at the end of the Second World War, Changchun was reconstructed in drab socialist style as an industrial city (automobiles, wood processing, and film production). The wide streets and many parks, however, remained; the largest park, *nanhu gongyuan*, lies along **South Lake**, to the south of the city. Between the train station and the **City Park** (*shengli gongyuan*) are attractive brick apartment blocks, constructed under the Japanese regime, which have an almost European look to them. The area above the "Imperial Palace," where you will see houses from the original Chinese period, is also delightful; the vibrant life of its market constrasts vividly with with the dullness of the planned city. However, the latter contains the very revealing **Museum of Mining** (near the People's Park) and the rather sad-looking **"Imperial Palace,"** the official residence of PuYi, which was used as the set for Bertolucci's film *The Last Emperor*. The **Film City**, with its special effects studio, prop store and the "Palace" of Emperor Pu Yi, can sometimes be visited with a CITS guide.

The chemical industry center bearing the name of the province, **Jilin**, lies 76 miles (123 km) east of Changchun. Like Harbin, Jilin has a festival of lanterns sculpted from ice, one of the town's few attractions – which, of course, melt away in the spring. The attractive **Lake Songhua** with its picturesque holiday area lies only 9 miles (14 km) southeast of Jilin; on the eastern shore of the lake is **Longtanshan Park**, with breeding grounds for sika deer and mink, as well as ginseng plantations.

The province of Jilin is most thinly populated in the east, where the autonomous Korean territory of **Yanbian** is situated. This stretches over the thickly wooded volcanic mountains of **Changbaishan**, which reach their highest point in the 9000 ft (2750 m) **Mt Baitoushan**. With its beautiful crater lake, the **Lake of Heaven** (*tian chi*) and its generally snow-capped summit, Baitoushan – meaning "mountain of the frontier" – is regarded by the Koreans as the most sacred of their mountains. The Changbaishan are splendid for hunting and hiking. To reach it from the southwest, you pass through **Tonghua**, capital of the province of the same name and center of Manchuria's

Right: Second-hand market in Harbin (Heilongjiang).

wine-growing region. From there the road goes via Fusong in a wide arc to reach the eastern slopes of the Changbai mountains and the Lake of Heaven, idyllic landscapes which also contain a number of different accommodations CK.

Continuing southwest from here along the North Korean border and across the **Laoling** mountain range, whose slopes are covered with fields of ginseng, you reach the frontier city of **Ji'an**, lying in the fertile flood-plain of the Yalu River. During the partition of the Chinese empire in the 3rd and 4th centuries, the northern Korean empire of Koguryo developed into a powerful state. The ancient city of Ji'an lies in the triangle formed by the Tongou river flowing into the Yalu. It resembles a well-tended Siberian garden-city, and one can still make out the ramparts of the former royal residence (*guonei cheng*, in Korean: *kungnae song*), once the center of government of Koguryo. The 20-foot-high (6 m) square stela, a monument to Yongle, the nineteenth king (posthumously named Guangkaitu/Kwanggaet'o), recalls the heyday of this city. It stands 3 miles (5 km) northeast of the city; at one time Korean kings and distinguished citizens of Ji'an were buried here.

A number of interesting tombs have been preserved, including the huge pyramid-shaped tomb of King Yongle and a general's tomb which resembles an Aztec ziggurat. Both of these probably date from the early 5th century, as does the **Tomb of Dances** (*wuyong mu*), in whose square burial chamber there are enchanting murals depicting genre scenes. The **Tomb of the Five Helmets**, No 5, is from the late Koguryo period and consists of two burial mounds built of granite and shaped like helmets (hence the name). The murals in the burial chambers depict animal motifs. Because of its well-preserved murals depicting scenes from the daily life of Korean society, the **Tongou Tomb** (No 12) is a valuable document for sociologists and art historians.

A mile and a quarter (2 km) above the river Tongou, the mountain fortress of

Hunducheng (*hwando song*) stands guard on a hillside terrace. Built in the year 3 AD, this strategically important building served as a refuge for the ruler from 299 AD on. The mountain fortress of **Guanma Shanncheng**, in a valley 22 miles (35 km) further to the northeast, was an important outpost controlling movement between the north and south of Koguryo.

HEILONGJIANG
China's Far North

Named after Manchuria's largest river (the Heilongjiang or Amur) and occupying more than half of Manchuria, China's most northerly province is unmistakably close to Siberia. Short, warm summers are followed by long severe winters, which freeze the waters for six months, and the earth all the year round in the very north.

Above: A winter's day in Harbin (Province of Heilongjiang).

70

More reminiscent of a czarist Russian city than a Chinese one, **Harbin**, its capital, lies on the south bank of the middle Sungari river, only a few hours from Changchun by rail. It grew up on the site of a tiny fishing village, as a junction on the Trans-Siberian Railway. After the October Revolution, Harbin became a haven for tsarist refugees and grew to have the largest Russian population of any city outside Russia. The city's favorite meeting place is, ironically, the Stalin Park, on the bank of the river where in winter the ice-festival takes place.

Here, as elsewhere, the ice-lantern celebration is a great attraction: enchanting figures from Chinese history and legend, flowers, lanterns and pavilions are skillfully fashioned from blocks of ice and lit up from inside.

Sun Island Park (*taiyangdao gongyuan*), an attractive holiday resort, complete with sanatoria, serving the city and the region, is situated opposite on the north bank of the Sungari. It is also worth taking a look at the **Children's Park** (*er-tong gongyuan*), east of the main station, where since 1956 a children's railroad has served the two stations of "Harbin" and "Beijing."

Walking through the contrasting neighborhoods of this city reminds one that it grew up under different periods of foreign rule. There's the port and industrial zone on the right bank of the river; a Russian-style commercial quarter, characterized by the distinctive soaring onion domes of Russian Orthodox churches; a residential district, which is very Japanese in character; and the administrative district.

A **Confucian temple** (*wen miao*; 1926) and the Buddhist **Jile Temple** (1924) are reminders of the more recent Chinese presence in the city. After the Second World War, they expanded it with drab, utilitarian buildings, and developed it into the economic hub of the province.

Bus Nr 338 brings you to the **Japanese concentration-camp** (Germ Warfare Experimental Base, *riben xijun shiyan jidi*). After 1939, the Japanese occupiers of Manchuria ruthlessly carried out medical experiments on Chinese and European prisoners-of-war; 4,000 of them died as a result.

Northwest of Harbin, beyond the town of Anda on the way to Qiqihar, are the oilfields of **Daqing**. During the Cultural Revolution, these were regarded as a model for China's industrial progress: "Learn from Daqing!" was the slogan.

Among the places worth visiting north-west of Daqing are the **nature reserves** of **Zhalong** near Qiqihar (approx. 80 miles / 130 km) and **Wudalianchi** near Nenjiang (approx. 224 miles / 360 km). In the east of the province is the holiday area around China's largest crater lake, the **Mirror Lake** (*jingbo hu*), which lies 68 miles (110 km) south of **Mudangjiang**; this in turn is 197 miles (317 km) east of Harbin.

LIAONING
Getting there
Express trains connect the capital, Shenyang, with Beijing, Russia (Trans-Siberia) and the North Korean border; you can fly to Shenyang from Beijing and other major Chinese cities.

Accommodation in Shenyang
LUXURY: **New World**, Nanjing Nanlu, Tel. 386 9888. **Phoenix Hotel** (*fenghuang fandian*), 113 Huanghe Nandajie, Tel. 684 6505.
MID-PRICE: **Huasha Hotel** (*huasha fandian*), 5 Zhongshan Lu, Tel. 273 5170. **Liaoning Guesthouse** (*liaoning binguan*), 97 Zhongshan Lu, Tel. 383 9166.
BUDGET: **Dongbei Hotel** (*dongbei fandian*), No 1 Qi Li, Section 3, Taiyuan Jie, Tel. 383 2031.

Tourist information
CITS, 113 Huanghe Nandajie, Tel. 684 6037.
Hotline: 684 6450.

JILIN
Getting there
The capital, Changchun, is an important transport hub, with connections similar to those of Shenyang.

Accommodation in Changchun
LUXURY: **Changbaishan Hotel** (*changbai shan binguan*), 12 Xinmin Dajie, Tel. 898 3551. **Nanhu Guesthouse** (*nanhu binguan*), 2 Nanhu Lu, Tel. 8983571.
MID-PRICE: **Changchun Hotel** (*changchun binguan*), 10 Xinhua Lu, Tel. 892 9920. **Jixiang Hotel** (*jixiang dajiudian*), 80 Jiefang Da Lu, Tel. 892 9246.

Tourist information
CITS in the Changbaishan Hotel, Tel. 898 2401.
Hotline: 890 9246.

HEILONGJIANG
Getting there
The capital, Harbin, the third of north-east China's major railroad junctions, is also a significant stopover on the Trans-Siberian, and has an international airport with flights to Moscow and Europe.

Accommodation in Harbin
MID-PRICE: **Friendship Palace** (*youyigong binguan*), 57 Youyigong Lu, Tel. 461 6146. **Modern Hotel** (*madie'er binguan*), 129 Zhongyang Dajie, Tel. 461 5846. **International Hotel** (*guoji fandian*), 124 Dazhi Jie, Tel. 364 1441. **Swan Hotel** (*tian'e fandian*), 73 Zhongshan Lu, Tel. 262 4041. **The Milky Way**, 230 Zhongshan Lu, Tel. 262 0707.

Tourist information
CITS is located in the grounds of the Swan Hotel (see above), Tel. 264 1020.

ON THE SHORE OF
THE YELLOW SEA

HEBEI

TIANJIN

SHANDONG

JIANGSU

THE YELLOW SEA

The **Yellow Sea** (*huang hai*) is a broad and very shallow inlet of the Pacific Ocean, with an average depth of between 150 ft (45 m) and 350 ft (100 m). It measures 400 miles (650 km) from east to west and 600 miles (1000 km) from north to south. To the north and west it is bounded by the Chinese mainland and to the east by the Korean peninsula. It stretches southwards as far as the Yangtse estuary and then merges with the **East China Sea** (*dong hai*, "east sea"). In the northwest the Liaoning and Shandong peninsulas enclose the **Gulf of Bohai**. The sea is named for the color of its water, muddied by the huge quantities of sediment from the Yellow River. The relatively young Yellow Sea was created at the end of the last Ice Age, some 11,000 years ago, when the melting ice-cap raised the sea-level. It is rich in fish, while its oil-reserves are now being exploited by offshore drilling.

With the exception of the south coast of Shandong the Chinese coast of the Yellow Sea is remarkably straight. In this it differs from the coasts of the East and South China Seas. The coastal provinces of Hebei, Shandong and Jiangsu, as well

Left: A junk in the port of Shanghai.

as the urban regions of Tianjin and Shanghai (which are directly administered by the central government in Beijing), are all situated between the mouth of the **Yangtse** and China's historic north-eastern frontier in Manchuria, where the Great Wall begins at **Shanghaiguan**.

HEBEI
The land north of the He

Between the Yellow River in the south and the Mongolian highlands in the north, the province of Hebei, with an area of more than 73,000 sq. miles (190,000 sq. km), covers the densely populated North Chinese plain and the hilly country around Beijing, with its rich deposits of iron ore and coal. The **lowland plain of Hebei** was created by alluvium from the **Yellow River** and the rivers feeding the **Haihe**, which flows into the Gulf of Bohai in the Tianjin area. To the north of the plain the peaks of the **Yanshan** ("swallow mountains") surmounted by the zigzag of the Great Wall, form a clear frontier. The **Taihangshan** mountains mark the western edge of the plain, which is linked by narrow valleys to the Shanxi highlands and then drops away eastward to the sea.

From Shanxi the rivers, flowing only during the hot rainy summers, wash their

PROVINCES ON
THE YELLOW SEA
0   100km

the rainless winter months, most river beds are dry. The major waterways, and even the sea along the coast, freeze over at this time of year.

The region is also threatened by severe earthquakes caused by the collision of the two mountain ranges of the Yanshan and Taihangshan, as well as the inward pressure of the Gulf of Bohai. The violent earthquake of 1976 killed nearly a million people and flattened Tangshan, the largest city in the province, to the ground. With its heavy industry, the city, situated northeast of Beijing, had been built up into a showplace during the Cultural Revolution.

Shijiazhuang

Ever since the two cities of Beijing and Tianjin were made into separate administrative entities, Shijiazhuang has been the provincial capital of Hebei.

After being linked with the rail network in 1905, this once remote market town grew into an important railroad junction. This boosted its economic development, which, after the Second World War, turned into an industrial boom. The chemical industry (fertilizers) and textile manufacturing owe their prosperity to the coal reserves in nearby Huolo and Jingxing, which have been incorporated into the administrative district of Shijiazhuang.

This drab industrial city and former showpiece of the Cultural Revolution has a monument honoring the grave of Norman Bethune (1890-1939), the Communist idealist from Canada, who served as a doctor in the famous Seventh Infantry Army during the Chinese civil war. Some 25 miles (40 km) to the west in the Pingshan district is Xibaipo, where Mao Zedong, Chou Enlai and Zhu De established their temporary headquarters in 1947-1948.

Other excursions from Shijiazhuang lead westwards to the mountains of Tai-

heavy load of sediment down to the plain which, for that very reason, is prone to flooding. Since time immemorial the people of Hebei have feared the twin scourges of drought and flood which they endeavor to mitigate with large-scale flood prevention schemes, soil conservation and afforestation.

In recent decades, numerous dams have been constructed where the rivers flow into the plain, as well as with reservoirs on their lower reaches. At the same time, new canals were built to divert water to the sea. The **Dulin Jianhe** is one of these. By diverting the water of the river Daqing, it prevents the marshland of the Wen'an from turning into a swamp and the Haihe from flooding near Tianjin.

The **Machang Jianhe** connects the Imperial Canal at Machang with the estuary of the Haihe, and feeds a network of canals whose waters wash the heavy salt content out of the soil and help transform it into fertile farming land. During

Right: Maize harvest in Hebei.

hangshan and the beautiful valley near the historic frontier town of **Jingxing**. It was here that a guard was kept on the road to Taiyuan in the Shanxi highlands. About 16 miles (25 km) further southeast you reach the **Hanging Pavilion of Canyangshan**. A steep path leads up to this 6th-century building, with its uniquely constructed double roof, built on an arched bridge over a ravine about 200 ft (60 m) deep. Once, pilgrims journeying to the many mountain temples in the area used it for overnight lodging.

Southeast of Shijiazhuang near Zhao Xian, you will find one of the "Four Wonders" of Hebei: the **Zhaozhou Bridge**. This was built to span the river Jiao at the beginning of the 7th century, under the Sui dynasty and at the time of the second unification of the empire. Dragons and other mythical figures embellish its stone arches. The bridge is 55 yds (50 m) long and 32 ft (9.6 m) wide; it blends perfectly with its natural surroundings and is considered a masterpiece of early engineering.

Since freight, in northern China, is carried by road rather than on waterways, the bridges are not arched but flat, and are built strongly enough to withstand the summer floods.

The second "Wonder" of Hebei, the **Longxing monastery**, is situated 6 miles (10 km) north of Shijiazhuang in Zhengding. The following halls should be seen: the Hall of the Turning Library, the Maitreya Hall, the Amitabha Hall and the main hall (*dabei ge*), with its famous 62 ft (19 m) high **bronze statue of Bodhisattva Guanyin**. The third "Hebei Wonder" is in the east of the province, 11 miles (18 km) southwest of Langzhou on the Imperial Canal: an **iron statue of a lion**, in a walking position, over 16 ft (5 m) tall. Made in the 10th century, it is one of China's largest and oldest iron sculptures and was intended to carry a statue of the Goddess of Mercy (Guan-yin).

The **Pagoda of Dingzhou** (*liaodi ta* or *kaiyuansi ta*), considered the fourth "Wonder," lies halfway between Shijiazhuang and Baoding, near Ding Zhou

**SHIJIAZHUANG
AND SURROUNDINGS**

0   10   20   30km

(Ding Xian). It belonged to the Kaiyuan Temple and in the 11th century, when this was the frontier between the Song empire and that of the Liao in northern China, served as a watchtower. Rising to 262 ft (80 m), the 11-tiered pagoda is one of the tallest in China. Unlike other pagodas of its time, it is built of brick rather than wood. Its austerely elegant design makes it a masterpiece of Chinese architecture.

In the period of strife between empires (475- 221 BC) the city of **Handan** in the south of the province was the capital of the Zhao empire. The remains of **Zhaowangcheng** ("the city of the king of Zhao") can be seen in the southwest of the modern city, and in the northern district you will see a raised plot of land (*cong tai*, the "elevated terrace"). Here, around 400 BC, the Zhao ruler Wu Ling is thought to have built a fortress or a belvedere for use on ceremonial occasions.

Right: The palace-like Puning Temple in Chengde.

An attraction today is the **Congtai Park**, laid out in traditional garden style with an idyllic lake and an ancient fortress from which you can glimpse the mountains of Taihangshan. In the Song epoch (10th-11th c.) Handan was famous for its delicately glazed porcelain; today, this is produced in replica.

The trading center of **Zhangjiakou** (formerly Kalgan) lies in the northwest of Hebei on the Great Wall, halfway between Beijing and Inner Mongolia/North Shanxi. Once a caravanserai and stagepost for camel-trains from Mongolia, Tibet and the Silk Road, the town is still permeated with an air of the exotic, the "wide world." The 14th-century **Monastery of the Source of the Clouds** (*yungqan si*) offers views of the parched uplands and the town below.

Chengde – summer paradise of the Manchu emperors

In 1703, Kangxi, the most outstanding of the Manchu emperors, wishing to escape the oppressive heat of Beijing, ordered the construction of a summer palace in the northeast of Hebei, about 140 miles (230 km) from Beijing and close to some hot springs.

Set against a delightful backdrop of mountains, this luxurious **Mountain Refuge from Summer Heat** (*bishu shanzhuang*) is second only to Beijing's Imperial Palace in size and importance. Under the emperor Qianlong the Lamaistic **Eight Outer Temples** were built to the east and north of the Summer Palace. The most beautiful of these temples in Chinese, Tibetan and Mongolian styles is a copy of the Potala in Lhasa. The imperial residence lies north of the town of Chengde and is surrounded by a wall 16 miles (25 km) long. It includes a charming park, the imperial apartments, a library and even some temples that have survived. In the lowest hollow of the park is a lake; the **Front Palace** still stands on

its southern shore. You can reach this through the **Lizhen Gate**, the main gate in the outer wall; before it, the palace buildings are aligned along a north-south avenue. The islands in the lake are adorned with gracious villas and gardens in the South Chinese style, reminiscent of landscaped gardens in the warm southern lands of the Yangtse delta. East of the Summer Palace, beyond the Wuliehe river, stands the **Temple of Universal Goodness** (*puren si*) and next to it the partially preserved Tibetan **Temple of Universal Sincerity** (*pushen si*). A little further on you see the rotunda of the **Temple of Universal Joy** (*pule si*), which resembles the Altar of Heaven in Beijing. From here a path leads to the idyllic **Hammer Summit** (*bangchui shan*), whose needle-like shape suggests a column holding up the sky. Next, further north, you come to the buildings that make up the **Temple of Distant Peace** (*anyuan miao*), whose name refers to the pacification of the Dzungares, a Mongol people who captured Lhasa in 1717.

There are even more beautiful temples to the north of the imperial residence. The **Putuo Temple** (*putuo zongsheng miao*, or "Potaraka Temple") is the most splendidly proportioned monastic building in Chengde, harmonizing perfectly with its lush, green valley setting. The walled group of buildings, whose name means "Little Potala," was built between 1767-71, on 54 acres (22 ha) of land, to serve as guest accommodation for visitors from Tibet, Sinkiang and Mongolia. With its many guesthouses, pavilions, gates and the main palace at its highest point, on the north side, it mirrors the style of a Tibetan monastery. Built like a fortress, the "Potala" is a hallmark of the Summer Residence, and illustrates the political and religious links between the Manchu rulers and Tibet.

The **Puning Temple** (*puning si*), built in a mixture of Chinese and Tibetan styles, resembles an imperial residence and stands on the slope of a hill at the northernmost point in Chengde. Also called the "Temple of the Giant Buddha,"

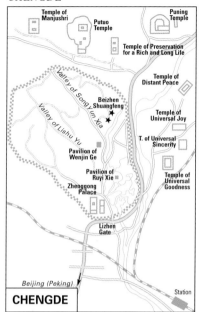

CHENGDE

Beijing (Peking)

Station

it was built to mark the victory of the emperor Qianlong over the Mongols and the unification of Mongolia with China. A **stele** inscribed in four languages (Chinese, Manchurian, Mongolian and Tibetan) commemorates this event. In the great **Mahayana Pavilion** (*dazhen ge*), in a commanding position to the north of the site, there is a towering, thousand-armed Guanyin Boddhisattva, more than 72 ft (22 m) high. It was carved from five species of conifer and weighs 110 tons.

East of the Potala you can see the **Temple of Preservation for a Rich and Long Life** (*xumi fushou miao*), which also imitates a Tibetan temple city. Built in honor of the sixth Panchen Lama, its gilded bronze roof decoration is typically Tibetan. The **Temple of Manjushri** (*shuxiang si*) lies west of the Potala. It is dedicated to the *Buddha of Wisdom* and shows the influence of a temple in Xiang-shan near Beijing.

Right: Shanhaiguan (Hebei) – "The pass between mountain and sea."

78

The Manchu emperors' cities of the dead

The **Western Tombs** (*xi ling*) are located about 68 miles (110 km) southwest of Beijing in the Yi Xian district. Resembling an imperial palace-city, the extensive complex is enclosed by a wall 16 miles (25 km) long. It contains the tombs and commemorative pavilions of the Manchu emperors Yongzheng (1723-1736), Jiaqing (1796-1821), Daoguang (1821-1851), and Guangxu (1875-1908).

The necropolis of the **Eastern Tombs** (*dong ling*) is even more crowded: five emperors, 14 emperors' wives and 136 concubines were laid to rest here. Dongling is 81 miles (130 km) east of Beijing, near the town of Malanyu. Like an immense residential palace, the necropolis spreads over the plain beneath the foothills of the **Yanshan** ("swallow mountains"). It was predominantly the early Manchu emperors who were buried in the 13 separate walled tomb complexes with their associated stelae, ceremonial halls, burial mound and subterranean palace. (See map of *xi ling* and *dong ling*, p. 57)

Shanhaiguan
"The Pass 'twixt Mountain and Sea"

For more than 25 miles (40 km) on the east side of Hebei, the Great Wall marks the boundary with the province of Liaoning. It reaches the sea near **Shanhaiguan**, situated since antiquity on the main route from northern China into Manchuria. After the second unification of the empire under the Sui dynasty in the 6th century, this strategically important outpost was expanded; in 618 AD, the year in which the Tang dynasty came to power, it was reinforced with a gated fortress (*yu guan*), often the scene of fierce fighting. The present gate, known as the **First Pass in the Empire** (*tianxia diyi guan*), on the main road through the walled inner city, was built in 1381 in the course

of the extension of the Great Wall, at the beginning of the Ming dynasty. The Wall once ran all the way to the sea, 2 1/2 miles (4 km) away at the beach of **Laolongtou** ("Old Dragon's Head"); a dragon's head stood here to symbolize the defence of the empire.

The ice-free oil port of Qinhuangdao and the nearby bathing-beach of **Beidaihe-Haibin** are about 9 miles (15 km) south of Shanhaiguan. There are good bus connections to the seaside resort of **Beidaihe**, from where you can walk to the **Seaview Pavilion** (*wanhai ting*) in the Liangfengshan Park, and the **Dove's Nest Park** (*geziwo gongyuan*).

TIANJIN
The Ford of Heaven

The city of **Tianjin** (known historically as Tientsin), with its 9 million inhabitants, is just 93 miles (150 km) from Beijing – three hours by train. It lies at the confluence of the Yongdinghe (the northern section of the Imperial Canal) and the Ziyahe, whose waters feed the both Imperial Canal and the Haihe river. It is the capital of the urban district of Tianjin, which ranks as a province. This highly developed industrial area extends from the dry plains around Beijing to the swamps, marshes and salt-beds bordering the Gulf of Bohai. After the silting up of the harbor of the old city of Tientsin a new one was constructed at Xingang on the Haihe estuary. During the 19th century it grew to be China's largest port; it also became a gateway for the entrance of the western powers, and a forced loading-station from which they shipped out Northern China's mineral wealth for their own ends. Since 1979 it has been able to take container ships of up to 40,000 tons.

After the signing of the Treaty of Tientsin, the way was clear for the establishment of foreign territorial concessions and therefore China's being opening up to foreign trade, including the importation of opium. Tientsin became a European colonial city, just like Shanghai and Canton. Beside the English and

French there were Germans, Austrians, Belgians, Italians, Japanese and Russians living outside the old Chinese city, which lay between the Imperial Canal (southern section) and the Haihe river, and whose walls were pulled down in 1900 during the Boxer Rebellion. Each nation endowed its district with its own institutions and the trappings of sovereignty. Pu Yi, the "last emperor," spent seven years in the territory leased by the Japanese before they appointed him to be puppet ruler of Manchukuo. The former Chinatown, with its picturesque alleyways, markets and traditional little houses, bounded by **North**, **South**, **East** and **West Streets** (*beima lu, namma lu, xima lu, dongma lu*) is still recognizable from its rectangular outline within the modern city. The modern city centers around the **Binjiangdao**. This boulevard of stylish shops, once called *Rue de France* when it was the main thoroughfare of the French concession, leads to the Haihe, across **Liberation Bridge** (*jiefang qiao*, built by the French in 1903) and on to the main railroad station. The two other principal shopping streets, which start from the North Station (Zongsham Street) and the West Station (Dafeng/Beimalu), meet at the northeast corner of the Old City, from where they continue as Dongmalu and Hepingen. Immediately to the north, **Jiefanglu** crosses Tianjin's administrative district, which was formerly the hub of the British concession and the location of the Hotel Victoria (now the Tianjin) and the Astor House. Tianjin is rather like a museum of European architecture, with echoes of London, Paris, Rome and Vienna. Extensive new housing developments grew up on the edge of the city after the earthquake in 1976, which also shook Tianjin severely.

Excursions around Tianjin

The Tianjin region has three ports, Hangu, Tanggu and Dagang, which are kept open by ice-breakers in winter. In

Above: Inside a Tianjin department store.

the northern corner of the region, 75 miles (120 km) from Tianjin, is the district capital of Jixian with its **Dule Temple,** which in the 7th century was the stronghold of the rebel An Lushan. Not far away is **Panshan**, also known as "the eastern Wutaishan," one of the fifteen famous mountains of China. From here roads lead up to the Huangya Pass on the Great Wall and to the **Eastern Manchu Tombs** in Hebei province (see p. 78 and map on p. 57).

SHANDONG PROVINCE

The name *Shandong* means "east of the mountains," referring to the mountains of Shanxi and Henan. This province, with an area of 59,000 sq. miles (153,000 sq. km), covers the broad floodplain of the lower reaches of the Yellow River (*huang he*) and the central range of ancient mountains that juts out to form the Shandong peninsula. These mountains have always stood in the path of the Yellow River, forcing it to detour now to the north, now to the south. Since 1933 this "Sorrow of China" has returned to its original northerly course. In the notorious marshland of Liangshan – the setting for the classic novel *The Robbers of the Liangshan Marshes* – the river meets the Imperial Canal, swings north around the provincial capital of **Jinan** and branches out into a broad delta where it flows into the Gulf of Bohai. The Yellow River connects Shandong with the continental interior, while the peninsula, with its long, indented southern coastline, brings it to the sea. Shandong has the longest coast of any province in China – over 1800 miles (3000 km). The climate is influenced both by the damp, warm air of the summer monsoon and the icy winter winds from Siberia.

Before the unification of the empire, the early centers of power and the spiritual cradle of Chinese culture were in Shandong. Finds from China's oldest ar-

chaeological layer, the Longshanan Neolithic culture, indicate the age of the first settlements along the lower Huanghe. This site, between the Yellow River and Mt. Taishan, near Jinan, dates back to the beginning of the 3rd millennium BC, and has yielded rich discoveries of delicate ceramics, polished stone axes, oracle bones and clay walls. The extension of the Imperial Canal (*da yunhe*, "Great Transport Canal") northward to Peking gave Shandong a new importance, and trading towns grew up at Dezhou, Linqing, Liaocheng and Jining.

Jinan – city of springs

At the place where 72 springs gush forth from an ancient loess terrace near Luokou on the south bank of the Yellow River, the prosperous trading city of Jinan grew up in the 7th century. In the 14th century it became the political nerve-center of Shandong. In 1899, construction of a railway link to the city made it the province's transportation

hub; together with Qingdao, it was also a commercial center which eclipsed the old trading town of Dezhou on the Imperial Canal. The design of Jinan's **central railway station** is a reminder that German engineers and architects built the line from Qingdao to Jinan. From here you pass through the middle of the modern city westward to the **Old City**, once walled. On its north side, you find the inviting **Lake Daming Park** with its pavilions, temples, museums and public library. In the center of the Old City is the **Park of the Pearl Spring** (*zhenzhu quan*). The **Spring of the Black Tiger** (*heihu quan*) bubbles up in the southeast corner below the Jiefangge Terrace; in the southwest corner, you can see the Earth Fountain, the city's most impressive spring, which sends water spouting up to a height of 10 ft (3 m). In Batuquan Park there are further springs as well as a memorial pavilion and a small

Above: The designer of the central station in Jinan (Shandong) was German.

82

museum devoted to Li Qingzhao, China's most celebrated poetess, who was born here in the 11th century.

From the Old City the **Street of the Hill of a Thousand Buddhas** (*qianfoshan lu*) climbs southwards up to a park of the same name. During the Sui dynasty innumerable sculptures of the Buddha, paid for by pilgrims, were carved in the rock walls of caves.

Not far from Liubu, about 19 miles (30 km) further south, **the Pagoda of the Four Gates** (*simen ta*) is one of the oldest stone pagodas in China, dating from 544 AD. It, and the somewhat more recent **Dragon Tiger Pagoda** (*longhu ta*), are part of the **Shentong monastery**. This stands on the slopes of Mt Baihushan, below the **Rock of a Thousand Buddhas** (*qianfo yan*), whose rock caves contain over 200 figures of the Buddha.

From Wande, midway between Jinan and Tai'an, there is a track leading up to the **Temple of the Rock of Souls** (*lingyan si*). A large Buddhist monastery stood here in the Tang period, forming a sort of gateway to Mt Taishan. The abbots of the monastery are commemorated in more than 200 *stupas*. The slender, nine-tiered **Pizhita Pagoda,** dating from the Tang period (8th century AD), towers 177 ft (54 m) over the landscape. Delicately carved *luohan* statues (of Boddhisattva) maintain a silent vigil in the **Hall of a Thousand Buddhas** (*qianfo dian*). Take a look at the 423 **stone stelae** inscribed with quotations from famous poets and from the emperor Qianlong.

The Shandong railroad takes you from Jinan to the district capital of **Zibo,** a coal-mining center 62 miles (100 km) to the east. In a place called Linzhi, not far from here, archaeologists unearthed an **equestrian tomb** containing 600 skeletons and royal coaches from the state of Qi (contemporary with the eastern Zhou dynasty, about 2500 years old).

Tai'an, gateway to Taishan

The city of **Tai'an** is the gateway to the sacred mountain of **Taishan** (*dai shan*) the most important of China's five "Mountains of the Gods." This was the cradle of Taoism, China's oldest spiritual school. Founded by Laozi (Laotse, born around 600 BC), Taoism has had a lasting influence on the Chinese attitude to life. In the middle of Tai'an, surrounded by a grove of acacias, gingkos and cypresses, stands the **Taishan Temple** (*dai miao*), destination of many pilgrimages. The prominent **main hall** (*tian gong*) was built in 1009 AD, (Song dynasty), and has a double roof; inside, a mural over 200 ft (62 m) long shows the path up to the summit of Taishan.

For the steep climb to the summit middle or west routes are recommended. Ancient **stone stelae** mark the paths and there is a confusing plethora of bridges, arches, pavilions, temples and caves. Inscribed on the stelae are the imperial prayers beseeching the "Supreme Emperor of Heaven" (*shang di*, the Chinese

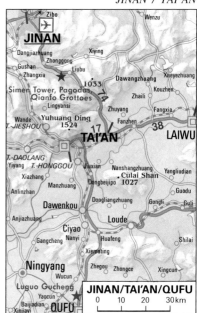

term nearest to "God"), to intercede and prevent earthquakes, floods and drought. The first group of buildings along the middle path is the **Temple of the Red Gate** (*hongmen gong*). Above it the **Gate-Tower of the Thousand Immortals** (*wanxian lou*) is followed by the **Temple to the Goddess of the Great She-Bear** (*doumou gong*), another Taoist temple that once served as a nunnery. From there you can reach the **Valley of the Stone Sutra** (*shiying yu*). The 6th-century *Diamond Sutra* (*jingang jing*) is inscribed on a rock face in perfectly formed characters. In the Ming period lines from the Confucian *Book of Great Learning* (*da xue*) were placed beneath it – a clear indication of the rivalry between the Buddhist and Confucian philosophies, which were now both taking their place beside Taoism. Continuing uphill you come to the **Tiger Heaven Pavilion** (*hutian ge*). Further up, at the **Bridge and Building on the Way to Heaven**, the path meets the western route; here, too, is the valley station of the cable-car

to the summit of Yueguan. After the **Bridge of Clouds** (*yunbu giao*), the **Little Tower of the Five Pines** (*wusong ting*) and the **Little Tower Facing the Pines** (*duisong ting*), steep steps lead up to the **Southern Gate of Heaven** (*nantian men*) on the ridge.

The climb continues to the **Summit of the Jade Emperor** (*yukuang ding*), Taishan's main peak, 5,000 ft (1524 m) high; or further, to the **Summit for the Comtemplation of the Sun**, from where you can enjoy the brilliant sunrises. The **Temple of the Clouds of Many Hues** (*bixia si*) from the Song period nestles at the foot of the two summits. It is consecrated to the daughter of the god Taishan and, from 1759 onwards, it was visited annually on the 18th day of the first month by emissaries of the emperor, who made sacrifices here to the Princess of Heaven.

Above: Temple of the Clouds of Many Hues on Taishan (Shandong). Right: Ceremony in the Confucius complex (Qufu).

Qufu – the city of Confucius

If you go 50 miles (80 km) south from Tai'an, through Yanzhou, you reach **Qufu**, the city of Confucius. Master Kong (Kongzi or Kung Fu-tse; 551-479 BC) was born in an era which later became known as the "Age of the Spring-Autumn Annals" (*chun qiu*), the title of one of the most important historical works. At that time, there was no longer a central royal authority in China; the land was divided into numerous independent states, each striving for supremacy. Like many other thinkers of the period, Confucius sought a philosophical basis for a centralized state. For 2000 years, his doctrines had a determining force on China's political, social and moral behavior, and they continue to influence Chinese thought. Thus, even today, the causes of social change are sought in the behavior of their leaders, who forfeit their authority if they fail.

Qufu, the town where Confucius, or Master Kong, was born and where he de-

veloped his ideas and influence, came to be an intellectual and spiritual shrine for China. Well into this century, the Kong family maintained a temple complex here (*kong miao*, "Confucius' temple"). Built only a year after the Master's death, the temple became the central point in the Qufu when the city was rebuilt in the 14th century. In the 16th century, it was fortified with a wall, and under the Qing Dynasty was enlarged to the size we see today. It was closed in 1948 and damaged during the Cultural Revolution. In 1979 its gates were opened once again.

The extensive residence of the Kong family resembles the Imperial Palace in Peking. China's most notable scholars and the descendents of Confucius lived in its 450-odd halls. The main building is the **Hall of Great Perfection** (*dacheng dian*), which, at a height of 105 ft (32 m), dwarfs the other temple buildings. The central temple precinct lies within a wall of its own, in the north of the complex of buildings and courtyards, and can be reached from the **South Main Gate**

(*lingxing men*). The complex is dotted with a profusion of gnarled, dwarf pines and cypresses; among them are more than 1000 stelae bearing inscriptions dating from the Han to the Qing dynasties. The final hall, also on the north side, is the **Hall of Sacred Documents** (*shenji dian*). It contains stone engravings from the Ming period depicting scenes from the life of Confucius. The **Street of the Drum Tower** (*gulou dajie*) leads northwards past the Yanhui temple and through the Wanguchangchun and Zishenglin gates to the **Forest of Confucius** (*kong lin*) outside the town. Hidden among some 20,000 pine and cypresses lies the modest burial mound of Kongzi himself.

Qingdao – China's Little Germany

The port and bay of **Jiaozhou** (Kiaochou) were for centuries an important destination for ships sailing to China and the major trading center for northern China. But due to a gradual rise in the

man colonial houses. For example, there are swimming beaches here, something you look for in vain in China's other big industrial cities. Behind the beaches rises **Laoshan** ("Old Mountain"), 3716 ft (1133 m) high. The mountain is the source of the famous Laoshan mineral water, a soft water which is supposed to be responsible for the fact that *Tsingtao* beer is known as the best in China. The mountain itself, a high granite massif, is an ideal destination for day-trippers; among its countless scenic and cultural attractions for walkers are the **Jiushui Waterfalls** and the Taoist **Taiqing Monastery**.

There is a rail connection across the peninsula to the port city of **Yantai** (formerly Zhifu) on the east coast, an embarkation point for ships to South Korea.

Further along the coast, 45 miles (73 km) west of Yantai, the legendary **Castle of Penglai** towers majestically on a rocky cliff. It commands a stunning view of the many islands in the Gulf of Bohai, which once formed a land-bridge to the present Liaoning peninsula. The first emperor of China set out from here in search of the Paradise Islands and the Herb of Immortality, which was eventually thought to be found in the ginseng root, a plant native to Manchuria and Korea.

The town of **Weifang**, halfway along the rail line from Penglai to Zibo, is said to be the home of Chinese dragons. It is true that there are impressive fossils to be seen near **Shanwang** and in the caves on **Mt Tuoshan**.

level of the coastline, the harbor silted up. Since 1860 its place has been taken by Yantai, on the north coast of the Shandong peninsula.

Soon thereafter, however, Jiaozhou again found itself in the spotlight of history. In 1895 the German imperial emissaries Admiral Tirpitz, G. Franzius, and Ferdinand von Richthofen, the great geographer of China, named the sheltered fishing port of **Qingdao** (Tsingtao) the new anchorage for the Imperial German navy and merchant marine. Two years later, Tsingtao was the administrative and commercial center of the German concession in Jiazhou. The building of a rail link in 1905 and the opening of coal mines in 1912 transformed Tsingtao into a flourishing port and commercial city until it was captured by the Japanese in 1914.

Qingdao today has more to offer the visitor than just the sight of its old Ger-

Above: The Catholic church in Qingdao (Shandong).

JIANGSU
The Netherlands of China

The province of Jiangsu, with an area of 39,000 sq. miles (102,000 sq. km), lies beside the Yellow Sea between Shandong, in the north, and the Yangtse delta to the south. It is named for two once-important prefectures, Jiangning (*jiang*, today, designates Nanjing) and Suzhou

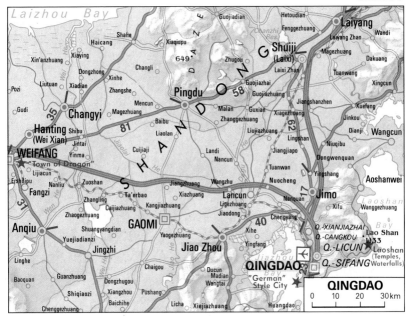

(*su*). The province extends over a large low-lying area between the Imperial Canal, the wide inland expanses of Lakes Hongzehu, Gaoyaohu and Taihu, and the flat, sandy sea coast. It is made up almost entirely of alluvial deposits from former branches of the Yellow River delta (the Xube or North Jiangsu), from the Huaihe and the Yangtse delta (Jiangnam or South Jiangsu), which for the past 2000 years have extended the coast an average distance of 30 miles (50 km) into the sea. A dense network of rivers and canals, interspersed with lakes, ponds and swamps, covers the alluvial plains which, for the most part, are no more than 130 ft (40 m) above sea level. The struggle to keep the sea at bay began in the 1950s with the construction of a system of dykes, drainage canals and polders – efforts which are comparable with the great achievements of Dutch hydraulic engineers.

The landscape around the **Great Lake** (*tai hu*), China's third largest lake, is especially notable as an example of this water-saturated region. There, roads and tracks have been replaced almost completely by man-made waterways, and nowhere are you more than 30 yards/m away from water.

The island mountains of the Yangtse delta, which give southern Jiangsu its unusual charm, soar up from the flat green carpet of the intensively cultivated rice-paddies and the roof of foliage of the mulberry plantations on which the silkworms feed. To the viewer, they look like a sunken mountain landscape, groaning under the masses of sediment carried down by the great rivers, which cut the coastal bays off from the sea and turned them into huge freshwater lakes.

The southern Song dynasty (1127-1279) saw an important stage in the historical development of the province. At that time, such famous garden-cities as Suzhou and Wuxi flourished under the protection of the imperial capital, Hangzhou (Hangchow). In the 20th century, Nanjing (Nanking) became the political capital of the new Republic of China, while Shanghai – today an autonomous

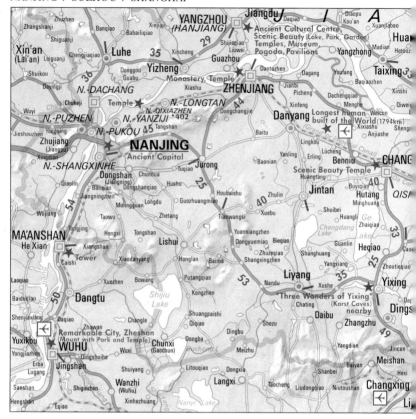

region administered separately from Jiangsu – grew in importance as the commercial hub of the Chinese economy and China's link with the outside world.

Nanjing (Nanking), the southern capital

During the "Spring-to-Autumn" period of the late Zhou era a strategically important frontier town grew up on the south bank of the Yangtse, where the river braces itself for its last great sweep to the east. The three states of Chu, Wu and Yue vied for its possession.

In 1386, the year in which the Ming dynasty was founded, the "Beggar King," Zhu Yuanghang (Hong Wu), who

had risen from a mendicant friar to the first Ming emperor, chose this town as China's capital. He built a new city which later functioned as a model for the imperial city of Peking. The third Ming emperor, Yongle, moved the imperial capital once more to the north. He called this *Bei*-jing, the "northern capital," to distinguish it from *Nan*-jing (Nanking), the "southern capital."

In 1842, Nanjing served as a proving-ground for the Europeans' forced military penetration into China. Through the *Unequal Treaties of Nanjing*, Britain obliged China to open up her ports, and took possession of the island of Hong Kong. In 1850 the Taiping Rebellion broke out, with the aim of toppling the

Manchu dynasty. In 1853 the rebel army captured Nanjing and set up a rival government in the city. However, imperial troops, backed by colonial army units, stormed the "rebel city" and reduced it to rubble. After this, Nanjing went into decline and became known as the "city of faded glory."

Nanjing bloomed again, briefly, in the 20th century: it was here, in 1911, that the end of the Chinese imperial age and the birth of the Republic of China were proclaimed. From 1927 to 1949, Nanjing was the first capital of the republic, until Chiang Kai-Shek fled with his retinue to Taiwan.

Oldest testimony to the city's existence is to be found about 12 miles (20 km) north of here, on the slopes of Mt Qixia, where a Buddhist monastery was founded in the 5th century AD. At the **Rock of a Thousand Buddhas** (*qianfo yan*), some 700 Buddha figures, carved in nearly 300 caves and grottoes, recall the great original examples of Yungang and Longmen.

South of here and east of Nanjing, **Mt Zijinshan** rises to a height of 1469 ft (448 m). It is also known as *zhongshan*, "Sun-Yatsen Mountain" (after the founder of the first republic). On its southern slope lies **Linggu Park** ("Valley of the Souls"), with its modern Linggu Pagoda and Linggu Temple. The original group of buildings, including the brick **Beamless Hall** (*wuliang dian*),

dates from the 6th century. A commemorative pavilion is dedicated to Xuan Zang, the famous pilgrim monk of the Tang period; it contains a miniature wooden pagoda with the holy man's skull in it.

The great triple-arched gate not far from the park proclaims Sun-Yatsen's fundamental ideal: *bo ai* ("universal love"). A wide avenue leads from here to the main entrance of the tomb of the founder of the republic. Four Chinese ideograms carved on it state his guiding principle: *tan xia wei gong* ("China belongs to everyone"). A long flight of steps leads to the top of the 518 ft (158 m) high hill on which stands the mausoleum of Sun-Yatsen (Sun Zhongshan). From a distance you can see the gleaming blue-glazed tiled roof of the building, which itself is 352 yds (323 m) wide and 239 ft (73 m) high. Inside, the "father of

the nation," (*guo fu*) is immortalized in white marble. He sits beneath the Chinese republican flag surrounded by flagstones on which his sayings are inscribed.

The first Ming emperor also had the reputation of being an innovator. His **burial mound** (*ming xiao ling*) is close by to the west, at the foot of Mt Zijinshan. The **Street of Souls**, which leads to the tomb complex, is inspired by the example of the Tang emperors' tombs, and was in turn imitated in the construction of the Ming tombs near Beijing. Stone statues of lions, elephants, horses, camels and mythical creatures are stationed along both sides of the avenue. These are followed by the loyal servants of the emperor: both civil and military officials. Massive stone figures also stand guard at the tomb of Xu Da, the first chancellor of the Ming dynasty, at the northwest foot of Zijinshan.

All that remains of the Palace of the first Ming emperor, which stood at the east gate (*zhongshan men*, "Sun-Yatsen

Above: Double decked bridge over the Yangtse in Nanjing (Nanking).
Right: Street life in Nanjing.

90

Gate"), are the marble **Five Dragon Bridges**, the former south gate (*wu men* or *niuchao men*) and the pedestals of the columns of the palace halls.

The **Provincial Museum** is near the Zhongshan Donglu; it offers a comprehensive survey of the earlier empires on the Yangtse as well as Nanjing in the Ming period. Of particular interest is a **burial shroud** made of rectangular plates of jade (eastern Han dynasty) found in north Jiangsu.

The layout of modern Nanjing is largely similar to that of its outline during the Ming period, when it was a residential city surrounded by a winding city wall nearly 40 miles (65 km) long and 40 ft (12 m) high and a wide defensive ditch. Of the remains of this strongly fortified wall, the China Gate (*zhongua men*), one of the 13 original gates, is particularly impressive. The southern gated fortress consists of four rows of gates and a bastion which once accommodated thousands of soldiers. From here a path runs south, away from the city wall, to the **Rainflower Terrace** (*yuhua tai*). In the 6th century, a shrine on this hill was a place of pilgrimage for Buddhists, today, there's a memorial here dedicated to the socialists and communists murdered by the nationalists in 1927.

In Bailuzhou Park, northeast of the southern gate, you can visit the **Taiping Museum** (*taiping tango lishsi bowuguan*). This former Prince's Palace, built by Xu Da, the first chancellor of the Ming dynasty, also contains the charming **Garden of Contemplation** (*zhan yuan*). Nearby is the atmospheric "old Chinese" **Qin Huai scenery**, a district in the old town.

By the Shuiximen gate in the southwest of the city is the **Chaotiangong**, a Ming palace which was converted into a Confucian temple in 1865. Passing from here beyond the city wall, you come to the beautiful **Mochou** ("Sans Souci") **Lake** which, like Xuanwu Lake northeast

of the city, lies in the midst of attractive parkland.

The huge double-decker **Yangtse Bridge** is an eyecatching symbol of modern Nanjing. Some 4 miles (6 km) long, it spans the river from the northwest corner of the Old City. It was started with Russian assistance, but ideological differences during the Cultural Revolution caused the Soviets to pull out, and the Chinese completed it on their own in 1968. The bridge provided the first direct rail link between Shanghai and Beijing.

Excursions around Nanjing

The day-trip from Nanjing to the Qinhai River is a rewarding one. Marvelous, colorful pageants on lantern-lit boats used to take place along the 6 mile (10 km) stretch of river between Dongshuiguan and Xishuiguan. There are organized boat trips along the Imperial Canal northwards as far as **Huai'an** and **Peixian**, and southwards to **Suzhou-Hangzhou**. Either by bus or boat you can

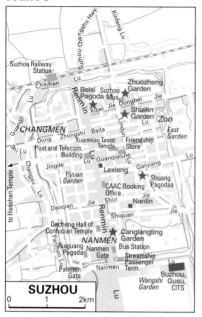

Map labels:
Xinfeng Lu, Suzhou–Changshu Hwy., Suzhou Railway Station, Chezhan, Lu, Renmin, Beisi Pagoda, Suzhou Mus., Zhuozheng Garden, Dongbei Jie, Xibei Jie, Shizilin Garden, Zoo, Lu, CHANGMEN, Zhongshi, Baita, Lindun, East Garden, Guangji, Shi Lu, Changshu, Xuanmiao Taoist Temple, Friendship Store, Dong, Post and Telecom. Building, Jie, Guanqian Jie, Lu, to Hanshan Temple, Jingde, Yiyuan Garden, Lexiang, Ganjiang, Lu, Shuang Pagodas, CAAC Booking Office, Daoqian, Jie, Shizi, Nanlin, Jie, Renmin, Shiquan, Dacheng Hall of Confucian Temple, Canglangting Garden, NANMEN, Panmen Lu, Ruiguang Pagoda, Nanmen Gate, Bus Station, Streamship Passenger Term., Panmen Gate, Nanmen, Lu, Suzhou, Wangshi Garden, Gusu, CITS, **SUZHOU**, 0 1 2km, Lu

The district capital of **Changzou** lies on the Imperial Canal between Zhenjiang and Wuxi, and is the center of the textile industry in Jiangsu province. Its canals are always bustling with activity, but tucked away among them is the idyllic **Red Peach Park** (*hongmai gong-yuan*) with its Yizhou pavilion.

The **Imperial Canal** (*da yunhe*, "Great Transport Canal"), was created in the 6th century by linking older stretches of canal. Attesting to the canal's busyness is the eyewitness report of a 9th-century Japanese monk named Ennin, who, in the course of a 9-day trip from Yangzhou to Kaifeng, saw an unbroken procession of boats laden with rice and salt. As early as the 3rd century, salt was being extracted on the coast of Jiangsu and carried inland.

Suzhou, the Heavenly Garden City

Suzhou is without doubt one of the most beautiful cities in China. There is a saying: *Shang you tian tang, xia you Su-Hang* – "above we have paradise, but on earth Suzhou and Hangzhou." Canals spanned by romantic bridges wind through this "Venice of the Orient," and today the city still depends on them for its water supply, sewage disposal, irrigation and transport. Suzhou was founded in the 6th century BC by He Lu, ruler of Wu, as his capital. His tomb is said to be on **Tiger Hill** (*hu qiu*), which rises out of the plain northwest of the city. In the 10th century an **octagonal pagoda** was built on top of this famous hill; known as the "Crooked Tower," it has become the emblem of Suzhou.

The building of the Imperial Canal put Suzhou at the very hub of the waterway network, and after the Song emperor had retreated to Hangzhou in the 12th century, Suzhou grew in prosperity as the center of silk-weaving in China. At that time this flourishing garden city boasted 14 canals, 359 bridges, 12 pagodas and over 50 temples. It was here that China's

reach **Yangzhou**, north of the junction of the Yangtse and the Imperial Canal. From the 7th century onward, this famous fortress of the Sui and Tang dynasties developed into an important city in the economically vital lower Yangtse region. During the last imperial dynasty, Yangzhou was the center of the salt trade. Like Suzhou, the city has a dense network of canals. In the northwest, the **Fajing Temple** (*fajing si* or *daming si*) stands on the shore of picturesque **Lake Shouxi**. The landscaped **Geyuan** and **Heyuan** gardens, in the northeast and southeast respectively, are a delight.

Zhenjiang, once a fortress facing Yangzhou across the river, is now known for its silk production, but has a beautiful Old Quarter. From there you can visit the monastery of **Jinshan** ("Golden Hill") and the cave temples of Fahai, Bailong Zhaoyang and Luohan, as well as the monasteries of **Jiaoshan** and **Beigushan**.

Right: A branch of the Imperial Canal in Suzhou (Jiangsu province).

first city map was published – or rather, engraved on a stone pillar. Here, too, the Chinese art of garden design was born: ponds, little hills, quaintly shaped rocks, terraces, trees and flowers were its principal elements. Paths lead past ornamental pavilions and bridges, ever opening up new vistas in the landscape, in which there seems to be a constant interplay of movement and repose.

From the central railway station, in the north of the city, our route leads across the outer moat and into the Old City. There, the **Pagoda of the North Temple** (*beisi ta*), 250 ft (76 m) high, affords a splendid panoramic view across the town and the surrounding countryside. This delightful 17th-century structure of brick and wood was modelled on a pagoda of the Song period, which forms part of the **Temple of Grace** (*bao'en si*).

Further east, Suzhou's **museum** vividly brings to life the history of the city, with exhibits on the Imperial canal, silk-making and the archaeological excavations in the country round about.

Next doors, the **Garden of Politics and Simplicity** (*zhuozheng yuan*) is – together with the gardens of the Summer Palace in Beijing, the Manchu residence in Chengde, and the Liuyuan garden (which is also here in Suzhou) – considered to be one of the four most beautiful gardens in China. Laid out in three parts, this garden looks as though it were painted in watercolors. It is thought to date from the early 16th century, and at one time to have belonged to an exiled official censor. From the **Hall of Distant Fragrance** (*yuanxiang tang*) in the middle of the garden, there's a sweeping view of a waterscape designed around many pavilions, bridges and rocks. Across the street to the south is the **Forest of Lions** (*shizi lin*), which was laid out by a Buddhist monk in about 1350 as a place of meditation, and named for its lion-shaped rock formations. The karst crags and cave entrances give the place a labyrinthine atmosphere; they are said to embody a landscape that the monk had seen in a dream.

93

The **Garden of Harmony** (*yi yuan*) was laid out as recently as the 19th century to a design by a Peking mandarin, but modelled on the other gardens of Suzhou.

The octagonal **twin pagodas** date from the 10th century and stand 98 ft (30 m) high in the southeast of the Old City. The attractive **Garden of the Master of the Nets** (*wangshi yuan*), further south, is the smallest of Suzhou's parks, with an area of just 1 1/4 acres (0.5 ha). This compact manorial garden, which achieves a perfect balance between grounds and buildings, is divided into three parts. The former owner's villa is in the east part; in the west, there's a pavilion.

Twice its size is Renminlu, a park surrounding the **Dark Blue Pavilion** (*canglang ting*), in the south, close to the main street, opposite the Confucian temple. It dates from the 10th century,

Above: Nature shaped by man in a landscaped garden in Suzhou. Right: A benign smile for the photographer.

which makes it the oldest surviving garden in the city. Unique in style and design, it charms the visitor with its atmosphere of simple beauty. The **Hall of the Pure Path** (*mindao tang*) is the most imposing part of this former prince's residence, and in the Ming period it was a venue for academic lectures.

Our route now takes us from the **Southern City Gate** (*nan men*), westward past the Ruigang Pagoda (10th c.) to the **Panmen Gate** and **Wumen Bridge**. The graceful, single-arched bridge, which spans the outer moat at the southwest corner of the Old City, blends harmoniously with the fortified gate, the best preserved of all the city gates.

Leave the Old City along atmospheric, tree-lined Jingde Avenue as far as the former Changmen Gate in the northwest corner. Nearby Shilu St is the departure point for the Nr 6 bus which takes you to the **Liuyuan garden**, the "Garden of Dalliance," laid out for a mandarin of the Ming period. In the center is an enchanting arrangement of hillocks and water.

Footpaths lead from the villas on the east side to other landscaped areas in the north and west. Some 300 stone tablets, engraved with famous examples of the calligrapher's art of various epochs, invite the visitor to "dally," and variously shaped windows (*huo chuang*, "living windows") provide ever-changing vistas of the ingenious landscaping. The Liuyuan was originally connected to the **Xiyuan** ("West Garden"), further to the west, but a later owner of the Liuyuan presented the West Garden to Buddhist monks who built the famous Jiezhuanglü Temple in it.

About 3 miles (5 km) west of Suzhou, near the docks on the Imperial canal, stands the 6th-century **Hanshansi**, one of the most famous temples in China, which bears the name of the Zen monk and poet Hanshan ("Cold Mountain"). On stone pillars in the main building are carved portraits of him and his friend Shide, both of whom appear detached from all earthly concerns.

Continuing westwards you come to **Lingyan Rock**, whose summit is crowned with a temple. Not far away rises the **Tianping** (or Baiyun Hill) with its intriguing rock formations and old maple trees. The landscaped parks of **Guangfu** and the legendary **East Mountain** (*dong shan*), with its temple dedicated to the Yellow Emperor, cling to the shores of Lake Taihu.

Wuxi – the "town without tin"

At one time, it is thought, there were deposits of tin beside Lake Taihu. However, it seems that by the 3rd century BC they were already exhausted – at least Wuxi, whose name literally means "without tin," has certainly been in existence since the Han dynasty (c. 200 BC). As recently as the 1930s, tinless Wuxi developed into the province's center for textile manufacture and is now a busy industrial city on the Imperial Canal. An at-

traction for visitors is to climb the 1080 ft (329 m) high Huishan hill, in the Xihui Park. The **Dragon Light Pagoda** (*longguang ta*) on the summit affords a fine view of the oval-shaped Old City, completely enclosed by the canal. A traditional tea-house near the **Second Spring on Earth** (*tianxia di'er quan*) is a welcoming sight. The **Plum Garden** (*mei yuan*), close to the Hotel Taihu, extends along the shore of the **Great Lake** (*tai hu*). In the springtime the blossom on the plum and cherry trees lends a touch of magic to the landscape. Opposite is the Hotel Hubin ("Lake-side"), with its Li Garden. From there you can walk to the **Tortoise Head "Island"** (*yuantou zhou*). Splendid villas and temples recall the time when wealthy mandarins and merchants lived here. A ferry trip to the **Park of Three Mountains** (*san shan*) makes you realize not only how beautiful the lake is, but also how richly stocked with fish. The fleets of traditional fishing-boats add greatly to the exotic charm of scene.

HEBEI

Getting there

Shijiazhuang, lies at the junction of two important rail routes: Beijing–Canton (northsouth) and Jinan–Taiyuan (Shandong–Shanxi, east–west). It can also be reached in comfort by direct flights from Beijing.

Accommodation

SHIJIAZHUANG: *LUXURY:* **Hebei Grand** (*hebei binguan*), 23 Yucai Lu, Tel. 601 5961.
MID-PRICE: **International Hotel** (*guoji daxia*), 23 Chang'an Xilu, Tel. 604 4321.
CHENGDE: *MID-PRICE:* **Yunshan Hotel** (*yunshan fandian*), 6 Nanyuanjie Donglu, Tel. 226171. **Shanzhuang**, 127 Lizhengmen Lu, Tel. 223501.
SHANHAIGUAN: *MID-PRICE:* **Jingshan Hotel** (*jingshan binguan*), Dong Dajie, Tel. 551130.
BEIDAIHE: *MID-PRICE:* **Jinshan Guesthouse** (*jinshan binguan*), Xijing Lu, Tel. 441768. **Zhonghaitan Guesthouse** (*zhonghaitan binguan*), 30 Xijing Lu, Tel. 441398.

Tourist Information

CITS in Chengde, Hebei Guesthouse.

Excursions

HANDAN: You can make an excursion to nearby Anyang (Province of Henan). This is the location of the **Ruins of Yin**, the earliest royal capital of the Shang dyanasty.
CHENGDE: The town can be reached from Beijing by train (a secondary line into Liaoning province) or with an organized bus tour. The temples scattered over a wide area (the **Eight Outer Temples**, *waiba miao*) can be reached by bus, taxi or bicycle. The southern main entrance to the park of the **Imperial Summer Residence** (*bishu shanzhuang*) is opposite the two hotels in town, Lizhengmen Fandian and Shanzhuang Binguan.

TIANJIN

Getting to and from the city

Tianjin, the capital of the urban region of the same name, lies on the main rail line Beijing–Nanjing–Shanghai and can also be reached by air from all the major cities in China. There are ship services from Tianjin Harbor (*tianjin tanggu*) to Yantai (Shandong) and Dalian (Liaoning).

Accommodation

LUXURY: **Astor**, 199 Jiefang Beilu, Tel. 339 0013. **Crystal Palace** (*shuijinggong fandian*), 28 Youyi Lu, Tel. 835 6666. **Sheraton**, Zijinshan Lu, Tel. 334 3388. **Tianjin Hyatt** (*kaiyue fandian*), 219 Jiefang Beilu, Tel. 331 8888.
MID-PRICE: **Geneva Hotel**, (*jinlihua da-*

jiudian), 32 Youyi Lu, Tel. 334 2222. **Yingbin Guesthouse**, Machang Dao 337, Tel. 24010. **Park Hotel** (*leyuan fandian*), 1 Leyuan Lu, Tel. 285966. **Friendship Hotel** (*youyi binguan*), 94 Nanjing Lu, Tel. 339 0372.
BUDGET: **Tianjin Nr.1 Hotel** (*tianjin diyi fandian*), 198 JiefangBeilu, Tel. 331 0707.

Tourist information

CITS 22 Youyi Lu, Tel. 318 0821.
China Travel Service, Jiefang Beilu 198.
Domestic Tourist Service, Chifeng Lu 52.
Fleet of the General Tourist Corporation in the Friendship Hotel.
Hotline: 331 8814

Museums and parks

Aquatic Park (*shui shang*) in the south-west of the city **Zhongshan-** (Sun-Yatsen-) **Park**. **Tianjin History Museum**; **Tianjin Natural History Museum**; **Tianjin Arts Museum**.

SHANDONG

Getting to and from the cities

JINAN: The provincial capital of Jinan is at the junction of the main lines Beijing–Nanjing–Shanghai and Qingdao–Dezhou–Shijiazhuang (Hebei) and is also served by daily flights from Peking and other major Chinese cities.
TAI'AN: The town can be reached by train (on the main Beijing–Shanghai line) or by bus from Jinan (journey-time about 80 minutes).
QUFU: Bus services to/from Yanzhou train station and Tai'an.
QINGDAO: Terminus of the Shandong rail line from Jinan; there are daily flights to/from Beijing and ship services connect it with Dalian (Liaoning) and Shanghai.

Accommodation

JINAN: *LUXURY:* **Qilu Hotel** (*qilu binguan*), Qianfoshan Lu, Tel. 296 6888.
MID-PRICE: **Nanjiao Guesthouse** (*nanjiao binguan*), 2 Ma'anshan Lu, Tel. 691 3931.
BUDGET: **Jinan Hotel** (*jinan fandian*), 240 Jingsan Lu, Tel. 691 5351.
TAI'AN: *MID-PRICE:* **Grand Hotel Taishan** (*taishan dajiudian*), Shanhongmen Lu, Tel. 224678. **Overseas Chinese Hotel** (*huaqiao daxia*), Dongyue Dajie, Tel. 338116.
BUDGET: **Taishan Guesthouse** (*taishan binguan*), Daizongfang, Tel. 334694.
TAISHAN: *MID-PRICE:* **Daiding Guesthouse** (*daiding binguan*).
BUDGET: **Zhongtianmen Guesthouse** near the Zhongtian Gate (halfway up the mountain).
QUFU: *LUXURY:* **Queli Hotel** (*queli binshe*), 15 Quelijie, Tel. 411300.

MID-PRICE: **Confucius Mansions Hotel** (inside the Confucian Temple complex), Tel. 412374.

QINGDAO: *LUXURY:* **Grand Regency**, 1 Taiwan Lu, Tel. 588 1818. **Huiquan Dynasty Hotel** (*huiquan wangqiao dajiudian*), 9 Nanhai Lu (on No.1 Beach), Tel. 287 9279. **Badaguan Hotel** (*badaguan binguan*), 19 Shanhaiguan Lu (on No.2 Beach), Tel. 387 2168. **Haitian Hotel** (*haitian dajiudian*), 39 Zhanshan Da Lu (on No.3 Beach), Tel. 387 1888.

MID-PRICE: **Zhanqiao Guesthouse** (*zhanqiao binguan*, built in the colonial style), 31 Taiping Lu, Tel. 287 0502. **Overseas Chinese Hotel** (*huaqiao fandian*), 72 Hunan Lu, Tel. 287 0731. **Yellow Sea Hotel** (*huanghai fandian*), 75 Yan'anyi Lu, Tel. 287 0215.

Tourist information
JINAN: CITS, 26 Jingshi Lu, Tel. 691 5858.
TAI'AN: CITS, Shanhongmen Lu 46 (near the Taishan Hotel), Tel. 333257.
QUFU: CITS in the Tourist Hotel near the bus station.
QINGDAO: OTC, Nanhai Lu 9 (near the Dynasty Hotel; the travel bureau also organizes tours of the Qingdao/Tsingtao brewery).

Tips and Trips
TAI'AN: The ascent of **Taishan** from the town center in Tai'an begins at the stone **triumphal arch** (*daizong fang*) and leads first of all to the temples at the foot of the hill. The Middle Path and the West Path meet at the **Zhongtian Gate**, at a height of 2930 ft (900m); this point can also be reached by road (minibus from the train station at Tai'an) and is the lower station of the cable car, which terminates at Wangfushan near the Nantian Gate.
QUFU: From Qufu there are various possible excursions: to the **excavation site of the Dawenkou culture**, to the **Temple of Mencius** in Zhouxian (the home of the great philosopher) and to the **Taibai tower** near **Jining** on **Lake Weishan.**
QINGDAO: The bathing season on the six beaches of fine sand runs from early June until the end of September.

JIANGSU

Getting to and from the cities
NANJING: The provincial capital, Nanjing, is served by regular flights from Beijing, Canton and other major Chinese cities. It is an important interchange station on the Beijing–Shanghai line and a port for shipping on the Yangtse river. Steamers going downstream reach Shanghai in about 19 hours and upstream they take two days to reach Wuhan.
WUXI: Wuxi lies on the Nanjing–Shanghai rail route and has a harbor on the Imperial Canal.

SUZHOU: Suzhou is a stop on the rail line from Nanjing to Shanghai and is also an inland port on the Imperial Canal.

Accommodation
NANJING: *LUXURY:* **Jinling Hotel** (*jinling fandian*), Xinjiekou, Tel. 445 4888.
MID-PRICE: **Nanjing Hotel** (*nanjing haohua dafandian*), 259 Zhongshan Lu, Tel. 663 4121. **Dingshan Hotel** (*dingshan fandian*), 90 Chaha'er Lu, Tel. 880 2888. **Hongqiao Hotel** (*hongqiao fandian*), 202 Zhongshan Beilu.
BUDGET: **Shuangmenlou Guesthouse** (*shuangmenlou binguan*), 185 Huju Beilu, Tel. 880 5961. **Xuanwu Hotel** (*xuanwu fandian*), 192 Zhongyang Lu, Tel. 330 3888.
WUXI: *LUXURY:* **The Pan Pacific Wuxi Grand**, 1 Liangqing Lu, Tel. 676 6789. **Taihu Sunshine Hotel** (*taihu fandian*), Meiyuan, Tel. 670 7888.
MID PRICE: **Hubin Hotel** (*hubin fandian*), Liyuan Lu, Tel. 670 1888. **Shuixiu Hotel** (*shuixiu fandian*), Liyuan, Tel. 676 8591.
BUDGET: **Liangxi Hotel** (*liangxi fandian*), Zhongshan Nanlu, Tel. 272 6812.
SUZHOU: *LUXURY:* **Bamboo Grove**, Zhuhui Lu, Tel. 520 5601. **New World Astor**, 156 Sanxiang Lu, Tel. 723 1888.
MID-PRICE: **Suzhou Hotel** (*suzhou fandian*), 115 Shiqian Lu, Tel. 520 4646. **Gusu Hotel** (*gusu fandian*), 5 Xiangwang Lu, Tel. 522 5127. **Nanlin Hotel** (*nanlin fandian*), 20 Gunxiufang, Tel. 522 4641.

Tourist information
NANJING: CITS, 202 Zhongshan Beilu.
SUZHOU: CITS and CTS, in the Suzhou Hotel.

Excursions
NANJING: The **Niu shou shan** (Ox head mountain) rises 12.5 miles south of the city. Attractions here are the graves of emperors and nobles of 10th-century dynasties with "soul paths", murals and reliefs. A pretty pavilion in **Ma'anshan** (37.5 miles/60 km) honors the Tang-poet Li Taibo.
SUZHOU: It is worth making a trip out to the 53-arched **Bridge of the Precious Belt** (*baodai qiao*) from the Tang period, on the Imperial Canal, southeast of Suzhou.
Other sights worth seeing:
Tianpingshan (Medicinal springs); **Guangfu** on Lake Taihu; **Purple and Gold Monastery** of Dongshan; **Baosheng Temple** in Luzhi; **Yushan** at Changshu.
In the Yixing district, west of Lake Taihu, the karst caves are particularly fascinating, e.g. at Shanjuandong, Zhanggongdong or Linggudong. The caves contrast strangely with the broad, verdant plains of the Yangtse delta.

WHERE CHINA'S PULSE BEATS

SHANGHAI

A JOURNEY INTO THE PAST

It is nearly 8 pm, and the bar of the Peace Hotel, furnished in the style of an English country house, has already filled with patrons. The regular evening performance of the "Old Time Band" is just beginning; it is one of those extraordinary but very telling experiences of a trip to China. With the help of Tsingtao draft beer, you can imagine that you have been transported back to pre-war Shanghai, especially when the band starts playing old favorites from the Thirties such as *Ain't Misbehavin', Dancing in the Dark*, or *Night and Day*. The Peace Hotel with its elegant Art Deco lobby was once called the Cathay, and formed part of Sassoon House (built 1923-26), which, with its dark green pyramid roof, is one of the landmarks of the **Bund**, Shanghai's spacious boulevard along the bank of the Huangpu river. If you drop in at the Peace Hotel you can still capture some of the ambience of colonial Shanghai. Apart from this, its central position it makes the best possible starting point for exploring the city.

And inevitably you will find yourself asking the question: what is there left of

Left: Tenements beside the Suzhou river in Shanghai.

the "Paris of the East?" Once as cosmopolitan as Casablanca or Alexandria, this city has been portrayed in classic Hollywood movies like *Lady from Shanghai* and *Shanghai Express,* and in the novels of Mao Dun (*Shanghai by Twilight*), Vicky Baum (*Hotel Shanghai*), and more recently J.G. Ballard's *Empire of the Sun* (which was made into a film by Steven Spielberg) as a glittering, legendary center of adventure and exoticism, pleasure and vice, splendor and squalor.

Looking back

The origins of Shanghai (literally: "over the sea") go back to the Song Dynasty. It was in 1554 that the first wall was built around what was, at the time, a mooring-wharf for junks, as protection against Japanese pirates. The course of this wall can still be seen in the oval of the ring-road surrounding the Old City. Of the **gates**, only the **Old North Gate** (*lao beimen*) still remains. It has been incorporated into the façade of a typical Chinese house (shop or workshop below, living quarters above). In the 17th and 18th centuries, the city was a textile center; 20,000 weavers are said to have lived here.

Modern Shanghai was born with the 1842 Treaty of Nanking (Nanjing),

99

which ended the first Opium War and prepared the way for the forcible opening up of China by gunboat diplomacy. The treaty granted foreigners the right of settlement and extraterritoriality in certain Chinese ports. Of the Treaty Ports that grew up in the wake of the enforced agreement, Shanghai quickly became far and away the most important, outstripping Canton (Guangzhou) as China's gateway to the world.

The century-long presence of foreigners in the International Compound made Shanghai the door through which modern life entered China: traders and missionaries, consumer goods and technology, and western ideas poured into the country. Both the British and the French concessions were extended westwards, in 1899 and 1914 respectively, and between them they covered an area of around 12 sq. miles (30 sq. km).

Their period of greatest prosperity was in the years 1900-1930, when the growth of industrialization brought factories and workers' settlements in alongside the commercial buildings, palatial banks and villas. The buildings that remain in the city and the outer districts to the west make Shanghai an open-air museum of European architecture; as well as various 19th-century pastiche "neo" styles (neoclassical, neo-Gothic, etc.), you can find Art Nouveau, Art Deco, Expressionism and Bauhaus.

GREATER SHANGHAI

Soon after the Kuomintang (Nationalist Party) consolidated its power in 1927, Greater Shanghai was established. Today, as a self-governing city, it covers an area of 190 sq. miles (495 sq. km), of which the historic Old City takes up 56 sq. miles (145 sq. km). In order to create a counterweight to the traditional city center, dominated by the influence of foreigners, the Kuomintang in the early 1930s endeavored to lay out a new down-town area in the **Jiangwan** district, with a main square in the form of a gigantic cross. Its vast expanse was supposed to outdo even the Square of Heavenly Peace in Peking.

The Japanese occupation during the Second World War (1937-45) put the brakes on this ambitious project, which can well be compared to the plans for the development of Paris or Berlin in the 19th century. Some of the public buildings erected in the classical Chinese style – such as the **Dundayu Town Hall**, completed in 1934 – have survived, surrounded by a wasteland of slab-sided concrete buildings.

The Communists, whose early organization was able to flourish in the French concession under the legal immunity afforded to foreigners, were driven underground in 1927 – those of them who had not already been butchered by the Green Brigade of Du Yuesheng (Du of the Big Ears) on the instructions of Chiang Kaishek. The Communists did not take Shanghai until the spring of 1949, after American marines had occupied the city for a short time. In order to clean up the "Shanghai cesspool," seething with organized crime, gambling dens, opium addicts, and thousands of prostitutes, the Communist Party set about its first radical re-education program in this Babylon of iniquity.

Even if Shanghai's feverish cosmopolitan atmosphere seemed finally to disappear as a result, the city has nevertheless remained the nerve-center of China's economy, as well as one of the largest cities in the country, with nearly 13 million inhabitants – in permanent rivalry with Beijing. It was one of the centers of the Cultural Revolution, and the political base of the "Gang of Four" in the 1970s. Today the metropolis is booming more than ever and its growth is accompanied by the "modernization" of the historic fabric of its buildings, which are being replaced by characterless concrete.

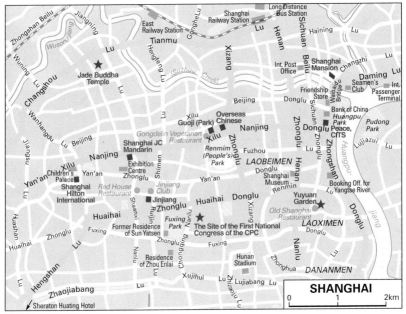

The historic Old City

Shanghai is definitely worth a journey. Its charms are not limited to its typical Chinese attractions, such as the **Jade Buddha Temple** (*yufo si*) in the Anyuan Lu, to which the statues were brought from Burma in 1882, or the **Longhua Pagoda** (*longhua ta*), 130 ft (40 m) high, in the south of the Longhua district. You certainly ought to visit the extensively restored Old City with its narrow streets and alleys. Here you can still get a feeling of life in pre-revolutionary China, bustling but at the same time confined. In the northern part of the Old City the **Yu Garden** (*yu yuan*), which was laid out as early as the 16th century, is also worth seeing; here the **Spring Pavilion** (*dianchun tang*) served in 1853 as the headquarters of the secret "Society of the Small Swords," when the society, simultaneously with the Taiping Rebellion, was plotting against the Manchu dynasty. Just in front of the main entrance, standing in the middle of a pool, is the **Huxingting Teahouse**. It can only be reached over a nine-section **Zigzag Bridge**, which is supposed to bar the way to evil spirits. On the left (looking towards the bridge) a restaurant serves delicious *baozi* (stuffed dumplings).

The Bund

Since the 19th century, the actual city center has been the former International Settlement to the north and west of the Old City. The imposing buildings of the colonial period are still ranged along the **Bund** (an Anglo-Indian word for quay), which has now been renamed **Zhongshanlu** in honor of Sun Yatsen.

If you take the road to the Bund from the north across **Waibaidu Bridge**, which was constructed of iron in 1907 and which crosses the Wusong (Suzhou) at its confluence with the Huangpu, you can see on your right the compound of the former British Consulate (No. 33). Today it houses, among other things, the "Friendship Shop". At No. 27 we see

what used to be the offices of Jardine Matheson & Co., the Hong Kong firm which provided James Clavell with the model for his novel *Taipan*. At No. 23 is the **Bank of China** with its impressive, 3-storey high banking hall. After passing the **Sassoon House** with its main entrance at No. 20 Nanjing Donglu, you notice the **Customs House** (No. 13), built in English Tudor style, with a clock which chimes like Big Ben. No. 12, with its tall dome, used to be occupied by the Hongkong and Shanghai Bank; then it was the seat of the city administration. Before the war the Shanghai Club at No. 3, reputed to have the world's longest bar, was considered the most exclusive address in town. In a contrast which is nothing short of sacrilege, this is now where Kentucky Fried Chicken has come to roost. From the next corner onward, the Bund was called Quai de France, as

strollers had now crossed into the French Concession. The best view over the city center is from one of the roof terraces of the **Shanghai Mansions** (*da sha* for short), which were built in 1934 on the far side of the Waibaidu Bridge. On the left is the **Astor House Hotel**, built in 1860; opposite that is the Russian Consulate, the only one to have continued in its original function without interruption. The nearby German, American and Japanese consulates were pulled down to make way for a soulless box of a hotel, which also accommodates the Seamen's Club, a dreary-looking establishment, in its grounds. During the prudish Cultural Revolution, it served as a locus for the supervised revelry of foreign sailors. To the right, as you look up the Wusong, stands the American-built, neo-Renaissance **Central Post Office**.

Nanjinglu (Nanking Street)

The *Nanjinglu*, Shanghai's main shopping street, meets the Bund at the Peace

Above: The skyline of Shanghai – the Bund and the Peace Hotel. Right: Family life out of doors – a typical scene in the Old City.

Hotel. Here are some large and small department stores from the 1920s and 1950s. All the side-streets off the Bund have been given the names of Chinese cities – such as **Beijinglu**, with the Friendship Shop at No. 40. On the right is **Suzhoulu** (once a place to go for entertainment, with teahouses, opium dens and brothels, but today lined with bookshops), and south of it **Yan'anlu**. The streets running parallel to the Bund are named after Chinese provinces, such as Sichuanlu or Henanlu (the old boundary of the International Compound). This neighborhood forms the actual city center, which stretches as far as Xizanglu on the edge of the People's Park.

After 1.25 miles (2 km) the Nanjing Donglu curves round and is from there on named Nanjing Xilu (formerly Bubbling Wells Road). This loop follows the final bend of the former race-course, on the site of which are now the attractions of the **People's Park** (with an admission charge) and a roller-skating rink; at party functions, parades are held here. The

brick building with a clock-tower, put up in 1935 at the start and finish of the race-course, has housed the city library since 1949. This is one of the largest libraries in China, well stocked with foreign as well as Chinese literature. Books published before 1949, however, are kept firmly under lock and key as *neibu* ("internal material") and can only be borrowed with special permission. North of the park towers the 18-floor **Park Hotel**, once the highest building in Asia. In the south, at the People's Square, are the new **Town Hall** and the **Museum of History**.

Outlying districts to the west

Exploratory tours through the western districts of the town as far as Hongqiao airport, 11 miles (18 km) from the city, can be eminently rewarding. In park-like grounds behind high walls are the old villas once owned by Shanghai's seriously rich, together with estates of terraced houses and apartment blocks in the Bauhaus style. Many restored buildings

now serve as head offices for various authorities; as children's or old people's homes; or, once again, as residential housing – but this living space is cramped and overcrowded, shabby, run-down, and wedged in between modern buildings.

In the southwest, not far from the Sheraton in **Xujiahui** ("Village of the Xu Family"), the French mission had its headquarters. Still standing are the cathedral, which is once more used for worship, and the weather-station. Its forecasts used to be hoisted on flags on the **Time Ball Tower** – also preserved – on the Bund, for ships heading out to sea.

The former French Concession

In the former French Concession, which surrounded the Old City of Shanghai on three sides, you can see evidence of China's more recent political history.

Above: Upper floor of the tea-house in the Yu Garden in Shanghai.

In the **Residence of Sun Yatsen** (Sun Zhongshan) in Xiangshanlu, the founder of the Kuomintang and "Pioneer of the Revolution" lived with his wife, Song Qingling. She was one of the sisters of the famous (or rather, notorious) and powerful Song clan; another sister married Chiang Kaishek. Inside the museum, Sun's extensive private library reflects the breadth of his intellect.

Not far from there, at No. 76 Xinggelu, the Chinese Communist Party held its highly secret First National Congress on July 1st, 1921. The number of cups on the table of the meeting-room, which has been furnished in appropriate style, represents the number of delegates. Among them was Mao Zedong. A small museum annex contains documents about the early phase of the Chinese Revolution. Once a place of pilgrimage for the Chinese "masses," it is mainly patronized by foreigners these days.

European food is served at the **Red House Restaurant** in Shaanxi Nanlu (No. 37), which was opened in 1935 and is one of the few restaurants to have survived from pre-war times. Those who prefer to eat in more exclusive venues can indulge themselves at the former Cercle Sportif Francais, now called the **Jinjiang Club,** or dine in the **Jinjiang Hotel** opposite, the oldest part of which dates back to 1909.

A trip around the harbor

You can take a boat trip round the harbor to where the Huangpu flows into the Yangtse. It is worth it just for the impressive view you get of the new Yanpu Bridge, the Pudong Quarter and the city rising on the skyline, as the boat returns to Shanghai.

Seeing this, you may well feel just what travellers felt in days gone by, when the normal means of access to Shanghai was the passenger steamer, rather than the jet.

SHANGHAI

Getting there

The international airport at **Hongqiao** lies 11 miles (18 km) from the city center (Information: Tel. 2536530). A shuttle-bus takes you to the **Air-China-Office**, Yan'an Zhong Lu 789. The **Central Train Station** on Tianmu Lu (in the Hongkou district) has direct connections to every major city in China. There are steamer services to ports all around the coast and up the Yangtse as far as Chonqing

Tourist information

CITS, Jinling Donlu 2, Tel: 6321 7200; office in the Peace Hotel, Tel. 6321 0032 (for reservations and airplane, train or boat tickets).

Visa extensions

Office of Public Security, Hankou Lu 221, 8.30–11.30am, 1.30–5.30pm, Tel. 63215380.

Consulates

Australia: Fuxing Lu 17, Tel. 6433 4604. **United Kingdom**: Suite 301, Shanghai Centre, Nanjing Xilu 1376, Tel. 6279 7650. **United States**: Huai Hai (Middle Rd.) 1469, Tel. 6433 6880.

Accommodation

LUXURY: **Shanghai Hilton International**, Huashan Lu 250, Tel. 6248 0000. **Huating Sheraton** (way out of the city), Chaoxi Beilu 1200, Tel. 6439 1000. **Shanghai JC Mandarin**, Nanjing Xilu 1225, Tel. 6279 1888. **The Portman Shangri-La**, Nanjing Xilu 1376, Tel. 6279 8888.
MID-PRICE: **Peace Hotel**, Nanjing Donglu 20, Tel. 6321 1244 / 6321 8050. **Jinjiang**, Maoming Nanlu 59, Tel. 6258 2582. **Shanghai Hotel**, Wulu muqi Beilu 505, Tel. 6248 0088. **Shanghai Mansions**, Suzhou Beilu 20, Tel. 6324 6260. **Park Hotel**, Nanjing Xilu 170, Tel. 6327 5225. **Huaqiao**, Nanjing Xilu 104, Tel. 6327 6226.
BUDGET: **Dongfeng**, Zhongshan Dongyilu 3, Tel. 321 8060. **Astor House**, formerly called **Pujiang** (dormitory), Huangpu Lu 15, Tel. 6324 6388.

Medical care

HOSPITALS: **Shanghai Diyi Yiyuan**, Suzhou Beilu 190, Tel. 6324 0100. **Ambulance**, Suzhou Beilu 410, Tel. 6324 0100. **Foreigners' hospital**, Yan'an Xilu 257, Tel. 6256 3180.
PHARMACY: **Pharmacy Nr. 1** (western medicine), Nanjing Donglu, opposite the Hualian department store.

Changing money

Bank of China, Zhongshan Dongyi Lu 23, Mon–Sat 9.00–11.45am, 1.30–4.30pm, Tel. 6329 1979. There are **bureaux de change** in the big hotels, which also accept all credit-cards.

Shopping

Friendship Shops, Beijing Donglu 40, 9am–10pm Tel. 63234600 (money-changing, credit-cards, overseas dispatch service).

DEPARTMENT STORES: **Department store Nr. 1**, Nanjing Donglu 830. **Hualian**, Nanjing Donglu 635. **Department store Nr. 2**, Huaihai Zhong Lu 889.
BOOKSHOPS: **Guoji Shudian** (foreign language literature), Fuzhou Lu 436. **Xinhua**, Nanjing Donglu 345 (all big hotels provide bookstalls, the Peace Hotel has foreign daily newspapers).
HANDCRAFTS: **Duoyunxuan**, Nanjing Donglu 422.
RECORDS / CASSETTES: Xizang Zhong Lu 365.
TOILETRIES: **Jessica Store**, Jinjiang Hotel. **Supermarket** in the Park Hotel.

Post / telecommunications

Central Post Office, Sichuan Beilu 1761, 7am–10pm, Tel. 6324 0135. All larger hotels have their own postal counter. **Telegraph office**, Nanjing Donglu 30; Tel. 6321 0022.

Museums

Museum of Art and History, Public Square. **Natural History Museum**, Yan'an Donglu. **Lu Xun Museum**, Hongkou Park. **Museum of the Founding of the Party**, Xingge Lu 76. **Sun Yat-sen Museum**, Xiangshan Lu. Opening times of the museums: 8.30am–5pm (closed for lunch, except Sundays).

Restaurants

Shanghai Laofandian (Shanghai cuisine; booking essential!), Fuyou Lu 242, Tel. 6328 2782. **Xinya** (Cantonese), Nanjing Donglu 719. **Meilongzhen** (Sichuan), Nanjing Xilu 22, Lane 1081. **Yangzhou** (Shanghai; must book!), Nanjing Donglu 308, Tel. 6322 5826. **Renmin** (Suzhou/Wuxi), Nanjing Xilu 226. **Yueyanglou** (Hunan), Xizang Nanlu 28. **Gongdelin** (vegetarian), Huanghe Lu 43. **Seaport** (Canton/Sichuan), Taixing Lu 89. **Wang Baohe** (first opened in 1744; rice wine), Fuzhou Lu 603. **Red House** (European), Shaanxi Nanlu 37. **Green Wave Corridor** (traditional), Yuyuan Lu 131. **Nanguo** (Canton), Beijing Zhong Lu 813. **Xijiaoting** (seafood), Nanjing Xilu 1333. **Deda Xicai He** (German), Sichuan Zhong Lu 359.

Excursions / Sightseeing

North of the city lies **Hongkou Park**, formerly a golf-course, with the **tomb of Lu Xun** (1881-1936), who dominated the literary scene in pre-war Shanghai, and the **Lu Xun Museum**.
Further north, along the disused railroad track to Wusong, where the German Medical College used to be, you come to **Jiangwan**. The **sports stadium** dating from the 1930s is clearly related in architectural terms to the stadium built in Berlin for the 1936 Olympic Games. Nearby is the campus of the **Fudan University**, which ranks as China's second most important academic institution after Beijing University.

YIN AND YANG
OF SEA
AND MOUNTAINS

ZHEJIANG

FUJIAN

ZHEJIANG

South of Shanghai lies **Zhejiang**, one of China's smallest provinces, with an area of 39,300 sq. miles (101,800 sq km); but also one of the most densely populated, with 40 million inhabitants. Its history goes back to the 8th century BC. In the 12th century, members of the Song imperial family fled south to escape the invading hordes and founded the Southern Song Dynasty (1127-1279) in the region of the modern province; and in the following centuries Zhejiang became a center of imperial culture. The steady rise that began in the Song period ended with the Taiping Rebellion in the 19th century. Only the northern part, an area almost detached from Zhejiang, lies within the fertile **Yangtse Delta**. The much larger southern part is characterized by mountain scenery and by a rugged coastline with some 18,000 offshore islands. Rice, tea, silk, brocade and satin have traditionally been Zhejiang's chief products.

Hangzhou

"*Shang you tian tang, xia you Su Hang*" ("Paradise is above; on earth are

Left: Tea-picking in the mountains of Zhejiang province.

Suzhou and Hangzhou"); so runs a Chinese proverb. Hangzhou's astounding palaces, magnificent temples, idyllic parks and broad avenues delighted Marco Polo in the 13th century. Situated between the lower reaches of the River Qiantang (also called *zhe jiang*) and Western Lake (*xi hu*), Hangzhou, Zhejiang's provincial capital, has for centuries attracted travelers from all over the world. Hangzhou experienced the first boost to its economic development in the 7th century with the completion of the **Imperial Canal** (*da yunhe*, "Great Canal"). The city really began to flourish, however, after the arrival of the Song imperial family, who built Hangzhou up as their imperial capital. The "City of Silk and Tea," and "City of Artists and Scholars" glittered like an urban jewel in the landscape, until it was almost totally destroyed in the Taiping Rebellion.

Hangzhou's prime tourist attraction is the Western Lake (*xihu*), so named because it lies west of the city. Poets have extolled this incomparable landscape as an "earthly paradise," with its lake and park, its temples, pagodas and pavilions, covering just over 2 sq. miles (5.6 sq. km). On three sides Xihu nestles beneath towering mountains; and all of its richly varied views make up a kaleidoscope of impressions.

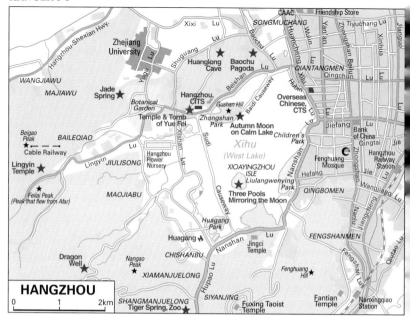

A good starting point for seeing the Western Lake is the 148 ft (45 m) high **Baochu Pagoda** (*baochu ta*) in northwest Hangzhou. Dating from the 10th century, it has been destroyed on several occasions, but rebuilt each time. The **Broken Bridge** (*duan qiao*) and the **Baidi** ("Bai's causeway", named after a poet of the Tang dynasty) link the largest island in the lake, the **Hill of Solitude** (*gu shan*), with the mainland. It was amidst this breathtaking scenery that the Song rulers began building a palace. Lovers can still enjoy the moonlight in the **Pavilion of the Autumn Moon by the Still Lake** (*pinghu qiuyue ge*), which contains a stele of Emperor Qianlong from 1699. The grounds of the former imperial residence encompass the present **Zhongshan Park** and the **Zhejiang Provincial Library**. On the northwestern shore of Xihu stands the **Temple of General Yue Fei** (*yue miao*). Advisers to the emperor

envied General Yue (1103-1142) his military successes in reconquering the northern territories, and intrigued against him until they succeeded in having him executed. Ever since his rehabilitation twenty years later, the Chinese have honored him as a model of loyalty and devotion.

A delightful walk along the **Sudi Causeway**, the sections of which are linked by arched bridges, leads straight to the park of the **Bay of Flowers** (*hua gang*).

The **Three Pools Reflecting the Moon** (*santan yinyue*) and the **Island in the Little Ocean** (*xiaoying zhou*), on the other hand, can only be reached by boat.

A few miles further west is the **Monastery of Refuge of the Soul** (*lingyin si*) at the foot of the **Peak that Flew There** (*feilai feng*). The path to the Lingyin temple leads past hundreds of Buddhist sculptures hewn from the face of the cliff. In a niche in the rock is a **Milefo** (Smiling Buddha of the Future) from the Song period, whose smile is irresistibly infec-

Right: The idyllic Western Lake near Hangzhou (Zhejiang province).

tious. His fat stomach bulges out of the folds of his robe, while, in a semi-reclining position, he casually props himself up on a cushion. Monks in the 10th century built the temple complex beyond it, part of which is dug into the rock. In the impressive, 108 ft (33 m) high **Sumptuous Hall of the Great Hero** (*daxiong baodian*) the Buddha Sakyamuni is seated on a lotus throne. The statue, carved from gilded camphor-wood, towers 30 ft (9 m) high. North of the temple, the **Northern Gao Peak** (*bei gaofeng*) commands a view of Xihu and the surrounding area. A stairway cut into the rock winds nearly 1000 ft (300 m) up to the summit. Exhausted sightseers can take a cable car to the top.

Between the Qiantang river and the Western Lake is the source of the former's most famous tributary, **Running Tiger Spring** (*hupao quan*). The surface tension of its water is so great that you can float coins on it – a restful pastime when accompanied by a bowl of Longjing tea.

Shaoxing

The origins of **Shaoxing**, one of the oldest towns in Zhejiang, situated 42 miles (67 km) southeast of Hangzhou, go back to the 7th century BC. In many of its narrow streets, time seems to have stood still. In the picturesque Old Town, crisscrossed by little canals, you can observe the inhabitants' way of life at close quarters. Then you can round off the evening with a bowl of yellow Shaoxing wine (a strong rice wine) that has been pressed in the same traditional way for centuries.

In the town center the **Pagoda of the Temple of Great Goodness** (*dashansi ta*) rises proudly to a height of 131 ft (40 m). The hexagonal brick pagoda, dating from the 6th century, was destroyed several times, and given its present form in the 13th century.

The **Qiu Jin Guju** ("Former residence of Qiu Jin") in the south of the town was the family home of the poetess and revolutionary Qiu Jin (1875-1907). She fought for women's emancipation and the over-

SOUTHEAST OF HANGZHOU

0   10   20   30   40   50   60km

throw of the Qing dynasty. After a failed rebellion she was publicly executed.

A few steps further on, the **birthplace of Lu Xun** and the **Lu Xun Exhibition Hall** remind us of an important Chinese writer of the 20th century. Lu Xun (Zhou Shuren, 1881-1936) castigated the social and political disorder of his time, for example in his grotesque and ironic story *Ah Q – Diary of a Madman.*

In the eastern part of town, the **Baziqiao Bridge,** built in 1256, makes the shape of the Chinese symbol for the number eight as it curves over a small canal.

Ningbo

Ningbo, some 97 miles (140 km) from Shaoxiang, was a market and hub of trade as early as the 7th century, but also had to open its gates to the foreign powers following China's defeat in the first Opium War. Although Ningbo has lost its former importance, eclipsed by Shanghai, the city has remained a significant center of commerce, with 400,000 inhabitants and a constant buzz of activity. On the west side of town the **Tian Yi Pavilion** (*tianyi ge*), built in 1561-66, houses China's oldest private library. Fan Qin, an official of the Ming dynasty, collected over 70,000 volumes here.

Ten miles (15 km) further north, on Mt Lingshan, stands the **Baoguo Si** ("temple that protects the land"). Its 11th-century main hall is thought to be the oldest wooden building in the province.

On Mt Taibaishan, about 21 miles (34 km) east of Ningbo, stands the **Tiantong temple monastery** (*tiantong si*). This was founded in the 3rd century and has been destroyed and rebuilt several times. The Japanese monk Dogen, one of the fathers of Zen Buddhism, studied here in the 13th century.

Putuoshan

From a small island in the East China Sea (about 25 miles/40 km from Ningbo as the crow flies) rises **Putuoshan,** one of the sacred mountains of Chinese Buddhism. According to legend, Guanyin, the goddess of mercy, appeared to a monk here. In the 11th century, monks founded the first monastery on the island. A secluded pinewood conceals **Puji Temple-monastery** (*puji si*) from the harbor. Its largest hall can hold a thousand worshippers. Further north you come to the 16th-century **Fayu Monastery** (*fayu si*). Closer to the summit – and to the gods – and reached by stone steps, is **Huiji Monastery** (*huiji si*), on Foding, 955 ft (291 m) high. If you are tired after this, you can relax on the sandy beaches of the island's east coast.

Wenzhou

The 2000-year-old port of **Wenzhou** in the south of Zhejiang Province was one of those which had to accept foreign occupiers after the Opium War. The colonial influence is reflected in some of the architecture in the town center.

The sights of Wenzhou are on **Jiangxi-nyu**, an island in the River Oujiang. Here are two eye-catching pagodas: the **East Pagoda,** built in 869 AD, and the **West Pagoda** of a century later. The older of the two temples on the island, the 9th-century **Temple in the Heart of the River** (*jiangxin si*), was built by monks. **Wen Tianxiang Temple,** dating from the 15th century, is dedicated to General Wen Tianxiang (1236-83), a loyal warrior of the Southern Song Dynasty.

Yandangshan

The enchanting mountain scenery of the Yandangshan in southern Zhejiang stretches for about 110 miles (180 km) to the coast. You can walk for miles among the peaks, caves, waterfalls, pools, temples and countless romantic pavilions in the part of this mountain chain which lies north of Wenzhou, and includes the 3467 ft (1057 m) **Beiyandang Shan**. The most beautiful place to head for is the

area around the **Peak of the Gods** (*ling feng*), 886 ft (270 m) high, which is reached from Wenzhou via Baixi. The immense **Peak of the Folded Hands** (*hezhang feng*) and **Peak of the Golden Cockerel** (*jinji feng*) tower beside the **Monastery on the Peak of the Gods** (*lingfeng si*, dating from 1023). Southwest of the Lingfengsi lie the 130 ft (40 m) deep **Cave of the Goddess of Mercy** (*guanyin dong*) and the waterfall of **Sanzhebao,** which tumbles over three cascades. South of the **Temple of the Rock of the Gods** (*lingyan si*) the **Dalongqiu Pubu,** one of the largest waterfalls in China, thunders down from a height of 623 ft (190 m), bathing the surrounding area in a mysterious light. At Daxue, near the border with Fujian, the neighboring province to the south, there is a monastery on the highest mountain in the Yandangshan chain, the 4057 ft (1237 m) **Nanyandang Shan**.

FUJIAN

The same contrast between mountains and sea marks the province of Fujian. Its largest towns are strung along the 2000 miles (3300 km) of rugged coastline like a necklace. Here, Fujian seems to be a verdant paradise; in fact, over 90% of its area is mountainous and barren. Its position on China's southeast coast facing the island of Taiwan ensured the rapid economic development of Fujian in the 11th century. However, during later years of decline, caused by overpopulation and the vagaries of the monsoon climate, many people left their homeland. Statistics show that nearly 40% of all overseas Chinese trace their origins back to Fujian. Today it has a population of 26 million.

Fuzhou

"City of the banyan trees" is what the Chinese call **Fuzhou,** Fujian's provincial capital. The shade-giving trees already

flourished here during the Song dynasty. In the 10th century, Fuzhou was the capital of the Min kingdom, and it has remained the center of the province ever since. Thanks to its position on the delta of the navigable **Min river** (*min jiang*) Fuzhou grew into an important port which, under colonial pressure, was declared another "open port" in 1842.

Among the sights of the city center is **Yu Hill** (*yu shan*), from whose summit, 190 ft (58 m) high, you get a bird's-eye view of the city. The **White Pagoda** (*bai ta*), 134 ft (41 m) high and rebuilt in brick in the 16th century, stands at the western foot of **Yushan**. Its counterpart, the older **Black Pagoda** (*wu ta*), nestles in the eastern side of the higher **Wushan**, 282 ft (86 m).

The **Western Lake** (*xi hu*), northwest of town, was created as early as the 3rd century by farmers burdened with heavy tribute duties in order to provide a con-

Above: Quanzhou's Old City (province of Fujian).

stant water supply for their fields. It is the twin, although smaller, of Hangzhou's Western Lake. Also in the north of the town is the **Tomb of Lin Zexu**, a Qing Dynasty general. General Lin (1785-1850) attempted to prevent the British from importing opium, but lost his life in the first Opium War.

Drum Mountain (*gu shan*) gets its name from an enormous flat stone on the summit, which makes a sound like a drum when it rains. It is 2194 ft (669 m) high and lies about 9 miles (15 km) to the east. Numerous terraces, springs, caves, pavilions and temples, including the famous 10th-century **Temple of the Bubbling Spring** (*yongquan si*), adorn its slopes. Most visitors come to see the **reclining Buddha** carved from white jade.

Quanzhou and its environs

Quanzhou, about 125 miles (200 km) south of Fuzhou, seems a quiet place now; starting in the 7th century, however, it long ranked among the world's largest and most important commercial ports. Marco Polo compared its busy harbor with that of Alexandria. Quanzhou's decline began in the 15th century, when the Ming Dynasty, after an interlude of expansionism, put a stop to trading with foreign nations.

There are few monuments to recall the city's former greatness and splendor. **Kaiyuan Temple** (*kaiyuan si*) in northwest Quanzhou, founded in the 7th century and enlarged in the 14th to an area of 17 acres (7 ha), is still one of the largest temple complexes in China. The main halls, the **Tianwangdian** and **Daxiong Baodian** (with five Buddha and 18 *luohan* figures), the **Terrace for the Ordination of Monks** (*ganlu jietan*) and the **Pavilion of the Holy Books** (*cangjing ge*) form the central axis. In the temple grounds stands the city's emblem, the **Double Pagoda** (*shuang ta*). The 157 ft (48 m) high **Zhenguota** to the east was built in the 9th century; the smaller **Pagoda of Goodness and of Long Life** (*renshou ta*) somewhat later.

A good 60 miles (100 km) northwest of Quanzhou, **Dehua** has a delectable surprise in store for connoisseurs of porcelain figurines. For this is the home of *Blanc de Chine*. Using no color or paint, this style shows the ivory or milk-white glaze to its best advantage and thus makes a pleasing contrast to other over-decorated styles.

The **Bridge of Peace** (*anping qiao*), is 1 1/4 miles (2 km) long, and links Anhai (19 mi./30 km south of Quanzhou) with Shuitou. It was built in the 12th century from blocks of stone 23 to 33 ft long (7 – 10 m), weighing up to 25 tons, and set on more than 300 piers.

Xiamen (Amoy)

The Song emperors were the first to appreciate the strategically favored position of the island of **Xiamen** (Amoy). Other offshore islands protect its spa-

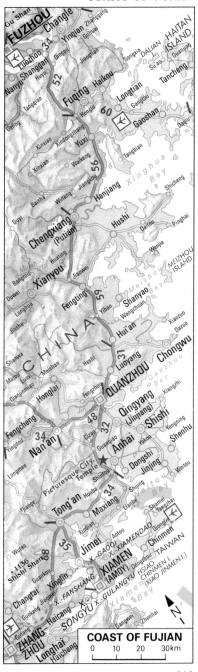

Above: View of the former European Concession district in Xiamen (Amoy).

cious natural harbor. Like many Chinese ports, the town, whose defences were built as early as the 14th century, had to be opened to the colonial powers. The causeway linking the island with the mainland was not built until the 1950s. The Special Economic Zone set up in 1980 for foreign investors is helping Xiamen to achieve a remarkable rate of growth.

The charm of the town lies in its narrow, winding streets with long arcades in front of the houses, to keep off the sun.

To the west of the town center a small ferry takes visitors to the island of **Gulangyu**. Its little town has an almost Italian atmosphere – a perfect place for strolling, undisturbed by motor traffic. It was here that the European colonial masters built their villas in the 19th century.

The highest point on the island goes by the apt name of **Sunlight Rock** (*riguang yan*). The panoramic view from the top richly rewards the effort of climbing up; the path takes you past **Lotus Flower convent** (*linhua an*), and the **General Koxinga memorial pavilion**. South of the hill, you can unwind in Shuzhuang Park or on the long sandy beach.

Some way out of the town to the southeast, below the **Five Old Men mountain** (*wulao shan)*, the **Temple of the Southern Putuo** (*nanputuo si*) was built by monks a thousand years ago. It is named after one of the sacred mountains of Buddhism, Putuoshan, in the province of Zhejiang. At the entrance to the **first hall** the *Buddha of the Future* smiles mischievously. The **main hall** contains sculptures of the *Buddhas of the Past*, *Present* and *Future*, and a wooden statue of the *Bodhisattva Guanyin* with the thousand hands.

In northeastern Xiamen, on the slopes of **Lion Mountain** (*shi shan*) lies the **Park of Ten Thousand Rock**s (*wanshiyan gongyuan*), which is also the site of the **Botanical Garden**.

ZHEJIANG

Getting there

Hangzhou, the centre of Zhejiang, is part of an extensive network of transport connections, which reaches as far as Hong Kong. The 125 miles (200 km) between here and Shanghai ares covered several times daily by train and bus services. If time allows you should take a boat along the Imperial Canal towards Suzhou.

Accommodation

In **HANGZHOU** there are numerous hotels offering accommodation in every category. Almost all of them are found in the west of the city (near the Xihu lake). *LUXURY:* **Dragon**, Shuhuang Lu, Tel. 799 8833. **Hangzhou Shangri-la Hotel**, Beishan Lu 78, Tel. 707 7951. *MID-PRICE:* **Huagang Hotel** (*huagang fandian*), Xishan Lu, Tel. 707 1324. **You Hao**, Pinhghai Lu 53, Tel. 707 7888. **Xihu**, Xishan Lu 7, Tel. 707 6889.

SHAOXING: *MID-PRICE:* **Shaoxing Hotel**, Huanshan Lu 9, Tel. 513 5881.

NINGBO: *MID-PRICE:* **Asia Garden**, Mayuan Lu, Tel. 736 6888. **Ningbo Hotel**, Mayuan Lu 65, Tel. 736 6334. *BUDGET:* **Shanghai Hotel**, near the train station.

PUTUOSHAN: Very basic sleeping facilities in the monastery or in one of the guesthouses. **WENZHOU**: *BUDGET:* **Huaqiao Dasha** (accommodation used by overseas Chinese).

YANDANGSHAN: Very simple accommodation can be found in the monastery.

Restaurants

HANGZHOU is famous for its fish specialities and fresh vegetable dishes: **Louwailou Restaurant**, Waixihu 20 (on Gushan Island), specialities here are the sweet-and-sour fish and the lotus soup. **Hangzhou Restaurant**, Yan'an Lu 52.

Tourist information

CITS (state-owned tourist bureau): **HANGZHOU**: Shihan Lu 1, Tel. 505 2888; there is a branch office in the Baochu Lu. In **NINGBO**: **OTC**, Ningbo Hotel, Tel. 736 4451.

Excursion

Along the road from Ningbo to Wenshou it is worth making a little side-trip (turn off near Gaojian, from there 19 miles/ 30 km) to Tiantai, where you can visit the 6th century Buddhist monasteries on **Mt Tiantaishan**; the Buddhism practised here bears marked Taoist characteristics. About 37 miles (60 km) south-west of Hangzhou you will find, near Pailing (Chun'an), the **Lake of a Thousand Islands** with many picturesque bays around its shores. In every city you can visit a Chinese opera. The *Nanxi* ("Southern Opera") is based in Zhejiang. (**HANGZHOU**: Hangzhou Theater, Tiyuchang Lu.)

FUJIAN

Getting there

The most convenient way to reach the province is by air to **Fuzhou**; from there you can visit nearly every coastal town by bus or ship. From Fuzhou und **Xiamen** there are also steamer services to Hong Kong.

Accommodation

FUZHOU: *LUXURY:* **Lakeside**, Hubin Lu 1, Tel. 753 9888. **Wenquan Dasha**, Wusi Lu, Tel. 755 1818. **Foreign Trade Center Hotel** (*waimao zhongxin jiudian*), Wusi Lu, Tel. 752 3388. *MID-PRICE:* **Minjiang Hotel**, Wusi Lu, Tel. 755 7895. **Overseas Chinese Hotel** (*huaqiao dasha*), Wusi Lu, Tel. 755 7603.

XIAMEN: *LUXURY:* **Holiday Inn Crown Plaza**, Zhenhai Lu 12, Tel. 202 3333. **Mandarin**, Huli Foreigners Residential Area, Tel. 602 3333. *MID-PRICE:* **Overseas Chinese Building** (*huaqiao dasha*), Zhongshan Lu 444, Tel. 202 5602. **Lujiang Hotel**, Lujiang Dao Lu 54, Tel. 202 2922. *BUDGET:* **Gulangyu Guesthouse**, Huangyan Lu 25, Tel. 202 2052.

QUANZHOU: *LUXURY:* **Jinquan**, Nanjunjiang Lu, Tel. 282 5078. *MID-PRICE:* **Overseas Chinese Hotel** (*huaqiao dasha*), Qingchi Xi, Tel. 282 2192.

Restaurants

The restaurants on or near the coast serve freshly caught fish and seafood. A special delicacy of **FUZHOU** is jasmine tea.

XIAMEN: Along the Zhongshan Lu (Sun-Yatsen Street) there are many restaurants specializing in seafood. Quite a number of them allow their customers to choose the dishes for their meal from a "living menu" – a large aquarium.

Tourist information

CITS (state-owned tourist bureau): **FUZHOU**: Dong Dalu 44, Tel. 755 5506. **XIAMEN**: Zhenxing Bldg., Hubin Bei Lu, Tel. 505 1822. **QUANZHOU**: In the Overseas Chinese Hotel, Tel. 282 2039.

Excursions

Zhangzhou, situated just a few miles from Xiamen is known as the "City of Blossom and Fruit", since these grow luxuriantly in the surrounding area. South of the town on Mt Nanshansi a monastery with thousand year old **Marble Buddha** and to the east the **Cave of Clouds** (*yundong yan*), whose walls are decorated with calligraphic poems. On the border with Jiangxi near Chong'an lies the enchanting mountain and river scenery of the **Wuyishan**. Rare plants bloom, and amphibians and reptiles of all kinds haunt this nature reserve. You should make a point of exploring the area around the green **River of the Nine Bends** (*juiqu xi*).

THE SENSUOUS SOUTH

**CANTON
(GUANGZHOU)
GUANGDONG
HAINAN
GUANGXI**

GETTING THE FEEL OF THE SOUTH

If you start your journey to China in Hong Kong, there is only one way of travelling that really allows you to get acclimatized: by train. Overcrowded carriages, hard seats and blaring loudspeakers – these are all part of the Chinese experience. Travelling by rail, you can soak up the atmosphere right from the start – on the way from Hong Kong to the Chinese border and through the province of Guangdong to Canton (Guangzhou), which is our first stopover.

From Hong Kong's **Kowloon** station, express trains and local services wend their way towards China, through the **New Territories**, with their labyrinthine housing developments that spread over the dwindling rice paddies. Near **Lowu** the once tightly-drawn bamboo curtain parts, with minimal border formalities, to allow travelers into the Kingdom of the Middle.

Within the first few miles, the People's Republic of China reveals an unwonted modern, almost "capitalist" side: the *Special Economic Zone* around **Shenzhen**, which is designed to attract large interna-

Left: Limestone mountains along the Li river near Guilin (Guangxi province).

tional companies, is scarcely distinguishable from the forest of high-rise buildings back in downtown Hong Kong.

In the mid-1980s Shenzhen was still something of a sensation. The Western lifestyle, as the Chinese imagined it, was paraded here on Communist soil under the very eyes of the comrades. During the day life was ruled by big business, but in the evening the workers could relax in discos or satisfy their curiosity about western life at fashion shows or at the Miss China Body Beautiful contest. That was in 1985. Today, this "exoticism" has disappeared from Shenzhen, and banking halls and office blocks set a more sober tone. There is nothing here to merit a stopover; no reason, in fact, to leave the train until Canton.

Canton (Guangzhou), the capital of Guangdong province, has a population of 2.7 million, but anyone expecting to find the "real" China here is usually disappointed. For Canton has always been – together with Shanghai – China's "gateway to the west." This has left many signs of Western influence, so that, at first sight, Canton is reminiscent of its economically much more powerful twin city of Hong Kong, only 68 miles (110 km) to the south.

If one wanted to try to sum up the Cantonese mentality, one would have to say

that, above all, they are born traders. At the same time, however, they take things less seriously than the Northerners and appreciate more fully the pleasures of everyday life. This easy-going attitude doubtless stems from a simple fact which all tourists become aware of almost the moment they arrive: the hot and humid subtropical climate of the south makes your clothes stick to your body after just a few minutes, and can put quite a damper on your plans for the day. For this reason you should choose the early morning to explore Canton and its environs.

CANTON (GUANGZHOU)

In the legend of the founding of the city of Canton, five goats play a major role. On their backs, it is said, five tutelary gods came down to earth. In their mouths the goats carried ears of rice which, from that day forth, would keep the inhabitants from hunger. The goats can still be seen in **Yuexiu Park** (*yuexiu gongyuan*) – carved in stone.

The city was first enclosed by a wall in 214 BC, and Canton later became an important seaport during the Tang Dynasty (618-907). From the mid-18th to the mid-19th century, the city enjoyed the unofficial distinction of being the only port linking China with the outside world. Admittedly, as time passed, Canton also earned the dubious reputation of being a market for opium, so it is no surprise that the Opium Wars of the mid-19th century were waged with particular ferocity in this area. As a result of European "gunboat diplomacy," Canton, like other major Chinese ports, was forcibly opened up to foreign shipping under the Treaty of Nanking, which was signed on August 29th, 1842.

However, the Cantonese would not let their hot-blooded fighting spirit be tamed so easily. Earlier in this century, the city was a hotbed of numerous revolts and uprisings, a fact which is commemorated in many monuments around the city.

Even after the People's Republic was proclaimed in October 1949, Canton, as a

trade and exhibition center, remained China's gateway to the world. Twice a year, in the spring and autumn, business people come from all over the world to fill their order books at the Canton Trade Fair. But today the impending repossession by China of the British Crown Colony of Hong Kong, due in 1997, looms large as a factor that will determine the future of Canton. For many years the city on the **Pearl River** (*zhu jiang*) has been regarded as a Communist counterweight to capitalist Hong Kong, and developed as such, to the considerable satisfaction of the Cantonese. Here the "emperor"–- or central government in Beijing – is far away, and economic and personal freedom is noticeably greater than elsewhere in China. So, between business and pleasure, the Party and the profit motive, life goes on in its calm southern way with a gradually increasing prosperity which the Cantonese take happily in their stride.

One person's gain is another's loss, however, and the traveller in China will find less of the typical Chinese atmosphere in Canton than in other cities. Nor is there much in the way of sightseeing. Yet there's something to touch the heart of every visitor to Canton; for they say the way to the heart is through the stomach. And Cantonese cuisine has a secret weapon in the form of *dimsum* (Mandarin Chinese: *dianxin*).

"Touch the heart" is the literal translation of the name of these tasty little bite-sized dumplings stuffed with delicious variations of fish and meat, prawns and chicken, savoury and sweet. No Cantonese would let her heart go untouched in the morning – so why should you miss out? There's opportunity on practically every street corner at stalls selling hot food and snacks, especially between 5 and 9:30 am. This is also the best time of day to get to know Canton. At the same time, you will be able to test for yourself, in part at least, the accuracy of the Chinese proverb that runs: "You should be born in Suzhou. You should live in Hangzhou. You should die in Luzhou. And you should eat in Guangzhou." Each of these cities has its own special claim to fame: in Suzhou you find the most beautiful women, in Hangzhou the most delicate silk, in Luzhou the finest wood for your coffin – and in Guangzhou, Canton, the best food.

Shamian Island and the Pearl River

If you arrive in Canton by train, don't expect to find the heart of the city near the station. All the same, you can benefit from the convenience of staying at the **Liuhua Hotel** right opposite the station. This is especially useful if you are leaving the city again by train a few days later.

Canton's real pulse beats along the **Pearl River** (*zhu jiang*), and the best place to start your tour of the city is Shamian Island. Here colonial buildings line the narrow avenues and remind us that in

119

the second half of the 19th century Shamian was an enclave under British and French colonial rule.

The Catholic church of **Our Lady of Lourdes** was built in 1890, and, after many years of inappropriately secular use as a warehouse, was reopened for worship in 1982. In the same year the **White Swan** luxury hotel opened its doors to reveal a waterfall splashing and murmuring in the foyer. This hotel is only a short walk from the church. In its coffee shop, you can pause for a snack while looking out through its long glass façade, which has a wonderful view of the Pearl River and the waterborne traders bustling to and fro between the junks and houseboats.

During rush hour, crowds of pedestrians and cyclists stream across the nearby **Renmin Bridge** to the south bank of the river. It was here, on June 23rd,

Above: The skyline of Canton on the Pearl River. Right: Qingping Market around the Qingpinglu in Canton.

1925, that British and French soldiers shot 23 Chinese workers who were demonstrating in favor of closing the rival port of Hong Kong. This regrettable event is recalled by the **Memorial to the Martyrs of the Shaji Massacre**, at the foot of the bridge.

The restorative peace of Shamian Island, however, will fortify you for the remaining tour of the city, which leads across Liu'ersan Lu to the **Qingping Market** (*qingping shichang*). Around Qingpinglu, Canton's famous, some would say notorious, market area buzzes with activity.

In the northern section, animal-lovers will be appalled to see creatures of every description being sold for consumption. Monkeys, cats and dogs are standard fare; more rarely, you can also see owls, anteaters and sloths cowering in small cages in front of fastidious gourmets. By contrast, the southern part of the market, with its trade in herbs and spices, compensates to some extent by dealing exclusively in vegetarian produce.

It would be a shame if visiting the market spoiled your appetite, because there are many inviting places to eat nearby. Among them is the **Shecanguan Restaurant** at 43 Jianglanlu, which has stood on this site for over a hundred years. You will not need an interpreter to understand its name. One glance through the window is enough: what you will see is a *snake* restaurant, and in fact the most famous one in Canton. Snake-meat is supposed to strengthen the body's natural immunity and stimulate the circulation of the blood. During the high season, in autumn and winter, up to a thousand snakes are eaten here every day.

On the menu can be found such dishes as: "Gallbladder of Canton snake cooked in rice wine" (prepared at the table), "Boiled cobra with smoked ham" and even "Snake, chicken and cat soup." Snake meat has a flavor that reminds one sometimes of fish, sometimes of chicken. Those who have by now lost their appetite for meat can take refuge in the **Caigenxiang Restaurant** nearby (167

Zhongshan-6-Lu). There they will be comforted by vegetarian dishes with poetic-sounding names such as "Ting Lake vegetarian delight" (seaweed, mushrooms, nuts and bamboo), "The power of Buddhism" or "The sweet scent of flowers."

Pagodas and parks

Walking north along Renmin Nanlu and Renmin Zhonglu you come to some of the town's beautiful temples and parks. The **Temple of Children's Piety** (*guangxiao si*) was founded in the 2nd century BC and is believed to be the oldest temple in the city. In 397 AD the Indian monk Dharmayasas gave readings from the Buddhist scriptures here. The temple was given its present name in 1151. Most of its buildings were destroyed by a fire in the middle of the 13th century and were not rebuilt until much later. However, the **Mahavira Hall** and the **Liuzudian Hall** are worth seeing. **The East and West Iron Pagodas**

(*dongtie ta* and *xitie ta*), which have survived intact, date from the 10th century. They represent the earliest examples in China of this technique of building.

To the east, in the Liuronglu, stands the **Temple of the Six Banyan Trees** (*liurong si*). The origins of the temple site date back to the year 537. The **Flower Pagoda**, (*hua ta*), appears from the outside to have nine storeys, but inside there are 17 floors. It is one of Canton's landmarks, towering above this Buddhist complex in the center of the city. The poet Su Dongpo gave the Liurongsi its name in the year 1099. It was he who executed the calligraphy for the name *liu rong*, which can be seen and admired in facsimile.

Continuing north on Jiefang Beilu you reach **Yuexiu Park** (*yuexiu gongyuan*), the largest green space in central Canton. The park, covering about 250 acres (100

Above: Statue of Buddha in the Temple of the Six Banyan Trees in Canton.

ha), stretches away beyond the **Sun Yatsen Memorial Hall** (*zhongshan jiniantang*), which is roofed in blue ceramic tiles and commemorates the founder of the Guomindang (Kuomintang), who died in 1925. It seats over 4,700 people and so ranks among Canton's most important public venues. In the middle of Yuexiu Park are three lakes, **Dongxiu** (eastern), **Nanxiu** (southern) and **Beixiu** (northern), as well as the **Tower Overlooking the Sea** (*zhenhai lou*), which is over 600 years old. Housed in this former watchtower is the **Guangzhou Museum**, where you can see the **Monument of the Five Goats,** celebrating the legend of the founding of Canton. On the opposite side of Jiefang Beilu, the **Orchid Garden** (*lanpu*) is worth a visit.

There are two other parks in the west of the city. **Liuhua Park** (*liuhua gongyuan*), on Dongfeng Xilu, contains several artificial lakes, while in **Liwanhu Park** (*liwanhu gongyuan*), at the end of Zhongshan-8-Lu, the great attraction for visitors is the **Panxi Restaurant**. On Zhongshan-8-Lu you will also find the **Ancestral Temple of the Chen Family** (*chenjia ci*). The woodcarvings and clay figures in this building, which was completed in 1894 and has since been restored, are outstanding examples of architectural decoration.

The **Huanghua Mausoleum of the 72 Martyrs** (*huanghua gang qishi'er lieshi mu*) on Xianlielu is an important monument. It commemorates the unsuccessful uprising led by Sun Yatsen (Sun Zhongshan) against the Qing rulers, on April 27th, 1911. In a garden on Zhongshan-3-Lu the **Memorial to the Martyrs of the Guangzhou Uprising** recalls the massacre of December 11th, 1927, when Chiang Kaishek ordered the killing of over 5000 Communists.

The city also holds memories of Mao Zedong. The Institute of the National Peasant Movement (*nongmin yundong jiangxisuo*) at 42 Zhongshan-4-Lu is

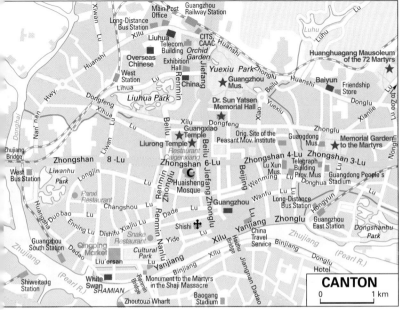

where the Great Helmsman instructed his comrades in the principles of guerrilla warfare, as early as 1926.

The **Huaisheng Mosque** (*huaisheng si*) is China's oldest mosque, dating from 627 AD. Its **minaret** (*guang ta*), 119 ft (36 m) high, towers above it. This center of worship for Canton's Muslims is situated in Guangtalu.

The Cantonese themselves usually like to relax in the park surrounding **White Cloud Mountain** (*baiyun shan*). Numerous lakes and tea-houses cluster around the foot of the 1256 ft (383 m) peak. If you are looking for action and excitement rather than tranquility, you should take a walk along the bank of the Pearl River, where there is hectic activity at all hours of the day, both on the water and ashore.

It's here that you'll find what is certainly the most delightful way to take your leave of Canton: the ferry that leaves from **Zhoutouzui Wharf** on the Pearl River and steams down the coast to Hainan Island.

TOURING IN GUANGDONG PROVINCE

Foshan ("Buddha Hill"), lying barely 19 miles (30 km) southwest of Canton, is one of the most popular destinations for a day's outing.

The Taoist **Ancestral Temple** (*zu miao*) has remained unchanged since it was damaged by fire in the middle of the 14th century. In a rectangular pool in the grounds of the temple you will find a **stone turtle with a snake** on its shell. It symbolizes happiness and blessings, which visitors ask for by throwing a coin on to the turtle's back. For many Chinese this little "game of chance" is the high point of their trip; but souvenir hunters may also strike it lucky in Foshan. The town is known all over China for its paper cut-outs and ceramics, on sale in various markets.

A little way off the well-trodden tourist routes through Guangdong province, but nestling among charming scenery in the northeast, is the port of **Shantou**. For-

123

merly called Swatow, it lies on the estuary of the Hanjiang River.

Only 27 miles (43 km) to the north you come to the old trading center of **Chaozhou**, which goes back 1700 years; the Buddhist **Kaiyuan Temple** dates from the Tang period.

One way to visit the 2000-year-old town of **Shaoguan**, about 125 miles (200 km) north of Canton, is to make a stopover on the train journey towards Beijing. Among its sights, the **Nanhuachan Temple** is by far the most rewarding.

The area around **Zhaoqing** on the **Xi River** (*xi jiang*) is notable for its scenery: the impressive landscape of mountains, cliffs and caves lies 75 miles (120 km) west of Canton. The dominant feature are the **Seven Stars Crags**, set in lakeland scenery.

Travelling overland (by bus or rail) from Canton to Hainan, you reach **Zhan-**

jiang, a gloomy, grey town on the sea. However, the bays and islands here offer refreshing opportunities for swimmers and divers.

HAINAN

"Soundlessly the hunter of the Li tribe follows the fresh spoor. In a quiet cove, fringed by a long white beach, he finally corners the mighty deer. But as he draws his bow, the animal turns its head – and changes into a beautiful girl." The way this legend ends can be guessed easily enough. But only a few people know the beach where it is supposed to have taken place.

The hordes of international tourists were long led right past the southern island of **Hainan** and its beach of **Luhuitao**. Nowadays, huge flocks of Chinese from the People's Republic, Hong Kong and Taiwan enjoy taking their seaside holidays on what used to be known as the "Island of Exiles."

In earlier days, no self-respecting

Above: Subtropical atmosphere in Shantou (Guangdong province).

Chinese citizen would have voluntarily chosen to spend time here. But the picture has changed quite drastically over the past few years, and now even leading Party members visit the island in search of rest and relaxation on the beach and in the water.

Hainan, which was not made an independent province until 1989, owes its late appearance on the tourist map principally to its geographical and militarily strategic position. Vietnam lies almost within shouting distance to the west, while the Philippines press in on the eastern flank and Taiwan on the northeastern. Hainan itself – to borrow the epithet usually reserved for Australia – is "down under": it's farther south than any part, any peninsula of the mainland of the People's Republic.

Although it can easily be reached from the mainland, the island province is nonetheless far removed from the preconceived picture of China held by most visitors. There are two ways of getting there. The voyage by ferry from Canton is restful, but time-consuming: it takes a total of 36 hours to reach the port of Haikou. Anyone with less time at his disposal can fly direct from Canton to Sanya in the southern part of the island, and can be relaxing on China's most beautiful beaches within little more than an hour. It has to be said, however, that despite its marvellous beaches and scenery, Hainan can't compare with Southeast Asia's more famous resorts in Thailand or Bali, since in many places large building sites obstruct access to the beaches.

Haikou and the North

The port of Haikou lies in the north of the island. To a first-time visitor, it might seem that this capital of Hainan, with a population of 250,000, has seen better days. Don't be deceived. Certainly it's true that, in the few streets of the old town, the paint is flaking off the last sur-

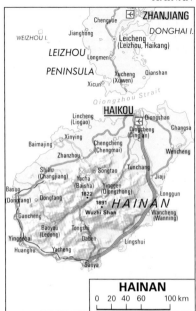

viving houses built in a Portuguese-Chinese style. But if you glance into the shops or through the open windows of the houses, you will be surprised to see luxuries which are generally unheard-of in other parts of China. Hainan owes its privileged economic position firstly to the many Hong Kong Chinese who have made the island their second home, and secondly to the *Hainan Scandal*. In 1985 some officials misappropriated a special provision of foreign currency amounting to nearly US $1.5 billion, which had been earmarked for developing the island as a Special Economic Zone; instead, they used the money to buy consumer goods and cars in Hong Kong for sale on the black market on the mainland. Nonetheless, enough money still flowed into Hainan. One positive side effect for tourists lies in the excellent public transportation between most of the island's towns and villages, which are served by Japanese minibuses.

Haikou itself is best explored on foot. A walk round Jiefang Xilu and Xinhua

Nanlu takes you through the liveliest part of the town center. Also worthwhile is a detour to the harbor to see the junks at anchor and fishermen landing their catches.

However, you will probably want to set off quickly for the south of the island. There are three possible routes for the journey, which is about 190 miles (300 km). In the west a road runs down through the coastal towns of **Dongfang** and **Yinggehai**.

The eastern route also takes you along the coast, by way of **Wenchang** and **Wanning**. Both these roads take more time than the route through **Dunchang** and **Tongshi**. Air-conditioned long-distance buses make this trip along a good road several times a day, crossing the middle of the island, where the Li and Miao minorities live.

All three routes, however, converge on one place: **Sanya**. The harbor area of this southern port is the scene of hectic activity, while in the market nearby you are struck by the plentiful supply of fish and vegetables.

However, the real attractions of the south, China's most beautiful beaches, are found in the area around Sanya. The place with the best facilities for tourists is Dadonghai, where Chinese girls show off the latest beachwear from Shanghai or Wuhan and take a dip in the gentle surf. This "shore of the great eastern sea" stretches as far as the rain-forest green of the hills on the horizon. By Chinese standards it is still relatively empty, and its sand is fine as powder.

A different kind of scenery is to be found west of Sanya at **Tianya Haijiao**. The poet Su Dongpo, whose footsteps we followed at the Liurong Temple in Canton, gave the beach its name. It means roughly: "Where the finger of the earth touches the sky."

This designation was given in the year 1097 – but even today, countless Chinese still seem to regard the place as a paradise on earth. The rocks on the beach, which

Above: Dadonghai Beach, near Sanya, is the one most developed for tourism.

have been worn smooth by the waves, are often photographed as a typical feature of Hainan.

The third beach worth a visit is on the **Luhuitao** peninsula. It was here that the deer in the legend turned its head and changed into a beautiful maiden. Hotel complexes and dense groves of palm trees extend right down to the shoreline. In the evening, the open-air restaurants put their tables and chairs right out on the beach. The range of dishes includes fresh prawns in a sweet-and-sour sauce and lobster in garlic sauce, with fresh bamboo-shoots as a side dish. Towards midnight the beach falls still. On the horizon the anchor-lights of the fishing junks sparkle, while in the large hotels and resorts the tourists dance.

Minorities and markets in the island's interior

Most of Hainan's population belong to the ethnic minorities of the Li and Miao. They live predominantly in the interior of the island and have made **Tongshi** the capital of their autonomous district. The surrounding landscape is dominated by the 6124 ft (1867 m) high **Five-Fingered Mountain** (*wuzhi shan*). After every hairpin bend you look down into another green valley. Remote villages nestle among fertile rice-paddies, in the shade of trees hung with lianas.

In the market of Tongshi, mangoes, papayas, watermelons, apples and oranges are piled high – proof of the fertility of this luxuriant countryside, where fields alternate with jungle and large plantations of rubber and tea. The export of latex, or "white gold," is the mainstay of Hainan's economy. The green tea harvested here provides a culinary trademark of the "southern island" (the meaning of *hai nan*).

Because of the town's beautiful location and its pleasantly cool climate, rich Chinese are increasingly attracted to

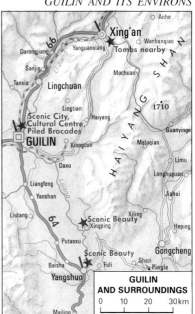

Tongshi. For tourists who want to get to know the minority peoples of the interior, the town makes a good starting point.

The members of the Li tribal group traditionally used to adorn themselves with tattoos. Today, however, the blue skin decorations are only seen on the old women of this hunter-gatherer society. The costume worn by members of the Miao tribe is recognizable by its glorious colors and its sequined embroidery.

GUILIN
Reality or dream?

It is the landscape around **Guilin** which practically every traveler carries in his or her imagination as epitomizing the beauty of the Kingdom of the Middle. There is scarcely another region which can be considered so "typically Chinese" as the karst (limestone) mountains which ring this rather featureless city with a population of 350,000, in the north of the **Guanxi Autonomous Region of the Zhuang Minority**.

127

Around 300 million years ago nature laid the foundations of Guilin's attraction for visitors. In that epoch the region was still covered by the sea. When the water receded it exposed a limestone plateau, which over the course of millions of years has been eroded away. What remain are the strange karst peaks which today rank among China's greatest tourist attractions, alongside the cosmopolitan cities of Peking and Shanghai and the terra-cotta army of Xi'an.

Tourists are usually lost for words to describe the scenery. Poets and calligraphers, on the other hand, have been moved time and again to extol Guilin in ever more enraptured terms. At the beginning of the 9th century the poet of the Tang period, Han Yu, expressed the experience in words that are still apt today: "The river is like a green ribbon of silk.

The mountains are like hairpins of blue jade!"

Without allowing this to dim the pleasure of anticipation, there are a few things you should be prepared for. First, terrible monsoon weather, with heavy clouds and days of unceasing rain, is not unusual in subtropical Guilin. But if travelling around is more difficult in these conditions, the landscape is nonetheless bathed in that strange aura that is so evocative of a Chinese watercolor. The other thing you should be prepared for is all the paraphernalia of Chinese mass tourism – tacky souvenirs, annoyingly insistent peddlers and busloads of tourists.

Nevertheless, there are still many peaceful refuges to be found among the broad rice paddies of the surrounding district, which is best explored by bicycle. And in the autumn the sweet scent hanging over Guilin itself – from the cassia trees to which the town owes its name – soothes away any tourism-induced stress that visitors might feel.

Above: Elephant Trunk Cave and Mountain near Guilin (Guangxi). Right: Boat-trip on the Li River near Guilin (Guangxi).

A town set amid mountains, lakes and caves

Guilin was founded in 214 BC, during the Qin dynasty. Guilin's destiny, like that of many Chinese towns and cities, was determined by the far-sighted action of the emperor Qin Shi Huangdi. In Guilin's case, a dramatic growth in its economy resulted from the building of the **Ling Canal** (*ling qu*). Because of the canal, Guilin rose to become an important point for the shipment of goods, a hub of transport routes between southern China and the center of the country. For this manmade waterway was the final link connecting the Yangtse in the north and the Pearl River in the south.

In 1647, the Ming Emperors made the town their defensive stronghold against the Manchus. Centuries later, during the Second World War, over 300,000 Chinese, fleeing from the Japanese army in Manchukuo, poured into Guilin.

Happily, most people nowadays have pleasanter reasons for coming to Guilin.

Anyone with limited time should take the one-hour flight from Canton; this is a strikingly beautiful journey, with breathtaking views from the air over the karst landscape with its steep hills. The train journey from Canton takes about 24 hours. It is even slower (but all the more atmospheric for that reason) to travel by steamer from Canton up the **river Xi** (*xi jiang*) as far as Wuzhou and then continue the journey to Yangshuo or Guilin by bus.

In the city itself, most tourists opt for the same routes. Even in the middle of Guilin there are several limestone hills, some of which can be climbed. A flight of more than 300 steps takes you up to **The Peak of Solitary Beauty** (*duxiu feng*). After descending again you can get your breath back beside this "Pillar under the Southern Sky" in the remains of a 14th-century **Royal Palace** (*wang cheng*). With renewed vigor, you can then make your way up the **Fuboshan** hill on the bank of the Lijiang. As you climb your eye will be caught by a bell

ing. Its highest point, **Mingyuefeng**, rises to 730 ft (223 m) and affords a wonderful view over Guilin from the north. South of the city, you can also climb **Elephant Trunk Hill** (*xiangbi shan*), which, standing at the edge of the river Li, looks strikingly like an elephant drinking (hence its name).

There are several parks whose outstanding beauty derives from the perfect harmony of their mountain and lakeland scenery. **Seven Star Park** (*qixing gong-yuan*), on the eastern, quieter bank of the Lijiang, gets its name from seven hills in a formation that recalls the constellation of the Great Bear. Several temples and caves, among them **Seven Star Cave** (*qixing yan*), add to its attraction.

The underworld can also be explored around Guilin: there are numerous caves with stalactites and stalagmites, which are open to visitors. **Reed Flute Cave** (*ludi yan*), which has eaten its way deep into the mountain, is particularly rewarding to investigate.

As evening falls, the distinction between appearance and reality, art and nature, becomes blurred. The sun sinks behind the karst mountains and the cormorant fishermen, with their birds trained to dive for fish, punt their slender boats over the still water. This is the moment when you should make yourself comfortable on a hilltop or a hotel terrace high above the city, for it would be hard to imagine a more idyllic close to the day.

from a former temple weighing 2.5 tons, or by a vast cooking pot from which over a thousand people were fed. Both these unusual objects are relics of the Qing period.

A further attraction is the **Cave of the Recovered Pearl** (*huanzhu dong*) at the southern foot of the hill. In it, a general of the Han period is supposed to have sharpened his sword while defending the city of Guilin against attackers. A legend has grown up to explain the name of the cave. A dragon once lived here; and in his cave was a pearl that gave him light. A fisherman robbed him of this jewel – only to bring it back again, filled with remorse, a little while later. On the eastern side the **Rock of the Thousand Buddhas** (*qianfo yan*) is decorated, not quite as its name suggests, by a "mere" 300 sculptures.

Near the city center, the **Hill of Many Colors** (*diecai shan*) is also worth climb-

Along the river Li to Yangshuo

There is almost no visitor who does not take a boat trip on the river Li while staying in Guilin. Starting at 7 am, the ferries leave from Zhujiang, 12.5 miles (20 km) to the south. All the tours have the same destination: Yangshuo, some 37.5 miles (60 km) away. The journey there takes you past about fifty karst mountains. They sport such elaborate names as "Father and son rock," "Five

Above: Fishing from a raft on the river Li near Guilin (Guangxi). Right: Cormorant-fisherman on the Li, Yangshuo (Guangxi).

tigers devouring a sheep," "Climbing tortoise" or "Skyscraper mountain." With a little imagination, you can see how the hills came by these names.

On the river banks beneath these mountains daily Chinese life goes on. Women do the washing, children play in the river, narrow ferry boats made of bamboo and laden with passengers, bicycles and baskets full of vegetables, ply at a leisurely pace between the opposite banks of the Lijiang.

After approximately five hours, the boat ties up at Yangshuo, which despite the steady influx of tourists has retained its village character.

However, anyone who wants to get away from the frantic city pace of Guilin should spend at least one peaceful night in Yangshuo.

NANNING

Nanning, the capital of Guanxi Autonomous Region of the Zhuang Minority, is China's southernmost city, with a population of some 650,000. Territorial disputes have plagued the area, inhabited predominantly by the Zhuang people, from time immemorial.

So Emperor Qin Shi Huangdi incorporated the city, which was founded in the Han period, into his empire. Thereafter the Tang Dynasty, the Ming Emperor and, much later the English and the French, all laid claim to it. Presumably the colonial powers were attracted by the city's geographical location – it is only about 100 miles (160 km) from the border with Vietnam.

Nanning lies rather off the beaten tourist track, despite the obvious attractions of its subtropical scenery.

The city itself does not have any major sights. Nevertheless, it is worth paying a visit to the **Guangxi Provincial Museum** (*guangxi bowuguan*) and the **Institute for Minorities**, as well as walking through the park with its **South Lake** (*nan hu*) or strolling around one of the markets where the ethnic minorities are much in evidence. In the surrounding

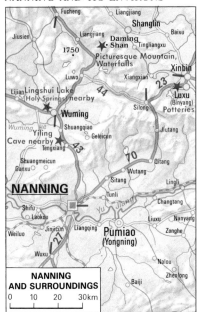

NANNING AND SURROUNDINGS

0   10   20   30km

area, in the direction of **Wuming** to the north, you can visit the **stalactite caves at Yiling** (*yiling yan*). Close to Wuming is **Lingshui Lake**, which is permanently warm. Rather further away, the **Daming Hills** (*daming shan*) entice you with their waterfalls.

Excursions into Guangxi province

At the confluence of several rivers, the town of **Wuzhou,** with its parks and markets, is a good place to break the journey from Canton to Guilin.

It is also worth stopping at **Liuzhou** on the railroad line between Guilin and Nanning, for its caves, parks and limestone landscape around the Lijiang.

About 118 miles (190 km) southwest of Nanning is **Ningming** (Chengzhong), near the Vietnamese border. From there you can get to the **Flower Mountain rock paintings** (*hua shan*), which are a thousand years old and have not yet been conclusively deciphered. The landscape there is enchanting.

GUANGDONG – HAINAN GUANGXI

Accommodation

GUANGDONG: CANTON (GUANGZHOU
LUXURY: **China Hotel** (*zhongguo dajiudian* Liuhua Lu, Tel. 666 6888 (1017 rooms; good, inex pensive bread and cakes; in the *Food Street* (open non-residents) there are various Chinese cuisine from Pekin to Canton). **White Swan Hotel** (*baiti n'e binguan*), Shamian Island, Tel. 888 6968 (a tractive location on the Zhujiang river; listed *Leading Hotels of the World* and one of China finest hotels). **Dongfang Hotel** (*dongfang bin guan*), 120 Liuhua Lu, Tel. 666 9900 (near th Yuexiu Hill). *MID-PRICE:* **Baiyun Hotel** (*bayu binguan*), 367 Huanshi Donglu, Tel. 333 3998 (op posite the Garden Hotel). **Liuhua Hotel** (*liuhua binguan*), 194 Huanshi Xilu, Tel. 666 8800 (centra location opposite station; established rendezvous fo independent travelers in China; since renovation th prices have gone up. *BUDGET:* A lot of cheap ac commodation can be found on Shamian Island, inc the **Guangzhou Youth Hostel** (*guangzhou qing nian zhaodaisuo*), 2 Shamian-4-Jie, Tel. 888 4298 and **Guangdong Youth Hostel** (*guangdong qingnian lüshe*), 26 Shamian Dajie, Tel. 888 761 (The rooms are usually dormitory style).
FOSHAN: *MID-PRICE:* **Rotating Palace Hote** (*xuangong jiudian*), corner Zumiao Lu / Lianhua Lu
SHANTOU: *LUXURY:* **International**, Jinsh Lu, Tel. 825 1212. *MID-PRICE:* **Jinsha**, Jinsh Lu, Tel. 823 1700.
ZHAOQING: *MID-PRICE:* **Overseas Chines Hotel** (*huaqiao fandian*), 90 Tianning Beilu, Te 232952.
HAINAN: HAIKOU: *MID-PRICE:* **Haikou** Haifu Dadao 4, Tel. 535 0221. **Haiku Tower**, Bin hai Dadao, Tel. 677 2990. **Nantian Hotel**, at th airport, Tel. 677 4888 (with swimmingpool an supermarket). **Overseas Chinese Hotel** (*huaqia dasha*), 17 Datong Lu, Tel. 677 2623 (central loca tion; good Chinese restaurant).
SANYA: *MID-PRICE:* **Jinling Resort**, Dadon ghai, Tel. 214081. *BUDGET:* **Sanya Holiday Re sort**, Sanya Wan, Tel. 273050.
TONGSHI: *MID-PRICE:* **Tongza Holiday Re sort** (*lüyou shanzhuang*) or **Wuzhishan Hote** (*wuzhishan binguan*), both in the center of town.
GUANGXI: GUILIN: *LUXURY:* **Holiday Inn** (*jiari guibinguan*), 14 Ronghu Nanlu, Tel. 28 3950. **Royal Garden**, Yanjiang Lu, Tel. 581 2411 **Sheraton Guilin Hotel**, 9 Binjiang Nanlu, Tel 282 5588 (all three hotels offer the expected interna tional standard but without any noticeable Chines ambiance). **Guishan Hotel** (*guishan jiudian*)

Chuanshan Lu, Tel. 484 3388. *MID-PRICE:* **Lijiang Hotel** (*lijiang fandian*), 1 Shahu Beilu, Tel. 282 2881. **Osmanthus Hotel** (*dangui fandian*), 451 Zhongshan Nanlu, Tel. 383 4300 (for many years this has been top of the list for independent tourists in China). **Overseas Chinese Mansion** (*huaqiao dasha*), 39 Zhongshan Nanlu, Tel. 383 5753. *BUDGET:* **Hidden Hill Hotel** (*yinshan fandian*), 97 Zhongshan Nanlu (along this street there is other reasonably priced accommodation).

YANGSHUO: *BUDGET:* **Yangshuo Hotel** (*yangshuo fandian*), in the center of town.

NANNING: *MID-PRICE:* **Mingyuan Hotel** (*mingyuan fandian*), 38 Xinmin Lu, Tel. 280 2986. **Yongjiang Hotel** (*yongjiang binguan*), 41 Jiangbin Lu, Tel. 280 8123.

Restaurants

GUANGDONG: **CANTON**: No list of restaurants in Canton can make a credible claim to completeness, since around every street corner you will stumble across an eating-place that would be well worth recommending. In any event, you should go out in the early hours of the morning to sample the delicious *dimsum*, which you can buy from mobile stalls that go from place to place, and where the food is cooked on the spot. Nevertheless, we will draw your attention to a number of gastronomic addresses which have proved their worth over the years: **Beiyuan**, 202 Xiao Beilu, Tel. 333 2460 and 32471 (one of Canton's oldest restaurants, situated in a beautiful garden; get a table in the old part, which has more atmosphere than the new annex). **Caigenxiang**, 167 Zhongshan-6-Lu, Tel. 334 4363 (a veritable oasis, and not just for vegetarians). **Guangzhou**, 2 Wenchang Lu, Tel. 888 7840 (the best-known restaurant in the city, justly famous for its Cantonese cuisine). **Panxi** (delightful atmosphere, set in parkland near a lake; a good place to go for *dimsum*). **Shecanguan**, 43 Jianglan Lu, Tel. 888 2517 (specializing in snake-meat recipes, but has a few dishes which even European palettes will find acceptable).

GUANGXI: **GUILIN**: When you are on the road you must be ready for some unfamiliar culinary experiences: the most exotic animals are displayed alive in small cages outside the restaurant, only to end up in the stew-pot at the whim of a diner.

Tips and Trips

CANTON: During the Spring and Autumn Trade Fairs there can be a severe shortage of accommodation. The rail journey from Hongkong to Canton not only offers the most evocative way of arriving in China, but is also considered – in comparison with Canton airport – to be less dangerous. A way to save money: foreign tourists who continue their journey by train from Canton through the People's Republic, are obliged to buy their tickets through the CITS office, which charges high prices. Concessionary fares (e.g. for students) are not generally granted. So it is advisable only to book short journeys from Canton, e.g. to Guilin.

HAINAN: There is a malaria alert on the island of Hainan and in other parts of southwestern China. You should equip yourself with anti-malaria medication before your leave your home country, since they are virtually unavailable on the island itself.

GUILIN: The steamer trip along the river Li is a real delight, even though the weather is unfortunately often very bad. The boats used by local Chinese tourists follow the same route and foreigners can also book seats on them. They work out significantly cheaper than the trips reserved for international tourist groups (though the latter provide considerable greater shipboard comfort and facilities).

Museums

CANTON: The **Guangzhou Provincial Museum** (*guangzhou sheng bowuguan*), Yan'an-2-Lu (fascinating insight into the history of the province). **Guangdong Museum**, Yuexiu Park, Zhenhai Tower (the city's past in a wider historical context, and a delightful physical setting). **Lu Xun Museum**, Wenming Lu (memorial to Lu Xun, the celebrated author and political thinker of the first half of the 20th century). **South China Botanical Garden**, Longyandong (rich variety of plants and shrubs). **Guangzhou Zoo** (*guangzhou dongwuyuan*), Xianlie Lu (with the obligatory panda). **NANNING**: In the Nanhu Park (information about the history of the province): **Guangxi Provincial Museum** (*guangxi sheng bowuguan*).

Festivals and events

NANNING: On the 5th day of the 5th month in the lunar calendar (during June) there is a dragon-boat race, famous beyond the borders of the province.

Tourist information

CANTON: **CITS**, 179 Huanshi Lu, Tel. 666 8808. **HAIKOU**: **CTS**, Overseas Chinese Hotel, Datong Lu, Tel. 677 5115. **GUILIN**: **CITS**, 14 Ronghu Beilu, Tel. 282 7427. **NANNING**: **CITS**, Mingyuan Hotel, Tel. 280 2042.

Excursions

CANTON: Hidden in the charming landscape are various monasteries, such as the **Luofu Monastery** (13th cent.) in the eponymous hills (44 mi / 70 km east), the **Nengren Monastery** at the Mountain of the White Cloud (*bai yun shan*, 6 mi / 10 km north), and the **Baiyun Temple** in the mountains of Xiqiao (37.5 mi / 60 km southwest).

GUILIN: In the district Xing'an, 41 miles (66 km) to the north, the **Graves of the Generals** and the **Shrine of the Four Sages** near the Ling Channel are worth a visit.

133

LANDSCAPE IN
WATERCOLORS

YUNNAN

GUIZHOU

YUNNAN

The provinces of **Yunnan** and **Guizhou** make up the southwest of the People's Republic of China. The name *Yunnan* means something like "Southern Land beneath the Clouds" – which suggests how remote the province was from the "Celestial Throne" in Peking. Until the end of the 19th century the region was thought of as a kind of Chinese El Dorado, of which scarcely anyone had any precise knowledge.

But times have changed. And now, even tourists flock to Yunnan. They are attracted to the province mainly by the beauty of its landscape – a vision of luxuriant tropical forests, steep mountainsides and fertile valleys, through which flow such mighty rivers as the **Langcang** (*langcang jiang*, better known as the Mekong).

No other province of China displays such a wide diversity of landscape: in the north, mountains rise gradually to the Tibetan plateau.

In the south, dense jungle has prevented many places from being invaded. The variety is matched by a multitude of plant and animal species.

Left: A woman of the Buyi ethnic minority in Huangguoshu (Guizhou province).

Centuries of contact with neighboring countries in Southeast Asia has ensured a rich cultural mix: Burma, Laos and Vietnam lie just over the border. The presence of these neighbors has led the Beijing government to class Yunnan as a politically explosive region. For the same reason, the ethnic minorities, who often form the majority of the local population, are still waiting to be granted the measure of autonomy which is already enjoyed in other parts of China.

In Yunnan there are 17 ethnic minorities of significant size. As well as the relatively large peoples of the Bai, Hani and Yao, each with over a million members, there are many other almost forgotten tribes, such as the Achang, Nu, Jinuo, Bulang, Dulong, and others, who generally number fewer than 50,000 people.

As disparate as their origins may be, these tribes all have one thing in common: for them, the region's political borders between provinces are boundaries that exist only on paper. In their hearts and minds, these arbitrary divisions mean nothing.

The most important tourist attractions in Yunnan are Kunming and the nearby Rock Forest of Shilin; Lake Erhai and the little town of Dali; and Xishuangbanna, the Autonomous Region of the Dai people in the far south.

135

Kunming

A city of two million inhabitants, **Kunming** is the capital of Yunnan province, and its position on a plateau, about 6500 ft (2000 m) above sea level, has earned it the nickname "City of Eternal Spring." With an average annual temperature ranging from 15° to 18° C. the climate here, many Chinese will tell you, is the best in the People's Republic.

The numerous city parks seem to be in bloom right through the year. Lovers of flowers in China appreciate Kunming chiefly for its magnolias, rhododendrons, primulas and camellias, as well as for the blossom which starts to bedeck the fruit-trees at the very beginning of March.

It's not only nature and the mild, consistent climate which give the city such a colorful aspect; another contributing factor are the bright traditional costumes of

Above: Street scene in Kunming (Yunnan). Right: Kunming – contrasts that create harmony? Far right: Lake view near Kunming.

the different ethnic groups who live in the country around Kunming.

Before setting out to explore the city, have a cup of freshly roasted Yunnan coffee and a crisp baguette at the **Nanlaisheng Bread and Coffee Shop** on tree-lined **Jinbi Street** (*jinbi lu*), where a "roof" of dense foliage shades the people cycling to work in the morning rush hour traffic.

Nearby **Dongsi Street** (*dongsi jie*) runs southwards to the former West Temple and East Temple. Built in the 9th century, the temples have long since disappeared, but two pagodas from the Tang period have survived: the 13-storeyed **West Temple Pagoda** (*xisi ta*) and the **East Temple Pagoda** (*dongsi ta*), which was rebuilt after an earthquake at the end of the 19th century.

A fascinating walk in the north of the city follows the history of Kunming, which stretches back to the time of the emperor Qin Shi Huangdi. Around the **Green Lake** (*cui hu*) lies the **park** of the same name, a favorite place for the local

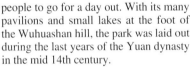

people to go for a day out. With its many pavilions and small lakes at the foot of the Wuhuashan hill, the park was laid out during the last years of the Yuan dynasty in the mid 14th century.

Close by, the Yuantongjie leads to the most beautiful temple in Kunming. The **Yuantong Temple** (*yuantong si*) dates from the Tang dynasty and has been restored several times in the past. At its center stands an octagonal pavilion, framed by a pond. The Yuantong temple is famous not least for the glory of its flower gardens.

Beyond it rises the Yuantongshan, whose slopes are the site of the city's **zoo.** The zoo's inhabitants reflect the wide variety of species living in southern China – including the ever-beloved panda bear.

Two cultural institutions are worth a visit: the **Provincial Museum of Yunnan** (*yunnan sheng bowuguan*) possesses some 50,000 exhibits relating to Chinese history, the Revolution, national minorities and crafts. If you want to learn more about the tribes of the region, you should seek out the **Institute for National Minorities** (*minzu xueyuan*) in the north of the city.

The country around Kunming

Soon enough, the visitor is drawn to the enchanting landscape around Kunming. To the south, **Lake Dian** (*dian chi*) lies close to the city. This, the sixth largest lake in China, is fed by 20 rivers which rush down from the mountains of the Yunnan plateau. The local people often also call it *Kunming Lake*, and love to relax on steamer trips over its 130 sq. miles (340 sq. km) of placid water.

Beside its northern arm lies the **Park with the Beautiful Outlook** (*daguan gongyuan*). It covers 148 acres (60 ha); construction on it started in 1690, during the Qing dynasty. In 1866, Wang Jiwen, who was governor of Yunnan at the time, had the park re-landscaped into its present form. Its emblem is the **Daguan Tower** (*daguan lou*) which stands on a

small island and is reached by walking through the Jinhuapu Pavilion. From the tower you can enjoy a breathtaking view over the lake to the nearby **Western Mountains** (*xi shan*).

The Western Mountains stretch for 25 miles (40 km) and rise to a height of 8200 ft (2500 m). They owe their nicknames, "Buddha Hills," and "Hills of the Sleeping Beauty," to their shape, which from a distance makes one think of a sleeping Buddha, or – as some would have it – a reclining woman.

One excursion into the Western Mountains leads to the **Dragon Gate** (*long men*). Like most of the Taoist temple complex to which it belongs, it was hewn out of the rock of **Mount Luohan** (*luohan shan*). From here, at a height of about 1500 ft (470 m) you have a view far out across the lake. As you climb, you first reach the **Huating Temple** (*huating si*), whose origins go back to the 11th cen-

tury. After that comes the **Taihua Temple** (*taihua si*), built in the shadow of the mountain which gives it its name (*taihua shan*), and which rises to a height of 7790 ft (2375 m). Later you reach the Taoist **Pavilion of the Three Pure Spirits** (*sanqing ge*) which has several halls. From here you only have to pass through some narrow passages – so low that you have to bend almost double – which the monks long ago cut through the rock walls, to come to the Dragon Gate and the realization, at last, that the climb has been worth while.

If this excursion into the Western Mountains has left you with aching muscles, you can ease them in the **hot springs of Anning**. The poet Yang Shengan, who lived in the Ming period, praised the mineral-rich waters more than 500 years ago as "the most invigorating springs under the broad heaven." But be warned; the temperature of the water is around 45°C (113°F). Nearby are the **Caoxi Temple** (*caoxi si*) and the **Pearl Springs**. To avoid disappointment, don't

Above: In the Western Mountains near Kunming, also called "Buddha Hills" .

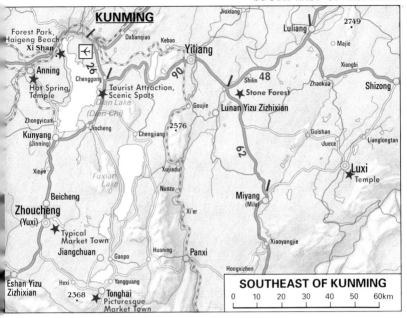

SOUTHEAST OF KUNMING

0 10 20 30 40 50 60km

expect too much of Chinese "spas" – you will find that neither comfort nor cuisine are given very high priority.

The **Bamboo Temple** (*qiongzhu si*), 7 1/2 miles (12 km) northwest of Kunming, is famous for its 500 clay *luohan* figures. Most of them were created, in an eclectic mix of various styles, by the artist Lu Guangxiu at the end of the last century.

North of Kunming there are two sights worth a detour: the **Golden Temple** (*jin dian*), 4 1/2 miles (7 km) from the city center, was built in 1602, but later transported to Dali.

The present building dates from the Qing period and is made, not of gold as its name suggests, but of bronze and marble. But the beauty of the temple is none the less remarkable for that. The camellia trees in the courtyard are said to be over 500 years old.

A further 2 1/2 miles (4 km) north of here lies the **Pond of the Black Dragon** (*heilong tan*) at the foot of **Mount Wulao** (*wulao shan*). It is ringed by Taoist temples and ancient trees. In the

vicinity you can also visit the **Botanical Garden** of the Botanical Institute of Kunming.

Excursions farther afield from Kunming

In the country round Kunming there are many picturesque, typically Chinese towns, with a bustling market life. Though some are quite remote, they are well worth seeking out. Among them are **Zhoucheng** (*yuxi*: about 87 miles/140 km to the south), **Tonghai** (about 118 miles/190 km to the south) and **Zhaotong** (326 miles/524 km to the north, in the panhandle of Yunnan that sticks up between Sichuan and Guizhou provinces).

Shilin and the Petrified Forest

In the region east of Kunming the **Rock Forest** (*shi lin*) is Yunnan's foremost tourist attraction. It's easy to make this journey of about 80 miles (130 km)

139

into the **Autonomous Territory of the Yi Nationality**, in the district of Lunan; many buses run there every day.

The history of the creation of the rock forest began 280 million years ago, when the raising of the Himalayas led to erosion which carved these strange rock formations out of the limestone plateau. Further upheavals of the earth's crust caused deep fissures in the rock which were enlarged by rainwater. Today, over an area of about 100 sq. miles (260 sq km), innumerable needles of rock soar to heights of nearly 100 ft (30 m). It is true that only some 250 acres (100 ha) are accessible to tourists, but here you can find a concentration of the most extraordinary rock shapes.

In **Shilin** the Chinese have given free rein to their fertile imagination in giving names to the rocks.

Along 3 miles (5 km) of well-marked paths take you past natural sculptures with names like "Lotus Hill," "Mother and Child," "Sleepwalking Rhinoceros," "Immortal Mushroom," "Baby Elephant" and "Bamboo." The **Wangfeng Pavilion** commands a fascinating view out over the whole area.

It is a good idea to wait until the many day-trippers from Kunming have left before trying to enjoy the delights of Shilin. Only then does peace fall over the village, and even the women of the Sani minority, who have been loudly crying their wares all day long, head wearily home.

Therefore, if time allows, you should really spend the night in Shilin. There are several hotels, mostly simple, as well as a number of restaurants. As the sun sinks behind the jagged needles of the rock forest, you can round off the day peacefully with a glass of the local liquor called *Meiguilujiu* ("Rose-dew"). Afterwards you walk back to the hotel under a night sky of such profound darkness that the stars seem to sparkle like diamonds.

Above: The Rock Forest near Shilin, one of the tourist attractions of Yunnan. Right: Dali, the most famous town on Lake Erhai.

Dali and Lake Erhai

Landscape and nature are also the attractions of **Lake Erhai** and its surroundings; its natural beauty is intensified by the patina of Chinese history and the local color of Yunnan's ethnic minorities.

To experience this, it is well worth making the 273 mile (440 km) trip to **Dali**, in the west of Yunnan, where the ancient and seemingly timeless China still slumbers.

You reach Dali, the tourist center on Lake Erhai, after what is usually a pretty exhausting bus trip. Depending on the state of the road surface, the mechanical condition of the bus and the – sometimes hair-raising – skill of the driver, the journey from Kunming can last for anything from seven to ten hours. Shortly before Dali, one normally has to change buses in **Xiaguan**. But this dreary-looking industrial town hardly invites one to linger.

In Dali, a good place to recover from the nerve-racking journey is the public **bath-house**, which, as is usual in China, has separate facilities for men and women. Here you will be given a relaxing massage, enveloped in a scented cloud of tiger-balm and eucalyptus oil. Whereas in much of China the bath-house has been consigned to history, here in Dali it is still very much alive and part of the of daily routine. Its many visitors are content to put up with the rather primitive accommodation in the communal guesthouses, Nr 1 and Nr 2 (*diyi* and *di'er zhaodaisuo*). Nr 1 is a little more comfortable.

To many backpackers, Dali is known as "the Kathmandu of China." For a long while now, the majority of visitors to this area have been lone travellers with rucksacks; fortunately, they have not made any significant impact on the atmosphere of the ancient town.

Dali lies at an altitude of 6475 ft (1974 m) and is entered through two old town gateways. Its history goes back a very long way: from 783 AD on, it was the capital of the Nanzhao empire of the Bai

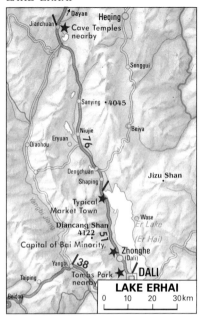

Dayan
Jianchuan
Heqing
Cave Temples
nearby

Songgui

Sanying • 4045

Niujie
Beiya
Eryuan
Qiaohou
16

Dengchuan
Jizu Shan
Shaping

Typical
Market Town

Diancang Shan
4122
Wase
Er Lake
(Er Hai)

Capital of Bai Minority,
Zhonghe
(Dali)

Yangbi
138

Taiping
Tombs Park
DALI
nearby
Beidou

LAKE ERHAI

0   10   20   30km

Despite the visible influence of the Islamic Hui minority, which include a mosque and a number of restaurants, it is the Bai who have had the most decisive impact on the town's appearance. The Bai who can usually be recognized by their colorful clothes, also inhabit the many little villages on the shores of Lake Erhai which lies some 2 miles (3.5 km) away from the town.

It is a particular delight to walk along the lake shore in the early morning or the evening. This is when the many fishermen set out in their boats to fish in a traditional and unique way: they use trained cormorants to dive for the fish, preventing the birds from swallowing their catch by means of a constricting noose around their necks.

Near **Xizhou**, about 16 miles north of Dali, the **Butterfly Springs** (*hudie quan*) bubble up beside the road to Shaping. Legend has it that a pair of lovers, pursued by their families, hurled themselves in despair into the bottomless pool – only to emerge again as butterflies. In the multicolored lepidoptera which flutter in the summer air you can see the descendants of the star-crossed pair.

If you take this road along Lake Erhai, the best day to go is Monday, so that you can take in the attractive peasant market in **Shaping**. For every Monday a mass migration of Bai converges on the little market town, some 19 miles (30 km) from Dali. From the deep valleys of the surrounding landscape, long caravans of traders and merchants make their way uphill. In the market-place, the timber merchant sets up his stall next to the barefoot dentist, the rope-maker next to the hairdresser. Basket-weavers, dressmakers, makers of nets and sellers of fish-traps – all sit waiting for customers.

people; and it later became capital of the Dali empire. Today the town dozes in the shadow of the towering **Mt Diancangshan** (13,520 ft/4122 m), dreaming of its former glory.

Dali is famous throughout China for the excellence of its white marble, which is processed in a factory beyond the town's western gate. You can admire the long-established craftsmanship applied to the marble in the **Three Pagodas** (*san ta*), which are the emblem of Dali. Ranging from 138 ft to 230 ft (42 to 70 m), they were built in the 9th century, largely from local marble, and are among the oldest buildings in southwest China. It is significant that these white pagodas were built by the Bai people (*bai* means "white").

It is also worth the strenuous climb to the **Zhonghe Temples** (*zhonghe si*), high above the town, and to visit the **Guantong Temple** (*guantong si*) in the village of Guanyin, 2 miles (3 km) south of Dali.

Right: Island temple in Lake Erhai (Yunnan).

The peasants' products offered on sale here range from fresh vegetables to squealing piglets. Thousands of people crowd between the makeshift stalls, to buy or just to look; their bright traditional

costumes add vivid splashes of color. And although a cloud of dust hangs over Shapin up on its hill, down below the lake gleams brightly. Not until the afternoon do peace and quiet return. In overcrowded buses and heavily-laden tractors, the local people and the tourists head for home. The former know for sure that they will be back next Monday – Shaping is not least a weekly trading-post for gossip and small vanities. The latter go away convinced that they have discovered one of the most exciting country markets in China.

In the mid-1980s, when restrictions on travel to Tibet were partially lifted, a number of independent travellers tried to reach Lhasa from Dali. One reason for this was that by taking this route you could avoid the police checks near Chengdu in Sichuan province. Due to the tense political situation in Tibet, however, the connection from Dali has now also become subject to strict control. What is more, the dangers of this illegal journey are difficult to cope with. Only

the first 80 miles (130 km) of the trip can be covered with relative ease. This brings you to **Lijiang** in the **Autonomous Territory of the Naxi minority**. The town is overshadowed by the 3477 ft (5600 m) **Jade Dragon Snow Mountain** (*yulong xueshan*).

Today, there's little in the lifestyle of the Naxi to remind one of their former historical importance; but from 1288 to 1730, Lijiang was the capital of the kingdom of Mu, which had been founded by the Naxi people.

Simao and Xishuangbanna

In the **Autonomous District of Xishuangbanna**, which occupies the southernmost corner of Yunnan province, a sultry and humid tropical climate prevails all year round, with an average temperature of 21°C. During the rainy season, from the beginning of June to the end of August, it often pours for days on end. The vegetation grows luxuriantly, and in many places one's progress is blocked by

143

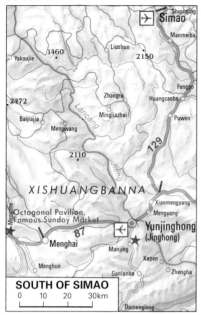

dense jungle. The soil is fertile; exotic fruit of all kinds bedeck people's tables and are stacked up for sale in the peasant markets.

Xishuangbanna is comprised of twelve administrative areas, which all have one thing in common: the Dai "minority" represents the majority of their total population of 650,000.

Until recently, the journey to the south of Yunnan deprived tourists of valuable holiday time. This was because, after the one-hour flight from Kunming to Simao, there was an agonizing bus journey of almost six hours to the administrative capital of **Jinghong**. But now you can take a plane to Jinghong and save yourself the bus trip from Simao, a decision made all the easier by the fact that there is nothing in Simao worth seeing.

You do not need to get your cameras out until you reach Jinghong. The first

Right: The White Pagoda of Damenglong south of Jinghong. Far right: Detail of a Buddhist temple near Jinghong.

tourist attraction is the Dai village of **Manjing** on the southern outskirts of the town. You can spend the night here in traditional surroundings. In the center of town there are some small temples to discover, and you can get an informative overview of the indigenous plant life at the **Research Institute for Tropical Plants** (*redai zhiwu yanjiusuo*), located to the right of the road leading out of the town towards Menhai. On Sundays, it is entertaining to stroll through the **market**, where traders from a wide surrounding area set out their stalls of colorful and vitamin-rich tropical fruits and vegetables.

Water plays a special role in the life of the Dai. All year round you can take boat trips on the **Lancangjiang** which, further south, takes on the name by which it is generally known to the outside world: the Mekong. The **Dai water festival**, however, only takes place once a year, in the middle of April, or, according to the Dai calendar, on the 24th day of the sixth month.

Visitors to this festival certainly can't be afraid of water, because, in their joy at the end of the dry season, the revellers spray each other liberally with water. This activity also creates a good omen for the coming rainy season, which will ensure the fertility of the land and their own prosperity. The festival also includes **dragon-boat** races. The boats which compete are up to 165 ft (50 m) long, and are paddled by as many as 50 men in pairs. The racing has a long tradition and attracts huge crowds of spectators. Because of the limited transportation possibilities to the area, it can be difficult to get an air ticket around the time of the water festival, so you may be forced to put up with a bus journey of nearly three days from Kunming.

Although you will only find a few temples in Jinghong, life in the Xishuangbanna district is strongly influenced by Buddhism; monks in their ochre-colored robes are a common sight.

Outside the town there are some scattered religious shrines which the population visits in large numbers. The best known of these is the **White Pagoda** (*bai ta*) **of Damenglong**, 37 miles (60 km) south of Jinghong, near the border with Myanmar (Burma). Beneath the building, which dates back to 1204, lie the feet of Buddha himself – that at least is the legend. To the west, in **Menghai** and **Mengzhe**, there are also some fine pagodas. But experience shows that most visitors on an excursion to Xishuangbanna restrict themselves to Jinghong and the surrounding area, with a side-trip to Damenlong. The oppressive heat sometimes becomes almost unbearable and this seems to put a damper on people's spirit of adventure.

GUIZHOU

Question: where can you see rice growing in the sky and not seem to see a single patch of level earth? Answer: in **Guizhou** province. A further question

might be: which is probably the least developed region in the People's Republic of China? Again the answer has to be Guizhou. And that sums up the chief problem of the 33 million inhabitants of the province. In many places here you can witness Chinese rural life in its untouched, and frankly poverty-stricken, state. There is an inadequate transport and communications infrastructure and many important commodities are in short supply. This has meant that Guizhou has preserved its predominantly rustic character. It is why the rice seems to grow heavenwards on steep slopes that can only be worked with difficulty. But it's only this hard-won self-sufficiency that makes survival possible.

The capital, **Guiyang**, is familiar to train travellers as the place where one changes on the journey from Guilin (in the neighboring province of Guanxi) to the city of Chongqing to the north, on the Yangtse. Guiyang is a typical Chinese provincial city, with all the damage left behind by the over-hasty introduction of

145

socialist measures to produce economic growth: air pollution caused by primitive industrial plants, and the incarceration of the people in concrete apartment blocks.

For this reason tourists make straight for the surrounding countryside, where there are some caves to be explored, including those in the **Huaxi Park** (*huaxi gongyuan*), which also has lakes and temples. Or you can breathe the fresh air of the **Qianling Mountain Park** (*qianlingshan gongyuan*) where the **Hongfu monastery** (*hongfu si*) dates from the end of the Ming period.

Like the whole of southwestern China, the province of Guizhou has since earliest times been settled by numerous ethnic minorities. The Miao, Yi and Dong have made their home here, as have the Hui, Bai and Zhuang. Fifty-one percent of the population of Guizhou belong to races other than the Han Chinese.

Above left: A girl of the Miao minority in Kaili (Guizhou). Above left: The Huangguoshu Waterfall (Guizhou).

Many of Guizhou's tourist attractions are famous beyond the borders of the province, such as the **Huangguoshu Falls** (*huangguoshu dapubu*), 93 miles (150 km) southwest of Guiyang. With a width of 266 ft (81 m) and a height of 243 ft (71 m), this is the mightiest waterfall in China.

On the way there, you pass through the town of **Anshun**, which has a Confucian temple; in the countryside outside of town, there are several caves you can explore.

Travelling eastward by train, towards Hunan, you reach **Kaili**, 118 miles (190 km) away. The town is set in picturesque country, surrounded by **Miao villages**. The colorful costumes of the Miao are a feature of the busy market, which stretches west from the bus station. From Kaili the railroad continues northeast to **Wuyang** (Zhenyuan), where temples grace the surrounding countryside. It is well worth the 19 mile (30 km) trip west from here to the idyllic, old-world Chinese town of **Shibing**.

YUNNAN AND GUIZHOU

Accommodation

YUNNAN: **KUNMING**· *LUXURY:* **Golden Dragon** (*jinlong fandian*). 575 Beijing Nanlu, Tel. 313 3104 (Kunming's top hotel). **Holiday Inn**, 25 Dongfeng Donglu, Tel. 316 5888. **Kunming Hotel** (*kunming fandian*), 145 Dongfeng Donglu, Tel. 316 2063 ("classic" stronghold of independent tourists in China; two separate buildings; centrally located with all necessary service facilities from CITS to the Bank of China).

MID-PRICE: **Green Lake** (*cuihu binguan*), 6 Cuihu Nanlu, Tel. 515 5788 (a little way from the center, but in a quiet location). **Begonia**, Dongjiao Lukou, Tel. 313 8761.

BUDGET: **Kunhu**, 44 Beijing Lu, Tel. 313 3737. **Yunnan Hotel** (*yunnan fandian*), Dongfeng Xilu (not far from the Yunnan Provincial Museum).

SHILIN: *MID-PRICE:* **Shilin Guesthouse** und **Yunlin Hotel** (*yunlin fandian*, Tel. 22081-221), in the Lunan Autonomous Region of the Yi Nationality (both hotels are located near the Rock Forest; as there is a lack of restaurants in the area, you have no choice but to eat at your hotel).

DALI: *MID-PRICE:* **Dali Hotel** (*diyi zhaodaisuo*), Fuxing Lu.

BUDGET: **Guesthouse No.2** (*di'er zhaodaisuo*), Huguo Lu. Simple, rustic Chinese atmsphere; anyone looking for more sophisticated comforts has definitely come to the wrong town).

JINGHONG / XISHUANGBANNA: *MID-PRICE:* **Tai Yuan**, Nong Lin Han Lu 8, Tel. 212 3888. *BUDGET:* **Banna Hotel** (*banna binguan*), Galan Rd.

Restaurants

Although Guizhou offers the western tourist less culinary variety than other provinces of China, its name is "on everyone's lips": the highly alcoholic *Maotai* spirit is distilled in a town of that name in the north of the province (near the border with Sichuan). This famous and overpriced liquor will simultaneously rot your guts and blow your head off. However, no official dinner in China is complete without it, and thus it is an essential element of Chinese politics.

KUNMING: **Workers', Peasants' and Soldiers' Restaurant** (*gongnongbing fandian*), 262 Huguo Lu, Tel. 312 5679 (typical Yunnan cooking; a nostalgia trip for westerners who went through a Maoist phase as students).

Beijing, 77 Xinxiangyunjie, the menu does not specialize in any particular regional cuisine.

Chuanwei, Xiangyunjie, Sichuan cuisine with fish, meat and chicken.

Yunnan Vermicelli Across the Bridge (*guoqiao mixuanguan*), Nantongjie (famed for its Yunnan noodle dishes).

Nanlaisheng Coffee & Bread Shop, 299 Jinbi Lu ("proper" coffee and "Chinese" baguettes – but you could hardly start a morning in Kunming in a more typically "French" style; otherwise, the typical breakfast in this southern province usually consists of a noodle soup – equally tasty in its way.

DALI: Numerous restaurants and coffee shops treat their customers to rich and varied fare; the choice of cuisine and ambiance in Dali really does remind the globetrotting backpacker of restaurants in Kathmandu (Nepal).

Museums

KUNMING: **Yunnan Provincial Museum** (*yunnan sheng bowuguan*), Wuyi Lu (50,000 exhibits relating to the history of the province of Yunnan).

Botanical Institute of Kunming, attached to the Chinese Academy of Sciences, situated in Heilong (north of the city; near the Pond of the Black Dragon; there are 13,000 species of plant in the Botanical Garden and over 30,000 books in the specialized library).

Zoo (*dongwu yuan*), Yuantong Hill (situated in the northern part of the city; here one can gain an overview of the great variety of animal and plant life in the whole of southwestern China).

Zoological Institute of Kunming, part of the Chinese Academy of Sciences, Huahongdong (in the western part of the city; can be recommended to all, not just keen animal lovers).

Events

DALI: Between the 15th and 21st day of the third month of the lunar calendar (usually in April) the people of Dali celebrate the **Festival of the Third Moon** (*san yue jie*), which has a long Buddhist tradition. During the rest of the year there are further festivals on varying dates.

XISHUANGBANNA: In the calendar of the national minority of the Dai people the **Water Festival** is held annually on the 24th day of the sixth month, which means it usually takes place in April. To keep the tourists happy, the celebrations now take place at a fixed date – between the 15th and 19th April. If possible, you should arrange your excursion at this time, but be sure to book your travel tickets both ways, well in advance.

Tourist Information

KUNMING: **Yunnan OTC**, 145 Dongfeng Lu, Tel. 316 811 (in the Kunming Hotel; there is also a branch office in the Golden Dragon Hotel).

FROM THE RED BASIN, DOWN THE YANGTSE

SICHUAN

HUBEI

ANHUI

SICHUAN
Where the pepper grows

During the Long March, so the story goes, Mao Zedong once declared: "Anyone who doesn't like red pepper isn't a real revolutionary." As one leafs through the annals of the Chinese Revolution, however, it emerges that Sichuan, while admittedly the base of the luckless Fourth Front Army under Zhang Guotao, has otherwise politically distinguished itself only by the fact that during the war against Japan (1937-1945) the government of "Free China" under Chiang Kaishek (Chiang Jieshi) had its seat in Chongqing (Chungking).

So let us restrict ourselves to considering the culinary aspect of the pepper, which gives the spicy Sichuan cuisine its distinctive fiery quality. The *yin* and *yang*, the balance of opposites in this gastronomy, lies in its combination of hot, spicy flavors with soothingly mild ones. The fire in the cooking of Sichuan suits the prevailing climate of the province, which is humid all year round and can be numbingly cold in winter. In summer the red pepper brings sweat to your brow and cools you by evaporation, in winter it is a substitute for central heating. In its taste,

Left: Sichuan, the rice-bowl of China.

the famous Sichuan pepper's hotness is tempered by its vaguely flower-scented aroma. In its classically pure form, the culinary harmony of opposites is found in the thick, reddish broth called *huoguo* or "fire-pot." Its unmistakable flavor comes from the hot spices and the Sichuan pepper. Particularly in **Chongqing**, it's hard to choose between the innumerable little **Huoguo restaurants**. Like a Swiss *fondue*, the broth is placed in a gas-heated pot set into the table; with it are provided bite-sized pieces of vegetable, fish, meat and *doufu* (soya-bean curd) which, with the help of a small woven sieve, you dip in to the brew to cook quickly before eating – this is one of those meals where preparation is half the fun!

The ingredients come chiefly from the "Red Basin," the geographical heart of China. This bowl of land in the middle of Sichuan province, is ringed to the north, east and south by mountain ranges which in places rise to 6500 ft (2000 m). In the west, towards the Tibetan border, the chains of mountains have been pushed together in a massive block, whose peaks, in the "Great Snow Mountains" south of **Kangding**, soar to a maximum height of 24,784 ft (7556 m). About 60 miles (100 km) before the border with Tibet lies the second-highest town in the world, **Litang**, at an altitude of 15, 400 ft

149

(4700 m). The diagonal distance across the Sichuan Depression, between the outer points of Chengdu and Chongqing is just over 168 miles (270 km); the average height above sea level is 1000 ft (300 m). The landscape might have been put there as a subject for traditional Chinese painting: red sandstone hills capped with pine trees or cloaked with terraced rice-paddies so picturesque that they recall the Hanging Gardens of Babylon. The alluvial flood-plains beside the southward-flowing rivers, chiefly the **Min river** (*min jiang*) near Chengdu, are among the most fertile and intensely cultivated areas in China. All these rivers join the **Yangtse**, which is navigable as far upstream as **Yibin**.

A Chinese proverb claims that wealth is not measured in pearls but in grains of rice, wheat, barley, millet and the shoots of the soya-plant. This wealth is provided by the agriculture of the **Red Basin**,

Above: Rush-hour traffic in Chengdu, the capital of Sichuan.

where as long as 2300 years ago a highly-developed irrigation culture was already established. Sichuan is known as the "Rice-bowl of China;" its flooded fields produce two harvests a year. Rape-seed is grown for edible oil; mulberry trees provide food for hungry silk-worms; tobacco is grown near Chengdu, cotton around Foling; and a wide variety of fruit and vegetables thrive in gardens everywhere. The mountainous, wooded west yields timber and bamboo for practical use and artistic carving and weaving. The young bamboo shoots in the western forests provide food for the giant panda, the symbol of all endangered animal species.

However, *homo sapiens* is not threatened with extinction in Sichuan. The population of the province, which is approximately the same size as France, long ago passed the 100-million mark and accounts for about 10% of the entire population of China. While the national minorities – Tibetans, Yi, Miao, Qiang and Hui – maintain their own languages, the great majority of the Han Chinese speak *guoyu,* the southwest Chinese variant of the Mandarin language.

The industrialization of Sichuan began during the Sino-Japanese War (1937-45), when the Guomindang retreated to this region, bringing factories with them. In the 1970s, after the fall of the "Gang of Four," the still largely agricultural province became a testing-ground for the break-up of collective farms, partial privatization and the creation of free markets. This may not be unconnected with the fact that Deng Xiaoping was born in Sichuan in 1904 and until 1952 was a local party leader.

Chengdu, "City of Brocade"

On the western rim of the Red Basin lies the capital of China's most densely populated province, a city of some 4 million inhabitants. Its history goes back about 2500 years. During the later Han dynasty (22-220 AD), **Chengdu** was famed for its silk brocade weaving, earning the nickname "City of Brocade." A rampart 12 miles (20 km) long encloses the rectangular Old City, in the exact center of which the viceroy's palace was built in the 14th century. The layout of Chengdu was based on that of Peking.

In the 1960s the modern barbarians of the Cultural Revolution destroyed what remained of the city walls and blew up the palace. In its place stands a hideous palace of Socialism in the ostentatious Soviet style.

The comparison with Beijing cannot be carried too far; Chengdu is much greener and has more old-world charm with its many little atmospheric drinking-houses and markets. A noisy counterpoint is provided by the live fowl on sale at the **poultry market** near the Jinjiang Hotel. The **People's Park** (*renmin gongyuan*) at the southwest corner of the Old City offers entertainment and a chance to relax in, for instance, a bonsai rock-gar-

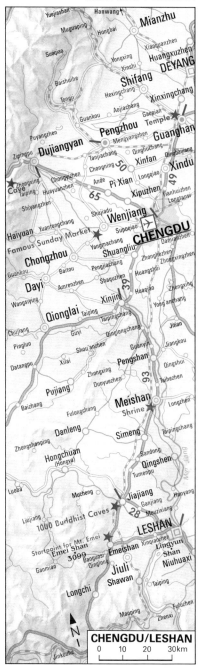

151

den or the famous **tea-house** (*cha guan*) by the lake, where you sit in comfortable bamboo chairs and allow the tea to have its soothing effect. West of the People's Park, the **Cottage of Dufu** (*dufu caotang*) turns out to be a charming little property in memory of the famous poet Dufu (712-770).

In the southwest of the city, the **Temple of Duke Wu** (*wuhou si*) stands in the **Nanjiao Park** (*nanjiao gongyuan*) with a lake and pavilion. It commemorates the Duke of Wu (181-234 AD), a great scholar and military strategist who lived in the age of the Three Kingdoms.

If you appreciate bamboo, the plant that, above all others, symbolizes the Far East, you should make for the **Tower Pavilion with River View** (*wangjiang lou*). It lies to the southeast (near the University of Sichuan) in a public park in the

middle of a grove of more than a hundred different species of bamboo. The bamboo-eating pandas would find a superb habitat in the thicket around the tower-pavilion. It is true that a number are kept – quite sensitively by Chinese standards – in the **zoo**, which, situated about 4 miles (6 km) northeast of the center, is worth visiting. Since Sichuan is the panda's natural habitat, this zoo exhibits the largest captive population of pandas in the world.

On the way back from the zoo, it is worth making a little detour to the **Wenshu Temple Monastery** (*wenshu yuan*) on the right-hand side of Jiefang Street. The original 6th-century temple was enlarged in the 17th century. It contains a large number of Buddhist devotional objects and is used for the training of young monks. Its special charm is due to the lively activity both inside and outside the gates: it includes both a tea-house and a picture gallery, and generally contains a plethora of soothsayers and traders selling joss-sticks, flowers and fireworks.

Above: Even in Chengdu the statue of Mao has now gone. Right: The panda makes his home in Sichuan's western mountains.

Over everything hangs the heavy perfume of flowers and aromatic smoke.

The **Museum of Sichuan University** (*sida bowuguan*) displays items of ethnological interest relating to the art and folklore of Tibet and the national minorities. If time allows, you should make a point of visiting the **Tomb of Wangjian** (*wangjian mu*), northwest of the center. Wangjian was an emperor of Shu (848-918 AD). The exhibition of its treasures includes jade jewelry, imperial seals, sculptures, books of the dead and much more.

Excursions in the country around Chengdu

About 12 miles (20 km) north of Chengdu, just beyond Xindu, lies the **Monastery of Sublime Light** (*baoguang si*). Around 1000 AD, it is said to have housed several thousand monks. In the Ming period the whole property – except for the pagoda, *sheli ta*, in the front courtyard – burned down but was rebuilt in the 17th century. Today pilgrims, monks, tourists and sellers of devotional objects fill the place with life. The monastery, picturesquely set among clusters of bamboo, is said to contain a relic of Buddha.

West of Xindu, and 40 miles (65 km) northwest of Chengdu) you come to **Dujiangyan** (Guanxian) and its **Temple of Two Kings** (*erwang miao*). It commemorates Li Bing and his son Li Erlang (3rd century BC), two masters of classical Chinese hydraulic engineering, who designed the irrigation system for the entire Sichuan basin. Below the temple the **Dujiangyan irrigation project** harnesses the **Min river** with dams and conduits. As far back as 2000 years ago its water made hundreds of thousands of acres fertile. In the nearby **Wulong Nature Reserve** ever-hopeful trekkers can keep an eye open for pandas.

About 300 miles (500 km) due north of Chengdu lies the **Jiuzhaigou Nature**

Park. High up in the "Gorge of the Nine Villages" unfolds a dream landscape become reality – a panorama of glaciers, crystal-clear lakes, deep forests, picturesque Tibetan villages and tinkling prayer-wheels. A helicopter pad, however, serves as a warning that this *terra* may not remain *incognita* for long.

Through Kangding to Dege

Kangding lies 200 miles (324 km) southwest of Chengdu in the **Daxu Mountains** (*daxu shan*). From this high point the northern stretch of the Chengdu-Lhasa road runs for 330 miles (530 km) through breathtaking mountain scenery and over the 15,088 ft (4600 m) **Chola Pass** to **Dege,** the last town before the official Tibetan frontier. The Buddhist-Lamaist monastery here is home to several hundred monks. In its workshop, monks are taught the craft of printing the sacred writings; there are over 200,000 hardwood printing blocks with texts in all fields of knowledge and mysticism.

153

The green guardian goddess, called Avalokitesvara in Sanskrit, protects this cultural treasure-house from fire.

Meishan and Leshan

About 50 miles (80 km) south of Chengdu you come to **Meishan** and the temple of the three men of letters of the Song period (960-1127), all of whom were members of the Su family. However, unless you can read Chinese you will not really be able to appreciate the calligraphy and documents in the shrine.

A further 50 miles (80 km) south lies **Leshan**, the town on three rivers. On **Mt Lingyung** (*lingyun shan*), overlooking the confluence of the three rivers, Buddhist monks in the 8th century took more than 90 years to carve the **Great Buddha** (*da fo*). Though he is sitting, he towers

Above: The foot of the Great Buddha of Leshan on Mt Lingyun (Sichuan). Right: The comfortable way to make a pilgrimage to Mt Emeishan, sacred to the Buddhists.

233 ft (71 m) high, his ears are 23 ft (7 m) long and the nail on his big toe measures over 5 ft (1.6 m). This colossus is the biggest statue of Buddha in existence and has been kept in good condition by its own internal drainage system. With his spiritual power the statue protected the boatmen on the three rivers and – in a more practical way – regulated the rivers' flow with stone rubble thrown down by the masons. Above the Great Buddha's head the mountain top is crowned by a temple. It is also worth visiting the monasteries of **Wuyou** (*wuyou si*) and **Wulong** (*wulong si*) and the little museum of calligraphy and paintings nearby, as well as a hall containing a thousand terra-cotta monks, no two of which are alike.

Emeishan

Mt Emei (*emei shan*) is one of the mountains in China that are sacred to the Buddhists. From the town of Emei, some 90 miles (150 km) south of Chengdu, buses take you to **Baoguo** at the foot of the mountain (altitude: 1800 ft/550 m).

From here you can tread the ancient pilgrims' path to the **Peak of the Thousand Buddhas** (*wanfo ding*) at a height of 10,165 ft (3099 m). Or take the bus up to 8330 ft (2540 m) and from there swing up in the cable-car to the **Golden Peak** (*jin ding*; 10,086 ft/3075 m). If you are going to tackle the climb, you should be properly equipped with hiking boots, a pullover and waterproof clothing. You can leave your heavy luggage near Baguo in the Hongzhushuan or Xixiang hotels.

The first Buddhist and Taoist shrines were erected on the mountain nearly 2000 years ago. In the course of time something like 150 temple-monasteries were built here, most of which have since fallen down. Yet there are still enough left to admire.

The 16th-century **Baoguo Monastery Temple** (*baoguo si*) at the foot of the mountain contains, among other things, a library of *sutras* and a huge porcelain Buddha. Above, hidden in the forest, is the **Monastery of the Lurking Tiger** (*fuhu si*) with its engraved copper pagoda 23 ft (7 m) high. It can provide accommodation for 400 visitors. Still higher up the mountainside stands the **Temple of the Ten Thousand years** (*wannian si*) the oldest of the surviving monasteries, dedicated to Puxian, the protector of the mountain, whose bronze and copper statue is said to weigh over 62 tons. The **Pavilion of Pure Sound** (*qingyin ge*) adorns an island in the middle of a fast-flowing river, in which perspiring climbers can cool themselves. The monastery beside the **Lake of the Bathing Elephant** (*xixiang chi*) lies at an altitude of 6790 ft (2070 m), at the point where the lower branches of the path converge, and so is usually overcrowded. Monkeys boldly demand food as an entrance fee. The final way-stations are the **Hermitage in the Bed of Clouds** (*woyun an*) and the **Summit Monastery**.

To experience a sunset on the summit of Emei is the fervent desire of every pil-

grim or secular tourist. Just as on Japan's Mt Fujiyama, the emotion of it all has caused many to hurl themselves from here into the depths.

Dazu

About 112 miles (180 km) west of Chongqing, in the **Dazu** district, are some of China's most important cave sculptures (comparable with those at Dunhuang, Luoyang and Datong). Since the 9th century, the caves of these forty hills were a place of refuge for Buddhists fleeing to Sichuan to escape religious persecution, who left their mark by carving sculptures in them. Two of the hills have been opened to the public. A half-hour walk brings you to the **northern hill** (*bei shan*) which alone contains thousands of religious figures.

Nine miles (15 km) further northeast, the **Treasure Chamber Hill** (*baoding shan*) lives up to its name, containing one of the largest of all collections of Buddha figures. Their number and size is almost

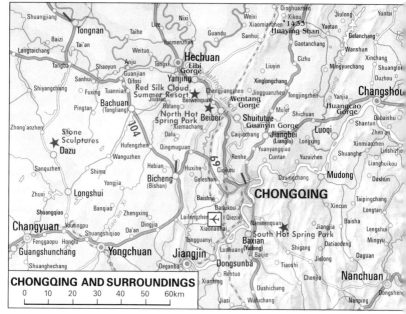

unbelievable; among them are, for example, a *guanyin* with more than a thousand arms, and a sleeping Buddha more than 100 ft/31 m long. Apart from these, the Baodingshan is itself a work of art, carefully designed to blend with such natural surroundings as a spring. O interest is its juxtaposition of Buddhist and Confucian motifs, suggesting that the persecuted Buddhists were "kowtowing" to the Confucian state authority.

Chongqing

An emperor of the southern Song dynasty (1127-1279) roguishly renamed the city, which had already existed for some time, "Twofold Happiness." Chongqing displays many twofold, contradictory or unusual qualities: in winter, it is Smog City, when the smoke from the numerous industrial plants mixes with fog drifting up from the Yangtse. In summer, the combined heat and humidity, aggravated by the ever-present smoke, make it difficult to breathe.

With a population of 14 million, Greater Chongqing is one of the largest cities in China, but is rather un-Chinese in that you seldom see bicycles here, since the city is built on steep hills.

The industrial city has grown up rapidly around its old core, which alone has 2 million inhabitants. This area, with its narrow alleys, steep stairways and "swallows-nest" style of building, still brims with traditional Chinese atmosphere. But the concrete blocks are advancing relentlessly.

Among Chongqing's few tourist sights is the **Luohan Temple** (*luohan si*). About a thousand years old, it contains 500 *luohan*, a large golden Buddha, and an Indian-style mural which shows Prince Siddharta having his hair shaved (a symbol of self-denial). The temple has its own excellent vegetarian restaurant.

In the **Chongqing Museum** (*chongqing bowuguan*) at the foot of **Pipashan** in the south of the city, dinosaur skeletons from recent excavations in Sichuan are on display.

In the western suburbs of Chongqing, the **Village of the Red Cliffs** (*hongyang cun*) is a group of buildings which has important links with the Revolution in China. Zhou Enlai was one of the representatives of the Communists based here during the alliance with the Guomindang in the struggle against the Japanese (the city was the seat of the Guomindang government in the years 1939-45). Also in the west of the city there is a memorial to the political prisoners of the Guomindang and its political and military cooperation with the USA.

About 30 miles (50 km) north of Chongqing the **Northern Hot Springs** (*bei wenquan*) bubble up on the bank of the river Jialing. They are surrounded by a park with a 5th-century Buddhist temple. Equally inviting for a hot dip are the **Southern Springs** (*nan wenquan*) about 16 miles (25 km) southwest of the Chongqing. The "Twelve Landscapes of Nanwenquan," as this most attractive park is often known, includes bridges, cliffs, gorges and luxuriant vegetation.

THE YANGTSE IN EASTERN SICHUAN, HUBEI AND ANHUI

The "Long River"

The name of the river Yangzi (traditionally spelled Yangtse in the west) comes from a town also called **Yangzi**. There, before the digging of the Imperial Canal, there was a ford which connected the north of China with the Yangtse Delta in central China; when the canal was completed in the 6th century, this grew to be the economic powerhouse of the nation. Yangzi become a fortified town whose name was transferred to China's greatest waterway. In the 16th century, when the Chinese discovered the actual headwaters of the Yangtse, they named them Jinshjiang ("Golden Sand River") and the lower reaches were henceforth to be **Changjiang** ("Long River").

From Tibet to the Pacific

The catchment of the Yangtse covers an area of some 770,000 sq. miles (2 million sq. km) whose climate is characterized by cold dry winters and hot, humid summers with frequent rainfall.

The headwaters of the Yangtse are fed by the glaciers of the **Tanggula**, 16,000 ft (5000 m) up in the northeast of the Tibetan plateau. The point in the center of China where the **river Min** (*min jiang*) flows into the Yangtse, was once thought to be in the upper reaches of the great river; in fact it is the beginning of its middle stretch.

Between Fenjie and Yichang the river breaks through the central Chinese highlands in the fascinating **Three Gorges** (*san xia*), where limestone strata, 4 million years old, have reached their highest elevation. Exposed rock, huge landslides, and the layers of detritus brought down by the tributaries once created serious obstacles in the winter when the water-level was low, and during the high waters of the summer they created a vicious current with dangerous whirlpools. Not until the advent of steamships, when rocks were blown up to clear the river bed and warning signals were installed, did the waterway become safe for shipping. The building of the Gezhouba Dam raised the water level, which also made navigation easier.

The center of attraction for tourists on the Yangtse, the Three Gorges, were first described in the 6th century by Li Daoyuan in his *Commentary on the Book of the Waters* (*shujing zhu*) :"One generally hears of the raging waters of the gorge, whose dangers we are warned of in written and oral tradition. Yet these reports say nothing of the beauty of the landscape. It is hard to describe in words how the chains of mountains with their beautiful peaks and strange shapes vie to outdo one another, and what a multitude of trees rise from the bank of mist."

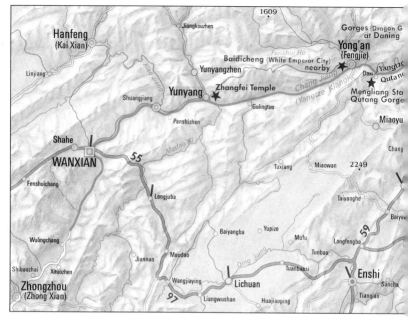

The **Gezhouba Dam** near Yichang marks the start of the lower reaches of the river, which winds in a broad stream between raised banks, through the lowlands of eastern China. In summer, in the lowland basin of Hubei/ Hunan, the great body of water fills the natural reservoir of **Dongtinghu**, increasing its surface area to as much as 1500 sq miles (4000 sq. km). In the second lowland basin, that of Jiangxi, **Lake Poyang** acts as a reservoir and in winter returns its water to the river. From here the next great bend continues to Nanjing and finally, after 3900 miles (6300 km), the river opens out into a 120 mile (200 km) wide estuary and flows into the East China Sea.

The Three Gorges of the Yangtse

The tourist steamer trip along the Yangtse begins in **Chongqing** (Sichuan) and ends 870 miles (1400 km) downstream in the city of **Wuhan** (Hubei). This shipping route was already thousands of years old when, in the 19th century, the Europeans forcibly opened it up to international trade, systematically surveying the river and linking the inaccessible province of Sichuan with the outside world. Until then, the dangerous business of towing ships upstream from the provincial border of Hubei, only as far as Chongqing, had taken more than a month. After 1922, the steamer trip all the way from Shanghai into the heart of China could be completed in a couple of weeks. Today a fleet of mail and passenger ships (mostly under the name *Jiang Han*) cover the 1550 mile (2500 km) distance, with various stops en route, in 8 to 15 days. The luxury vessels of the Yangtse Shipping Company and of western hotel groups ply between Chongqing and Wuhan on a 3- to 4-day schedule.

The first sight to look for downstream from Chongqing is near **Fuling**, where the river **Wu** (*wu jiang*) emerges from the limestone of Guizhou to join the Yangtse. In midstream stands the **stone fish**, which has been a famous water-level mark for more than 2000 years.

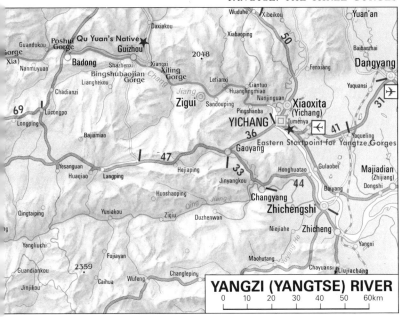

Further downstream, on the left bank, the town of **Fengdu** has been notorious since the Han period as the "Entrance to Hades." In honor of two well-known mandarins, Yin and Wang, the town was nicknamed *Yin-Wang*, which also has the meaning of "King of the Underworld." It later became a place of pilgrimage, where, especially after the 7th century, a number of temples were built. They are approached along a wearying mountain track which ends high up at a number of **halls** with representations of the *King of the Underworld*, the *Last Judgment*, and the Buddhist vision of Purgatory or Hell. Also here is the **Pavilion of the Son of Heaven** (*tianzi dian*).

Near **Zhongxian** an 11-tiered pagoda-shaped temple soars 100 ft (30 m) up from a rocky shore. It was built in the 18th century as the refuge for a monastery and named the **Refuge of the Stone Treasure** (*shibao zhao*). After this, the river narrows and flows straight as far as **Wanxian**. The industrious city on the slopes of the left bank has long been the main transshipment point for river-borne freight from the lowlands of eastern China, and today is still the gateway to the Three Gorges (*san xia*). The river now turns toward the next-largest city, **Yunyang**, and starts flowing west to east, to do battle with the central Chinese mountain range which lies across its path. Where the river becomes narrow once again, a **temple** with a large number of **stone inscriptions** from the Han to Qing period commemorates the 3rd-century military commander, Zhang Fei.

At the entrance to the Three Gorges, **Fengjie** once formed the western bulwark of the Yangtse state of Chu (3rd century BC). Here, on the north bank of the confluence with the river Tongxi, in the 1st century AD, stood the palace of the *White Emperor* (*gong sunshu*), a Chinese "counter-emperor" who attempted to found his own empire from his power-base in Chengdu. For strategic reasons he built a hilltop fortress over the river; this was to play an important part in the defence of the Shu state against that

159

of Wu in the 3rd century. One can still climb the prominent hill and admire the temple of the **City of the White Emperor** (*baidi cheng*) as well as the museum commemorating Liu Bei, king of Shu, and his loyal chief minister Zhuge Liang. Stone tablets tell of the legendary age of the Three Kingdoms.

At the **Kui Gate** the Yangtse flows into the 20 mile (33 km) long **Qutang Gorge** (*qutang xia*). In the first section it narrows to just 330 ft (100 m). It seems here as if the ships are sailing down "beneath the earth." One's gaze is caught by the **Bellows Gorge** (*fengxiang xia*) and the **Wall of White Salt**, where the **Menglian Steps** hewn in the rock indicate the line of the old tow-path.

Near Wushan the 125 mile (200 km) long **Daninghe** flows into the Yangtse. The lower reaches of this clear, fast-flow-

ing river has created the perhaps even more impressive **Three Small Gorges** (*xiao sanxia*) with their strange rock walls. Despite the difficulties presented by numerous shallows and strong currents, the **Dragon Gate Gorge** (*longmen xia*), **Misty Gorge** (*bawu xia*) and **Emerald Gorge** (*dizui xia*) can be negotiated in a small boat.

Below the confluence of the Daninghe the Yangtse flows through the 25 mile (40 km) long **Enchanted Gorge** (*wu xia*), which is named after the twelve-peaked **Enchanted Mountain** (*wu shan*). Even at the entrance one can make out the point of the **Fairy Peak** (*shennü feng*), which resembles a slim woman gazing into the distance, and because of the fate of many boatmen is also known as the "Lorelei of China." According to old writings there was once a lookout place (*yang tai*) here, on which Yao Ji, the daughter of the fabled Red Emperor, is said to have been turned into a four-leafed clover – or it may have been a pillar of stone. A ruler of Chu (Gao Yang) is

Above: A junk on the Yangtse near Chong-qing (Sichuan). Right: The Yangtse Gorges, one of China's greatest natural spectacles.

said to have fallen in love with Yao Ji, here where clouds (*yun*) and rain (*yu*) often envelope the mountain. From this, the term *yun yu* is to this day used as a synonym for secret love.

On the bank you can recognize yet another stone inscription carved in the rock – *kongming bei* or **Stele of Zhuge Liang**, on which Zhuge Liang is supposed to have recorded his views on the unification of the states of Shu and Wu.

Between Guandukou and Zigui the river valley broadens until finally the busy city of **Badong** appears on the south bank. Near **Zigui** the first two Chinese communities on the Yangtse grew up in the 9th century BC. These were Gui and Danyang, from which the Yangtse state of Chu later evolved (4th and 3rd centuries BC). A loyal Chu minister named Qu Yuan fell from favor as a result of slander, and was exiled to Zigui. In spite of sisterly comfort (*zi gui* means "the sister returns"), he took his life in Lake Dongting – an event which is recalled by the Dragon Boat Festival in May.

Beyond Zigui, and opposite the confluence of the river Xiangxi we reach the **Temple of Quyuantuo**. It marks the beginning of the **Xiling Gorge** (*xiling xia*), 47 miles (75 km) long and still dangerous because of the many shallows. It consists of a series of sheer-sided ravines, including the **Gorge of the Sword and the Military Manual** (*bingshu baoqian xia*) with its Green Sandbank, the perilous **New Bank** (*xin tan*) and the **Gorge of Buffalo-liver and Horse-lungs** (*niugan mafei xia*) with its Kongling Sandbank. In the **Gorge of the Yellow Ox** (*huangniu xia*) there is a temple dedicated to the Yellow Emperor. In the **Lamp-shadow Gorge** (*dengying xia*) you can recognize shadowy figures from the novel *Journey to the West*. These are followed, on the left-hand wall opposite, by the **Caves of the Three Travellers** (*sanyou dong*), recalling 9th-century scholars who came seeking protection.

Before the Yangtse enters its lower reaches in the plains of central China near **Nanjinguan**, you pass China's largest building site. Here a controversial dam closing three gorges is being built. In 1986 the largest dam on the Yangtse was completed downriver near **Yichang**: the Gezhouba, 154 ft (47 m) high and 1.6 miles (2.6 km) wide. Every second a staggering 3 million gallons (14,000 cu. m) of water roars through three canals to drive the 21 generators of the 2715 MW power-station.

In the lowland of the "Nine Rivers"

The historic **Yichang** was probably founded as early as the 6th century BC as a military stronghold on an island in the Yangtse, which today serves as the base for the Gezhouba Dam. The availability of electric power led to the rapid growth of the industrial city, which played a key role in the Second World War.

The red-brown waters of the river trace broad bends through the Hubei basin and create a watery landscape with lakes in the north and marshes in the south, which is known as *yun meng* ("Cloud-dream"). It was here that the legendary Nine Rivers (*jiu jiang*) were often sought.

Not until the 20th century was the course of the Yangtse fixed and levelled by means of cuttings. To protect the newly established irrigation schemes and guard against the frequent floods, artificial dykes had been built as early as the 3rd century AD.

The most famous example of these is the 112 mile (180 km) long Jingjiang Dyke, which rises 52 ft (16 m) above the surrounding land and runs as far as Shangzhewan. It chiefly protects the estuarial plain between the Hanjiang and the Yangtse.

Jiangling, capital of the Jingzhou region, was founded in the 3rd century BC as a river stronghold on an island in the

Right: The broad, stately expanse of the Yangtse as it passes Wuhan, capital of Hubei province.

Yangtse; 600 years later, it was fortified with a town wall which now contains a museum.

In the vicinity the present town of **Sha shi** ("Sandtown") grew up on the site of an old Yangtse ford (*jiang jin*) and is now known for its crafts and for producing thermos-flasks. Its landmark, visible from a long way off, is the 16th-century **Treasure Pagoda of Long Life** (*wan shou baota*), which is decorated with brickwork designs of landscapes and genre scenes. Nearby stand the **Pagoda for Observing the River** (*wangjiang ta*) and the **Spring-Autumn Pavilion** (*chunqiu ge*), built in memory of Guan Yu. In the town center the **Zhanghua Temple** contains valuable scriptures and Jade Buddhas. South of the main street the **Jiangdu Palace** has been reconstructed in memory of the statesman and poet Qu Yuan.

The charming little town of Jiangling (formerly Jiangzhou) is today still surrounded by a completely preserved town wall from the Song period, nearly 6 miles (9.3 km) long. Near the west gate, interesting finds in the Taoist **Kaiyuan Temple** (*kaiyuan si*) tell the story of ancient Jiangling (*jinan cheng*). Outside the town wall in the northwest the **Taihui Temple** (*taihui si*) was built in the 14th century as the luxurious residence of an extravagant ruler.

To the north lie the excavation sites of **Ying** and **Jinancheng**. Both towns were capitals of the Yangtse kingdom of Chu (6th – 3rd centuries BC). Chu, together with Qin, was once the last independent territorial state left before the first unification of the Chinese empire.

Near Chenglingji the Yangtse takes up the water stored in the reservoir of **Lake Dongting** (*dongting hu*) in the winter when the river's water-level is low. Opposite **Yueyang**, where there is a beautiful lookout tower, the island of **Junshan**, famous for its tea-bushes and unspoilt bamboo thickets, rises from the lake.

Further downstream on the left bank of the Yangtse, the large **Lake Hong** (*hong hu*) serves as a reservoir.

After the 3rd century AD, settlements began to grow up at the confluence of the **Hanjiang** with the Yangtse, which later became the towns of Hankou, Hanyang and Wuchang. They were later amalgamated to form the city of **Wuhan,** capital of Hubei province. In 1957, the first bridge over the Yangtse between the industrial town of **Hanyang** and the administrative town of **Wuchang** was built under difficult conditions. It runs for 1065 yds (1.16 km) from **Snake Hill** (*she shan*) on the right bank, where the **Tower of the Yellow Crane** (*huanghao lou*) stands as a landmark, to **Tortoise Hill** (*gui shan*) in Hanyang on the left bank. At the foot of this hill the temple of **Guishansi** welcomes visitors. Its hall contains 500 *luohan* figures, a Guanyin Bodhisattva and a statue of Buddha weighing 105 tons. In the 19th century, Hanyang was a center of colonial industry and also played a key role in the revolution of 1911.

The heart of the trading city of **Hankou** looks rather grand with its well maintained houses from the colonial era, once tenanted by British, French, Russians, Americans and Japanese. However, the buildings most worth seeing are those of the **University of Wuhan**, built in the traditional style on the shore of the **East Lake** (*dong hu*) in the Wuchang district. Not far away, the **Provincial Museum** displays a unique collection of ancient musical instruments, including bronze bells from the Zhou period and lithophones (made of resonating stone).

The Yangtse in Anhui

The tourist center of gravity of **Anhui** province (pop.: 50 million) lies in the south. It is easier to reach from Shanghai and Hangzhou in the east, or from Wuhan in the west, than from the provincial capital, **Hefei**. This latter is an industrial city to the north, which can be ignored.

The Yangtse ports of Guichi and Wuhu are suitable starting points for excursions

into the country, especially to the Huang-shan. In Wuhu itself, the **Zhe Hill** (*zhe shan*) with its park and temple pagoda is worth a visit.

In Wuhu, the railroad branches off down toward **Tunxi** in the far south of the province. This town seems to live in the timeless atmosphere of the Chinese backwoods. The main sources of income here are tea-plantations and forestry. Buses go from here to the Huangshan.

These **Yellow Mountains** (*huang shan*) consist of a chain of 72 peaks running parallel to the northwesterly course of the Yangtse through Anhui for 56 miles (90 km) as the crow flies. Thirty-one of the peaks exceed 5000 ft (1500 m) and the highest of them, the **Lotus Peak** (*linhua feng*), has an altitude of 5900 ft (1800 m). Ever since the Tang emperor Tian Biao gave the range its present name, back in the 8th century, Huang-shan has been a place that promises beau-

tiful, dreamlike visions of nature. It is especially haunting when thick clouds roll in beneath you and veil the trees clinging dizzily to the steep crags. The famous poet of the Tang period, Li Bai, sang the praises of the Lotus Peak. All the same, the visitor should not expect to find nature completely untouched here. Innumerable flights of steps and well-maintained paths guide the feet of the nature lover – and if the feet get tired, there is a cable-car to the top.

With the same orientation and landscape, though nearer to the Yangtse, the **Mountains of Nine Flowers** (*jiuhua shan*) have almost a hundred peaks. Here, too, Li Bai was impelled to draw a comparison with lotus flowers. The Jiuhua-shan is one of the mountains that are sacred to the Chinese Buddhists. It is said that at one time more than 300 temple monasteries stood here. One of the main attractions for walkers (or should that be stairway-climbers) is the **Huacheng monastery temple** (*huacheng si*) with a library dating back to the 15th century.

Above: View of the city of Wuhan. Above right: A path in the Yellow Mountains.

164

SICHUAN

Accommodation

CHENGDU: *LUXURY:* Chengdu, Shudu Donglu, Tel. 444 8888. **Jinjiarg Hotel** (*jinjiang binguan*), 36 Renmin Nanlu, Tel. 558 2222.

MID-PRICE: **Tibet Hotel** (*xizang fandian*), 10 Renmin Beilu, Tel. 334001.

BUDGET: **Jiaotong Hotel** (*jiaotong fandian*), 77 Linjiang Lu, Tel. 555 4962.

CHONGQING: *LUXURY:* **Holiday Inn Yangtze**, 15 Nanping Beilu, Tel. 280 3380. **Chongqing Hotel** (chongqing fandian), 41-43 Xinhua Lu, Tel. 380 9301.

MID-PRICE: **Renmin Hotel** (*renmin binguan*), 175 Renmin Lu, Tel. 385 1421 (Palace built in traditional Chinese style).

BUDGET: **Huixianlou Hotel** (*huixianlou binguan*), 186 Minzu Lu, Tel. 384 5027.

LESHAN: *MID-PRICE:* **Jiazhou Hotel** (*jiazhou binguan*), Baitajie, Tel. 22301 (comfortable; good, cheap hotel meals).

BUDGET: **Daduhe Hotel** (*daduhe fandian*), Wuyouba, Tel. 33286.

EMEISHAN: *BUDGET* **Hongzhushan Hotel** (*hongzhushan binguan*), At the foot of Mt Emeishan, Tel. 33888. The temple monasteries also provide sleeping accommodation and meals for a ridiculously small charge.

Restaurants

CHENGDU: **Chengdu** (*chengdu canting*), 642 Shandong Dajie (very popular with tourists). **Rong Le Yuan** (*rongle yuan*), 48 Renmin Zhong Lu (pleasant atmosphere, good natural ventilation.)

CHONGQING: Local speciality is the "fire-pot" (*huoguo*). The Wuyi Lu is locally known as "Fire-pot Street" (*huoguo jie*) – a happy hunting-ground for lovers of this dish. The **Chungking** (next to the Chongqing Hotel) is reckoned to be the best restaurant in town.

EMEISHAN: Restaurant of the Hongzhushan Hotel; the monasteries also provide simple meals.

Tourist information

CHENGDU: **OTC**, 19 Renmin Nanlu, Tel. 667 2369.

CHONGQING: **CITS**, in the grounds of the Renmin Hotel, Tel. 385 1665.

THE YANGTSE IN SICHUAN, HUBEI AND ANHUI

Getting there

WUHAN: Rail junction on the main line from Peking to Canton with frequent connections to Yueyang on Lake Dongting. International airport with flights to Hong Kong and all important Chinese cities.

By ship along the Yangtse

The state-owned Yangste Shipping Company based in Wuhan currently operates about twelve luxury vessels which ply between Chongqing (Sichuan) and Wuhan (Hubei) at an average speed of 15 knots (27 k.p.h.) Facilities on board include: outside cabins with single or twin beds; TV, swimming-pool, bar, ballroom; hairdresser, laundry, clinic; restaurant with very good Chinese cuisine; bureau de change, shopping facilities, telegram and telephone service, as well as a first-class crew. Meanwhile, stiff competition comes from joint-venture companies with five Holiday Inn ships and three ships from Regal Cruises. A **four-day cruise** with one day spent going through the **Three Gorges**, as the main attraction, includes excursions on shore. The regular scheduled river-boats, which run all the way to Shanghai, stopping at various places, only have 2, 8-12, or 20-40 bed cabins. You can also sleep out on deck. There are communal toilet and washing facilities.

Tourist information and ship reservations

CHONGQING: **CITS**, in the Renmin Hotel, Tel. 51449. Ticket office, Chaotianmen, Tel. 384 1001.

WUHAN: **HUBEI OTC**, Jianghan Yi Lu 48, Tel. 382 3505. **Changjiang Steamship Corp.**, Yanjiang Dadao 89, Tel. 581 2576.

Accommodation

HUBEI:

SHASHI: **Jianglin Hotel** (*jianglin binguan*), Gongyuan Rd., Tel. 33491. **Zhanghua Hotel** (*zhanghua binguan*), 100 Zhongshan Rd., Tel. 33401.

JINGZHOU: **Jingzhou Hotel** (*jingzhou binguan*), 4 Yingbinguan Lu, Tel. 467600.

WUHAN: *LUXURY:* **Asia**, 300 Jiefang Dadao, Tel. 586 8777. **Jianghan**, Shengli Jie, Tel. 581 6076. **Qingchuan Hotel** (*qingchuan fandian*), Hanyang, 88 Ximachangjie, Tel. 484 1141. **Yangzi Hotel** (*changjiang dajiudian*), Hankou, 539 Jiefang Dadao, Tel. 586 2828. *MID-PRICE:* **Lijiang Hotel** (*lijiang fandian*), Wuchang, 1 Tiyuguan Rd., Tel. 781 3668. *BUDGET:* **Victory Hotel** (*shengli fandian*), Hankou, 11 Siwei Rd., Tel. 283 2531.

ANHUI:

HUANGSHAN: *MID-PRICE:* **Taoyuan Hotel** (*taoyuan binguan*), Wenquan, Tel. 212381 (there is a branch of CITS in the hotel). **Xihai Hotel** (*xihai fandian*), Xihai. *BUDGET:* **Beihai Guesthouse** (*beihai fandian*), Beihai, Tel. 2550.

The two last hotels are located on the mountain.

CRADLE OF THE
RED REVOLUTION

HUNAN

JIANGXI

HUNAN

As early as the 3rd century BC, the Han Chinese migrated from the north into the region which is the present-day province of Hunan. The Miao and Yao peoples, who were long-time inhabitants, were either assimilated by the Han or driven westward. By the Yuan and Ming dynasties, the fertile land of Hunan was already an important source of rice for the Chinese empire. In the 19th century, however, overpopulation, scarcity of land and the impoverishment of the small farmers and tenants led to near-starvation among a large portion of the population. The result of this poverty was that revolts frequently broke out among the peasantry, culminating in 1850 with the mass uprising of the Taiping Rebellion, though this ended in defeat. Even after that, there was little change to the miserable conditions of the rural population. It was inevitable that in the 1920s Hunan would become a power-base for the Chinese Communists. Its name is closely linked with that of Mao Zedong: he was born here, received his education here, and here began his rise from village schoolteacher to leader of the Chinese Revolution. As well as Mao, several other famous personalities of the Chinese Communist Party came from Hunan, including Liu Shaoqi, Li Lisan and Hu Yaobang.

Situated in southeastern China, the province has an area of 81,000 sq. miles (210,000 sq. km) and a population of 55 million. Today Hunan is still predominantly agricultural and an important rice producer.

Changsha

The capital, **Changsha** – population: 800,000 – is the political, cultural and economic nerve-center of Hunan. For centuries, Changsha has owed its prosperity to its trade in rice and other agricultural produce. Mao Zedong lived in this city, first as a schoolboy and student, later as a teacher and revolutionary. Hua Guofeng also served as provincial party chairman in Changsha before he succeeded Mao.

Changsha's principal attraction is kept in the **Hunan Provincial Museum** (*hunan sheng bowuguan*): the mummy of an aristocratic lady, over 2100 years old, who belonged to the Western Han dynasty. Her untouched tomb was discovered near **Mawangdui** in 1972. What was interesting about the mummy was that – unlike mummies found in Egypt –

Left: Thinning out the young rice-shoots.

167

the internal organs had been preserved. This enabled scientists not only to diagnose the dead lady's illnesses, but even to analyze her eating habits.

Some of Changsha's most important historical sites lie on the 900 ft (275 m) **Yuelu Hill** (*yuelu shan*) on the west bank of the river Xiang. The Buddhist **Lushan Temple** (*lushan si*), half way up to the summit, was built in 286 AD. Standing on top of the hill is the **Yunlu monastery** (*yunlu si*). There the **Pavilion of Enjoyment of Dusk** (*aiwan ting*) creates a mood of tranquil contemplation.

Shaoshan

About 60 miles (100 km) southwest of Changsha, in the village of **Shaoshan**, Mao Zedong was born on December 26th, 1893. At that time it was just one of the many peasant hamlets that one finds in Hunan, nestling among gentle hills and

Above: The house where Mao Zedong was born (Hunan).

hemmed in by rice fields. But the fact that "The Great Helmsman" first saw the light of day here raised the village to the status of a national shrine once the Communists had seized power. In the late 1960s, at the height of the Cultural Revolution, millions of Chinese made their pilgrimage here from every corner of the land. Today, Shaoshan has once again sunk into sleepy obscurity. The **House of Mao's Birth** (*maozedong jiuju*), with four rooms, kitchen and bathroom around a central courtyard, would have been the typical home of a well-to-do freeholder in this region. A short walk along the village street brings you to the **Mao Museum** (*maozedong zhanlanguan*).

Yueyang

The town of **Yueyang** is situated at neck of Lake Dongting, where the Yangtse flows out of it, and looks back on 2400 years of history as a trading town. Near the quayside rises Yueyang's landmark, visible from a long way off,

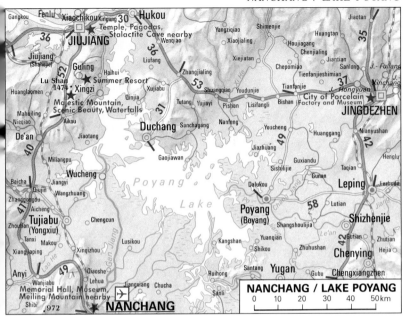

NANCHANG / LAKE POYANG
0 10 20 30 40 50km

the 66 ft (20 m) high **Yueyang Tower** (*yueyang ta*) from the Tang period. One of the three famous historic towers south of the Yangtse, it is built entirely of wood. From the top your eye sweeps far across **Lake Dongting** (*dongting hu*), China's largest fresh-water lake, with an area of 1500 sq. miles (3900 sq. km). The little **Junshan Island,** southwest of Yueyang, covers less than half a square mile (1 sq. km), but contains the **Erfeimu Tombs,** in which two princesses lie buried. The *Junshan Silver-needle tea* comes from this island.

Mount Heng

Mount Heng (*heng shan*, also called *nan yue*), is over 4000 ft (1225 m) high and one of China's sacred mountains. As well as delightful scenery, it offers the tourist a chance to visit numerous **Buddhist temples** (including the **Nanta** and the **Fuyan**), the **Cangjing Hall** (*cangjing dian*) where *sutras* are kept, and the 15th-century **Zhurong Temple** (*zhurong dian*)

perched on the summit. And the **Pavilion for Admiring the Moon** (*wangyue tai*) fulfils the promise of its romantic name.

JIANGXI

The southeastern province of Jiangxi has a population of 35 million living in area of a little under 66,000 sq. miles (170,000 sq. km). It is the region of Chian which is least known to tourism. Nevertheless, it's worth taking the time to see – and not just because of the porcelain factory in Jingdezhen, which has been famous for centuries.

The most important event in the history of Jiangxi took place in 1927 in the Jinggang mountains: the setting up of one of the largest soviets of the Chinese Revolution. After their unsuccessful revolts in the big cities of China, the Communists were forced to retreat to this remote and inaccessible mountain region. The troops of the Guomindang mounted a bitter campaign against them, but it was several years before they succeeded in

driving the Communists out of the Jinggang mountains. This evacuation led to the terrible *Long March*, in which the Communists covered 7,500 miles on foot and finally reached Shaanxi.

Nanchang

Jiangxi's provincial capital, Nanchang, was founded during the Western Han dynasty, some 2200 years ago.

However, Nanchang did not enter the pages of Chinese history until August 1st, 1927, when the Communists, led by Zhou Enlai and Zhu De, with an army of 30,000 men, captured the city and were briefly able to hold out against the Guomindang. This day is officially held to be the date of the founding of the Chinese Red Army, which was later renamed the People's Liberation Army.

Today Nanchang appears as a drab but hard-working industrial city of 2.5 mil-

Above: Jingdezhen (Jiangxi) – home of the Chinese art of porcelain.

lion inhabitants. Many of its sights recall the rebellion of 1927. Among these are the **Memorial Pagoda of the Nanchang Rebellion** (*"bayi" nanchang qiyi jinianta*) the **Martyrs' Memorial Hall** (*geming lieshi jiniantang*) which commemorates the most important battles of the Chinese Civil War, as well as the former **headquarters of the leader of the Nanchang Rebellion of August 1st, 1927** (*bayi qiyi jinianguan*) in the street named Zhongshanlu.

Exhibits from the cultural history of the province are on display in the **Jiangxi Museum** (*jiangxi bowuguan*). This is to be found on the south side of **Renmin Square,** an area designed in the modern monumental style.

Lu Mountains and Lake Poyang

The road from Nanchang to Jiujiang takes one through some of the most attractive landscape in Jiangxi. The massive, mist-shrouded mountains of the **Lushan** soar up from the steamy lowlands of northern Jiangxi, reaching a height of 4835 ft (1474 m).

Driving for about three hours from Nanchang up steep hairpin bends, you reach **Guling**. This welcoming little town is a refuge from the summer heat of the lowlands and a base for hiking on the thickly wooded mountainsides.

At the eastern foot of the Lushan lies **Lake Poyang** (*poyang hu*). It is fed by the **river Gan** (*gan jiang*) and is one of China's largest inland lakes; it also serves as a seasonal reservoir for the Yangtse. You can best enjoy the beautiful scenery from the deck of a boat, on an organized boat trip such as the one from Taihe to Ganzhou.

Jiujang

Just a stone's throw from here, north of the Lushan mountains, lies **Jiujang**, a picturesque and bustling little port on the

Yangtse. Throughout its 2000-year history it has been an important trading center for tea and porcelain.

Though small, Jiujang has a number of things to interest the tourist. In the middle of the town the charming **Pavilion of Mists** (*yanshui ting*) stands on an island in a lake. It can only be reached across a zigzag bridge, intended to confuse evil spirits, and today houses a **museum** of prehistoric finds.

Further south lies the **Palace of Heavenly Flowers** (*tianhua gong*) on the shore of Lake Gantang. The emblem of Jiujang, the seven-tiered **Suojianglou Pagoda**, in the northeast of the town, dates from 1585. It stands on a small hill beside the Yangtse and can be seen for miles around.

Jingdezhen

One of the high spots of a journey through Jiangxi is surely a visit to the town of **Jingdezhen**, for centuries famous for its porcelain.

As early as the Song dynasty (960-1279) the world-famous *rice-pattern* porcelain was being manufactured here. But the full flowering of the art of porcelain was achieved during the Yuan and Ming dynasties, when the factories concentrated above all on the priceless *blue and white* porcelain.

In its time, this was sought after not only in China but also by the aristocratic families of Europe.

The fine clay from which the precious porcelain is made has been dug up around the nearby village of **Gaoling** (Kaolin) since time immemorial. Today the chimneys of Jingdezhen's porcelain factories are still smoking and most of the town's 250,000 inhabitants are employed there. To arrange a guided tour you should contact CITS.

A notable sight in the south of the town is the **Red Pagoda** (*hong ta*), which dates from the Tang period.

HUNAN
Accommodation
CHANGSHA: *LUXURY*: **Huatian**, 16 Jiefang Donglu, Tel. 444 2888. *MID-PRICE*: **Xiangjiang Hotel** (*xiangjiang binguan*), 2 Zhongshan Lu, Tel. 446 8888. *BUDGET*: **Rongyuan Hotel** (*rongyuan binguan*), Bayi Lu, Tel. 426 7806. **SHAOSHAN**: *BUDGET*: **Shaoshan Binguan**, near the Mao Museum. **HENGYANG**: *MID-PRICE*: **Hengyang Hotel** (*hengyang fandian*), 54 Xianfeng Lu, Tel. 222 201. **YUEYANG**: *BUDGET*: **Yunmeng Hotel** (*yunmeng binguan*), 25 Chengdong Lu, Tel. 24498. **DAYONG**: *MID-PRICE*: **Dayong Hotel** (*dayong binguan*), Jiefang Lu. *BUDGET*: **Yuping Hotel**, near the bus station.
Restaurants
CHANGSHA: Well-prepared Hunan cuisine is served in the **Youyicun**, 116 Zhongshan Lu.
Tourist information (CITS)
CHANGSHA: 9 Wuyi Donglu, Tel. 440 1294. **YUEYANG**: In the Yunmeng Hotel, Chengdong Lu. **HENGYANG**: In the Hengyang Hotel. **DAYONG**: In the Dayong Binguan.
Excursions
The **Wuling Mountains** (*wuling shan*) stretch across western Hunan. From Dayong you can organize trips into the exciting scenery of the **Zhangjiajie Region**.

JIANGXI
Accommodation
NANCHANG: *MID-PRICE*: **Jiangxi Hotel** (*jiangxi binguan*), 56 Bayi Dadao, Tel. 626 7891. *BUDGET*: **Hongdu Hotel** (*hongdu fandian*), Bayi Lu. **LUSHAN**: *BUDGET*: **Yunzhong Hotel** (*yunzhong binguan*), 549 Henan Lu, Tel. 822 2547. **Lushan Binguan**, Hexi Lu, Tel. 828 2860. **JIUJIANG**: *MID-PRICE*: **Nanhu Hotel** (*nanhu binguan*), 28 Nanhu Lu, Tel. 822 5041. *BUDGET*: **Dongfang Hotel**, Xunyang Lu. **JINGDEZHEN**: *MID-PRICE*: **Jingdezhen Guesthouse** (*jingdezhen binguan*), 68 Lianhuatang, Tel. 225015. *BUDGET*: **Jingdezhen Hotel** (*jingdezhen fandian*), 1 Zhongshan Lu, Tel. 222301.
Tourist information (CITS)
NANCHANG: In Jiangxi Hotel, Bayi Dadao, Tel. 622 6681. **LUSHAN**: 443 Hendong Lu, Tel. 2497. **JIUJIANG**: In the Nanhu Hotel Tel. 822 3390. **JINGDEZHEN**: 8 Lianhuatang, Tel. 222939.
Excursions
In the **Jinggang Mountains** (*jinggang shan*), on the border with Hunan, the Communists established an important soviet in 1927. **Ciping** is the starting-point for tours in the Jinggangshan.

THE HEART
OF THE MIDDLE
COUNTRY

SHANXI
SHAANXI
HENAN

LAND OF YELLOW EARTH

"Loess" is the geologists' name for that fertile "Yellow Earth" (*huang tu*), which formed the cradle of Chinese civilization. The loess was created in the last Ice Age, when dry, cold winter winds from Siberia carried massive quantities of dust southward from the Mongolian desert. In northern China's Ice Age tundra, the dust was caught in tussocks of grass, and layers of it began to build up – the coarsest grains laid down in the north, with increasingly finer grains the further south it got. The steppe was stifled under the dust and became the graveyard of countless generations of grasses. However, these in turn provided the rich content of a soil which is unique in the world: the Yellow Earth. So long as there is a guaranteed minimum rainfall, loess country offers the best basic conditions for the prosperity of an agricultural society. The soil is easy to work; what is more, people have no difficulty in digging underground dwellings in the loess, which are unequalled in their solidity and natural air-conditioning.

The strength of the summer monsoon, which brings rainfall up from the south-

Left: The terra-cotta army of the emperor Qin Shi Huangdi in Lingtong, near Xi'an.

east, fades as it moves northwest, which means that the rain which falls on the loess lands is not always sufficient. Thus, since time immemorial, the inhabitants have been obliged to irrigate their fields artificially. In these fields they grow beans, peanuts and buckwheat, and at higher altitudes, *gaoliang* (cob millet), poppies, cotton and – in the highest cultivable areas – mainly wheat and other grain crops.

The most massive loess deposits lie in the southern part of the great bend in the Yellow River, between the Qingling mountain chain in the south and the Great Wall of China in the north.

The Yellow River,
northern China's lifeblood

The **Yellow River** (*huang he*) rises in the northeast of the Tibetan plateau, at a height of 14,600 ft (4455 m), between the Qaidam basin and the sources of the Yangtse. From **Zhongwei**, at an altitude of only 4000 ft (1230 m), its middle section flows in a wide arc around the Ordos plateau, leaving the traditional homeland of the Chinese. It swings south again, forming the long frontier between the provinces of Shaanxi and Shanxi. Below the **Hukou Falls**, the Yellow River reaches the heart of the loess region, flowing

173

through it in a narrow canyon. Along a stretch of only 30 miles (50 km), between Hukou and **Longmen**, the river picks up half its burden of sediment from the easily eroded banks of loess and carries it in suspension through the Longmen Gorge, just 165 ft (50 m) wide and 820 ft (250 m) deep. After leaving the **Dragon Gate** (*long men*) the mass of water and sediment is augmented by its two largest tributaries, the **Fenhe** (from Shanxi) and the **Weihe** (Shaanxi). Then, near Tongguan, the Yellow River is diverted eastward by the mountain wall of Qinling, and, passing through a last mighty gorge near **Sanmen** ("Three Gates"), finds its way to the lowland plain of northern China. Here, the lower reaches of the Yellow River flow in a broad stream between high embankments across the alluvial plain it has itself deposited, and which has grown to be China's most densely populated agricultural area.

How often in the past 2500 years have the lower reaches of the Yellow River altered their course! In doing so it has created the largest delta landscape in the world. How often have its dykes been breached, and devastating floods laid waste the land, claiming the lives of millions of people!

When the dyke burst at **Kaifeng** (Henan) in 1334, the mass of water swept southward again into the Yellow Sea; the result was a flowering (in the literal as well as figurative sense) of the provinces of Shandong, Henan, Anhui and Jiangsu. In 1938, during the Civil War, the dykes near **Zhengzhou** were blown up for military reasons; 12 million people in central China were left homeless by the resulting floods. In the plains of northern China, meanwhile, there was drought and salination of the water.

The battle against the "Great River" (*da he*) made it necessary for the Chinese

Right: A ferry crossing the Yellow River.

to become masters of hydraulic engineering, with which from earliest times they controlled the flow of the river. In 95 BC so it is said, they began work on an enormous canal between the upper and lower reaches of the river, in order to short-cut the great bend. In the Han period (around the beginning of our era), long stretches of the lower reaches were already embanked – with main dykes, inner dykes overflow and circular dykes, and reservoirs to store water in the rainy season.

SHANXI
west of the mountains

The province of Shanxi covers an area of 61,000 sq. miles (157,000 sq. km) in the loess hills that run between 3500 ft and 6500 ft (1000-2000 m) from the Yellow River in the west and south to the northern Chinese lowlands in the east. The central artery, the river Fenhe, flows into the dammed Yellow River below the Longmen Gorge. To the east, the **Taihangshan** mountain range, which reaches its highest point in the 9800 ft (3000 m) **Wutaishan**, separates Shanxi from the north Chinese plain. In the north, its border runs along the Great Wall, beyond which stretches the Mongolian plateau. The hill country, which rises from 1600 ft to 4000 ft (500-1200 m) is covered with a layer of loess up to 100 ft (30 m) thick. It is deeply eroded, and movements of the earth's crust have broken the loess into jagged slabs, creating a landscape dotted with small lakes and ponds.

The strange face that nature has given to this province has historically led it to forge its own political destiny, a fact which sets it clearly apart from other provinces of China. As early as the Zhou period, autonomous territories in Shanxi built walls to ward off attack by nomads from the north. The first emperor of the Qin dynasty combined these smaller fortifications to form the Great Wall.

Shanxi, therefore, took on the key role of a bulwark which could serve as a defense of imperial unity, but which could also be turned against it.

Shanxi produced champions of the unified empire which the great Tang dynasty had founded, but it also produced destroyers of the empire. Among these were the non-Chinese Kitan, who, in a prelude to the Mongol invasion, gained sway over northern China.

Because of the link to the north there grew up in Shanxi a very able business community, who, from the Ming period on, controlled banking in every city in China. The fertile valley of the Fenhe and the uplands with their many lakes, were sites of settlements of the earliest Chinese cultures; like magnets, they have continually attracted foreign migrants ever since.

Today, the province's economic importance is based on its mineral deposits and its extensive seams of coal, which are second only to those of Manchuria in size.

Datong – China's gateway to the north

Datong ("Great Harmony") lies on a dry plateau in the center of Shanxi's coal-mining region and is the largest city in the province. As the frontier city facing (Inner) Mongolia it has, since the 5th century AD, held a key strategic and economic position, and represents the most important link between northern China and Central Asia. During the Tang and Ming dynasties Datong was one of the most strongly defended frontier towns on the **Great Wall**.

Datong is spaciously laid out on a rectangular grid, and its surviving temples recall the heyday of Buddhism as the national religion. Particularly fine are the **Upper and Lower Huayan monasteries** (*huayan si*)**,** which date from the Liao period and can be found in the southwest corner of the Old City. Unusually, their huge prayer halls face east and contain valuable Buddhist statues from the 12th and 13th centuries. In the southeast quar-

ter of the Old City lies the **Shanhua Monastery** (also known as the *nan si*, "South Monastery"), dating from the 8th century. It was rebuilt by the Jürchen and possesses a magnificent library.

Nearby, the Confucian temple and the **Wall of Nine Dragons** (*jiulong bi*) were built at the beginning of the Ming period. The 150 ft (40 m) long wall is decorated with nine dragons made of brightly colored glazed tiles, which are said to bring protection and blessings to the city.

Also well worth a visit are the **Datong Locomotive Works**, where, until 1990, the last steam locomotives in China were built.

Yungang, a blend of Indian and Chinese cultures

Initially, the Toba-Wei people, who had penetrated as far as Shanxi, employed Buddhism as a weapon against

Above: Cave-temple in Yungang. Right: The Hanging Monastery on the Hengshan.

Chinese Confucianism and Taoism; later, they elevated it to be their official religion.

Among the cultural achievements of the Toba-Wei were the introduction of a just system of land distribution and the advancement of art and science. A pinnacle of these achievements is the artistic decoration of the cave-temples of **Yungang**. The carving and painting of the rock walls were carried on even after the Toba-Wei had withdrawn from Datong. In them one can discern a variety of influences from India (Vishnu, Shiva, elephants, clothing, coiffure), the Byzantine empire (beards, weapons, lions) and Greece (acanthus-leaves, trident). The caves were rediscovered in 1903. They have been heavily eroded by dust-storms and were a favorite target for art-thieves.

At the entrance you will notice the wood**en Shifogu Temple** (*shifogu si*) dating from 1652. It is the only remaining building of several monasteries which once stood outside the caves. Where the great Lingyan monastery formerly stood, you will now find **Cave Nr 3** with an unusual representation of three Buddhas in high relief. The principal attraction of Yungang is provided by **Cave Nr 5**, whose Buddha statues are a particularly fine reflection of the style and spirit of the Toba-Wei dynasty. In **Cave Nr 6** there are illustrations of episodes in the life of Buddha, from his birth to his passing. **Cave Nr 8** is decorated with a three-headed, eight-armed Vishnu on his steed Nandi, a bull, as well as the five-headed and six-armed Shiva riding an eagle. In **Nr 12**, celestial musicians play in honor of Buddha, who has achieved enlightenment. The walls of **Nr 14** are decorated with over 10,000 Buddhas. In **Nr 16**, the visitor could believe himself in a paradise of contemplation. One cannot fail to be impressed by the 46 ft (14 m) high statue of a striding Buddha. In **Cave Nr 18** an imposing Buddha sitting in a lotus position reaches a height of 53 ft (16 m). And the **triple cave, Nr 19,** ontains a 36 ft (11 m) high Buddha, whose stern and impassive expression is perfect example of early Wei art.

Hengshan and Wutaishan, the sacred mountains of Shanxi

About 44 miles (70 km) southeast of Datong, in the Hunyan district, rises **Hengshan**, the most northerly of China's sacred mountains. Clinging to its sheer cliff is the **Hanging Monastery** (*xuanong si*), which was built into the rock face during the Toba-Wei dynasty in the 6th century. The cliff face behind the 40 or more attractive wooden buildings has been hollowed out to form prayer-caves. Inside them, you should look at the well-reserved clay, stone, iron and bronze sculptures of Buddhist holy men, dating from the Tang dynasty. From the monastery you can climb the endless stone stairway to the twin summits of Hengshan, a little over 6,500 ft (2000 m) high.

Parallel to the Hengshan mountain chain, the peaks of the **Five Terrace Mountains** stretch southwards. They reach their highest point in the 10,000 ft (3058 m) **Wutaishan**, whose name also means "Mountain of the Five Terraces," and which is another of China's sacred Buddhist mountains. During the Toba-Wei and Tang dynasties it was one of the most important places of pilgrimage in China. Until well into the 20th century it was the most venerated burial-place of the Mongols. Once there were hundreds of temples here, which amassed considerable wealth from the sacrificial gifts of rich merchants; now, only about 18 of them have survived which are worth visiting. The **Xiantong Temple** (*xiantong si*) is a complex of 400 buildings and is the oldest of the five great Zen monasteries of Wutaishan. The **Foguang Monastery** (*foguang si*) contains two very fine buildings, the **Manjushri Hall** (*wenhu dian*) and the **Main Prayer Hall** (*zheng dian*); both were originally built in the Tang period and reflect the typical Chinese style of palace construction. Another crowning achievement of Tang architecture is the **Main Prayer Hall** (*da dian*) of the **Monastery of Southern Zen** (*nanchan si*).

Taiyuan

At the southwest point of Wutaishan lies **Taiyuan**, capital of the modern province of Shanxi. It stands in the center of the oldest culture in China and was a fortified city as early as the 5th century BC. In the Han empire Taiyuan played a strategic role as a bulwark against migrating invaders. It reached its first cultural flowering as capital of the Northern Qi dynasty (550-577 AD), when many temples, palaces and gardens were constructed. Taiyuan lived through another glorious period during the Tang dynasty. But this came to an end with the fall of the empire in the 10th century, when almost the entire city was destroyed. Not until the 20th century did the city regain a

period architecture contains a statue of sacred mother figure, surrounded by 4 women who embody the manners and behavior of their age.

From the Jinci, your route leads westward to the **Dragon Mountains** (*long shan*). There you will find the **Tongz Temple** (*tongzi si*), with the oldest ston lanterns in China, and the Taois **Haotianguan Monastery** (*haotianguan si*). Southwest of Jinci rises the **Moun tain of the Celestial Dragon** (*tianlong shan*) in which there are 21 Buddhi caves from the 6th to 8th centuries.

About 43 miles (70 km) south of the Jinci, not far from the Pingyao train station, you will find the **Temple of the Two Forests** (*shuanglin si*), whose price less sculptures from the Song and Yua periods are greatly admired by visitors.

SHAANXI
Cradle of Chinese civilization

The province of **Shaanxi** lies in the heart of China's loess country and cover an area of 75,000 sq. miles (195,000 sq km). It stretches along both sides of the Weihe valley: northwards beyond the **Great Wall**, and southwards over the great dividing range of the **Qinling**, with its peak of Taibaishan rising to 12,356 f (3767 m), and down to the headwaters o the **Hanshui** river. Shaanxi's position between the Ordos Desert and centra China, between the foothills of the mountains bordering Tibet and the lowe reaches of the Huanghe, has given it the role of crossroads between west and east north and south. Thus Shaanxi has in herited the name of Guanzhong, the "Land within the Passes," which is con sidered to be the cradle of Chinese civi lization. The core of *Guanzhong* wa once formed by the fertile loess plain o the Weihe river, where indeed the earlies traces of settlements have been found. T the north it extends into the loess plateau of Shaanxi. To the south it is bordered b

little of its former importance. This was when it was the seat of the dictator Yan Xishan, who ruled Shanxi as a virtually independent state until 1949.

You can get a comprehensive overview of the eventful history both of the city and its province in the two sections of the **Shanxi Provincial Museum** (*shanxi sheng bowuguan*).

One of the most famous temples in Shanxi lies about 16 miles (25 km) south of Taiyuan, nestling in an enchanting landscape thickly wooded with cypress trees. The **Temple of the Ministers of Jin** (*jin ci*, or *jindaifu ci*) was built in honor of the ministers of the state of Jin. These men earned the admiration of Confucius, since they had elected their ruler according to the prescribed custom. Here, slightly west of the center of a garden laid out in the classical Chinese style, stands the **Hall of the Holy Mother** (*shenmu dian*). This superb example of Song-

Above: Detail from the Temple of the Ministers of Jin (near Taiyuan).

the granite massif of the Qinling. This forms a frontier between northern and central China, separating them climatically, culturally and w th respect to vegetation and landscape. Even today, the Weihe valley is the center of population and agriculture; half of the province's population lives on just 8% of its total land area. Thanks to irrigation, it is sometimes possible to raise two crops a year of winter wheat, maize and millet, despite the cold, dry winter climate. Cultivation of cotton led to the first industrialization, though now mechanical and electrical engineering predominate.

Xi'an – once the Golden Capital

No Chinese city is richer in history than **Xi'an**. From the second millennium BC until the 10th century AD, it served as a royal and imperial capital. The earliest traces of habitation can be found in the village of **Banpo** east of the city. In 1953 a neolithic settlement was excavated here, whose fine colored ceramics are proof of the advanced development of early Chinese civilization in the *Yangshao* culture. A modern roof structure protects a completely exposed village, with well-preserved house foundations, ovens for firing clay pottery, storage caves and a cemetery with an urn-field.

In 221 BC, the small state of Qin (Chin) succeeded in uniting the whole of China under its name and ruling it from the Weihe valley. On the banks of the Weihe the first imperial capital, Xianyang, was established; in it, Qin Shi Huang ruled as the first supreme emperor. In the modern city of **Xianyang**, a cotton manufacturing center on the north bank of the Weihe, the **City Museum** (*xianyang shi bowuguan*) provides a survey of the age of the Qin empire (221-206 BC).

The rulers of the Han founded their new capital south of the Weihe, not far from Xianyang and Xi'an, and named it **Chang'an** ("Everlasting Peace").

An irregular city wall runs for 16 miles (25 km), protecting the palaces of the Imperial City and the residential houses. The city, comprised of 160 districts, enjoyed its greatest prosperity under the emperor and conqueror Han Wu Di (140-86 BC). Brick walls and the outlines of the imperial palace survive from that time. In the fields of the loess hill country north of the city, circular mounds the size of small hills mark the tombs of the Han emperors, as well as of early Zhou kings and several Tang rulers.

On the site of Xi'an's Old City, the rulers of the Sui dynasty (581-618) built their new imperial capital, which also bore the name Chang'an. What is today the Old City was at that time merely a district of the imperial city. The whole walled city covered an area of 31 sq. miles (80 sq. km). It was designed to accommodate a population of a million on a spacious chessboard ground plan. It symbolized a rebirth of hope following the fall of the Han dynasty and offered space for the growing population. According to

179

the ancient Chinese science of town planning, the new Chang'an corresponded to the principles of cosmic order.

This Chang'an was taken over by the emperors of the Tang dynasty (618-907). The tenth Tang emperor, Xuan Zong, under whom China's Golden Age reached its zenith, transferred the government buildings to a residential quarter in the southeast of the city. There the **Xing-qinggong Park**, with its delightful little lakes and wooden buildings in the Chinese palace style, reminds one that this was once the most beautiful city of the Tang period, and later served as a model for the imperial city of Peking.

Sadly, the old Chang'an was completely destroyed when the Tang dynasty fell. Historical documents of the period speak of Chang'an being the "political and economic heart of China," the "center of art and scholarship," and the "beginning and end of the Silk Road," where

Above: The subterranean loess dwellings of Shaanxi – warm in winter, cool in summer.

"rich merchants and missionaries of every religion" gathered.

Today, only a few reconstructed buildings recall the glory of the Tang epoch. Among these is the emblem of Xi'an today, the **Great Wild-goose Pagoda** (*da yanta*). The huge brick pagoda dates from 647 but was rebuilt in 1580. It belonged to the great monastery of Daci'an in the south of the Tang city, where the famous monk Xuan Zang translated the Buddhist canon (the *tripitaka*) into Chinese. From the 13th storey one can enjoy the view for miles. In the north you can recognize the truncated tower of the **Little Wild-goose Pagoda** (*xiao yanta*). This was part of the Jianfu monastery, another center of Buddhist teaching.

South from here, in the **Daxingshan Temple** (*daxingshan si*) Indian monks taught in the 8th century. It was from there that the Japanese monk Ennin took the script and customs of China to Japan, where the spirit and culture of Tang-period China has been preserved down to the present day.

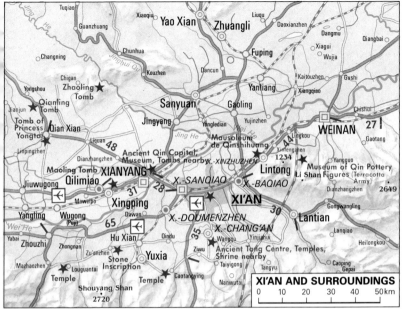

XI'AN AND SURROUNDINGS
0   10   20   30   40   50km

Particularly impressive is the **Quing-long Temple** (*qinglong si*) in the southeast of Xi'an, where Japanese monks studied Buddhism in the Tang age.

At the beginning of the Ming dynasty (14th century), the new city of Xi'an was built on the ruins of the first imperial city of Chang'an. Its impressive city wall and mighty gateway, restored in an exemplary manner, enclose the present Old City on all four sides. In the center, traffic from both main thoroughfares circles round the **Bell Tower** (*zhong lou*). Northwest of it rises the **Drum Tower** (*gu lou*), which houses an exquisite antique shop and points toward the Moslem quarter which clusters round the **Great Mosque** (*qingzhen si*), built in the 14th century in the Chinese style.

Within the Old City lie the ruins of old temples. Destroyed during the Cultural Revolution, they are now being restored again. Housed in a former Confucian temple is the famous **Forest of Stelae** (*bei lin*). It contains the oldest and, with 1095 items, the richest collection of stone stelae from the Han period up to the 17th century. In the 9th century, the classic books of Confucius were engraved on 114 stelae. One stele from 781 AD, in the Chinese and Ancient Syrian scripts, tells of the arrival of Nestorian Christianity in China. Stelae from the Song period display the oldest known maps of China.

In the southeast of Xi'an the interesting **Provincial Museum**, designed in the style of the Tang era, opened in 1991.

Excursions from Xi'an

EAST: The road eastward runs beside the Qinling range. After 19 miles (30 km), at the foot of **Mt Lishan**, you come to the **Park of Huaqing** (*huaqing gong-yuan*), whose hot springs were known to the kings of the Zhou dynasty, nearly 3000 years ago. Qin Shi Huangdi had a palace built here, and the emperors of the Tang dynasty laid out a magnificent summer residence. The buildings you see today in the park are, however, only an attempt at reconstruction.

Further eastward you reach the burial-mounds of the first emperor and see the great hall of **Lingtong**, which contains what is probably the most famous museum in China. It was here that Qin Shi Huangdi ordered the creation of a huge **army of terra-cotta warriors** (*bungma tong*), which was rediscovered in 1974. The 7000 or more life-size clay figures of soldiers and horses have been reassembled into a military formation 230 yds (210 m) long and 66 yds (60 m) long. The first division consists of 210 bowmen, followed by armored spear-carriers and battle-chariots. Most of the weapons which the warriors once carried are displayed in a separate exhibition beside the museum, where some of the finest chariots of Chinese antiquity can be seen. They carried two men armed with lances and had wheels 6 ft (1.80 m) in diameter, for travelling fast on smooth ground.

Above: The Bell Tower in the center of modern Xi'an. Right: A fresco in the Tang tombs at Qianling.

Going further east toward Shanxi, you pass **Mt Huashan**. This granite rock, 6550 ft (1997 m) high is the most westerly of the five sacred mountains of China. Its summit can be reached only after an arduous climb, but it is worth it for the unique view across the plain where the Weihe flows into the Yellow River.

WEST: About 50 miles (80 km) west of Xi'an you will see **Maoling**, one of the largest imperial tombs of the Han dynasty and resting-place of Han Wu Di. A few miles to the north, in the Qianxian district, lie the **tombs of the Tang emperors**. In a natural hill at **Zhaoling**, the second Tang emperor and his family were laid to rest, and in **Qianling** the third Tang emperor, Gao Zong, lies with his wife, the famous empress Wu Ze Tian. The tomb can be found in the **Liangshan** hill, which is approached along a magnificent processional avenue, lined on both sides with stone beasts, stelae and statues. In the Fufeng district, 56 miles (90 km) west of Xianyang, the

Famen Temple guards relics of Buddha. Beneath it a **Tang-period palace**, with valuable treasures, was excavated in 1987.

SOUTH: South of Xi'an, in the direction of the Qinling mountains, you will come across many other temples in a beautiful scenic setting. Most of these date from the Tang period and are gradually being restored to their former glory. Among them is the **Temple of the Grass Hall** (*caoting si*) in the southwest. From there you go west again to the **Terrace of the Belvedere** (*louguan tai*) with an inviting, panoramic view of the Wei valley. Heading south again, the **Temple of the Perfumed Loft** (*xiangji si*) and the **Monastery of Flourishing Education** (*xingjiao si*) lead on to **Mt Cuihua** and **the Five Southern Terraces** (*nanwu tai*).

NORTH: About 168 miles (270 km) north lies **Yan'an**. It was here, in 1936, that the legendary Long March of the Communists, which had led from Jianxi through Tibet and Gansu, ended. From 1936 until 1945 they established their headquarters in caves dug into the loess.

Halfway between Xi'an and Yan'an, near **Huangling**, is the tomb of the fabled Yellow Emperor (*huang di*).

HENAN

The province of **Henan**, with an area of 65,000 sq. miles (167,000 sq. km) and a population of 80 million, lies at the heart of classical China. The word *henan* describes its location and means "south of the (Yellow) river." The western part is dominated by the foothills of the **Qinling Mountains,** whose granite peaks are more than 6500 ft (2000 m) high. They tower above the hill country, covered with a thick layer of loess, which runs eastward down to the floodlands of the north Chinese plain.

Henan has the oldest known history in China. Between the Huanghe, the valley of the Luohe and the highlands of Shanxi, excavations have found evidence suggesting that in the neolithic period this was the most densely populated part of China. And in the north, near **Anyang**, archaeologists have discovered the early capital of the Bronze Age Shang dynasty (13th-11th centuries BC). In the 8th century BC, when the Zhou pushed their way eastward from the Weihe valley, they founded their new capital near the modern city of Luoyang, which, right up until the 10th century AD, was again and again to be chosen as China's capital. Henan and Shaanxi together formed the region in which the first "States of the Middle" grew up in the last 500 years before our era. The came to be known as *Zhongguo*, the "Kingdom of the Middle" – which is still the Chinese name for China.

Protected from the cold winter winds by the mountains to the west, Henan has a milder climate than the rest of northern China. This advantage is admittedly spoiled by an often very long dry season. Thus, from earliest times, it was necessary to base the economy on water; this both provided irrigation and at the same time protected the densely populated plains of the Yellow River from flooding. The most recent great achievement in hydraulic engineering is the **Canal of the People's Victory** (*renmin shengli qu*) between Zhengzhou and Xinxiang. Inaugurated in 1953, it takes off most of the floodwater from the Huanghe and carries it north to the Weihe. After the Mongol invasion in the 13th century, China's political center shifted permanently to the north, where Peking became the new "Middle of China." Not until the 20th century did Henan, which lay at the intersection of transport routes across China, join the national rail network and thus regain some of its economic importance.

Zhengzhou, capital of the province since 1949 and principal railway junction, provides a clear example of this economic development – in 40 years its population has increased tenfold and now exceeds one million. Socialist blueprints and meager resources have produced one of the ugliest cities in China – and is perhaps worth visiting just for that reason.

If so, you should also visit the **Henan Provincial Museum** (*henan sheng bowuguan*) in the Renminlu, which has finds from the Shang period as well as documents about the Railroad Workers Strike of February 7th, 1923.

Luoyang – city at the Dragon Gate

The one-time capital of China is today a quiet provincial town on the north bank of the Luohe, a tributary of the Huanghe. Its sheltered position between the **Mang Hills** (*mang shan*) in the north and the **Dragon Gate** (*long men*) in the south attracted the regents of the Eastern (or Late) Han dynasty (1st-2nd centuries AD), who succeeded the Zhou rulers and established their new capital east of the old Zhou city.

At a time when Buddhism was reaching China along the Silk Road, the first temples of this religion was built in Luoyang. A reminder of that period is the **Temple of the White Horse** (*baima si*), which the emperor Ming Di (58-76 AD)

ordered to be built outside the west gate of his capital after having had a prophetic dream. This monastic complex was enlarged in the Ming period and restored in 1957. At the entrance, two stone horses recall the legend, according to which two Indian monks, mounted on white horses, brought the holy Buddhist scriptures to Luoyang. The temple's **seven great prayer-halls** (*tianwang dian*) are dedicated to the *Celestial Guardians*, among others. A 13-storey brick pagoda is the central feature of the Baimasi, and in the fields round about you can still see the remains of Luoyang's city wall, built from fine clay bricks in the Han period.

During the Sui dynasty (6th century) Luoyang was the capital of a reunified China, and the construction of the Imperial Canal linked it with the agricultural regions of the Yangtse delta. The residential city extended in a large rectangle north and south of the Luohe river and represented the most important center of economic, commercial and cultural activity in China.

During the Tang period (7th-10th centuries) Luoyang declined to the status of a secondary capital of the empire and finally lost its political and economic importance. But the romantic Old City of the 10th century has remained. With the development of industries – tractors, engineering, glass – a New Town was built to the west of the Old City to accommodate a workforce which had been drawn in from all parts of the country. In the New Town's Zhongzhou Street, you will find the **City Museum** (*luoyang bowuguan*) which has interesting exhibits from the city's early history.

Excursions from Luoyang

NORTHEAST: Near **Anyang** in northern Henan, about 120 miles (200 km) from Luoyang, lie the excavations of **Yin**, a walled royal city of the Shang dynasty. From there, 32 miles (52 km) to the west, you come to the district capital of **Linxian** – and the **Red Banner Canal**: a canal network 930 miles (1500

185

km) long, which has been constructed across extremely inhospitable terrain.

NORTH: A few miles to the north, near **Mangshan**, you can find reconstructed tombs dating from the Han up to the Song dynasty.

WEST: The route west into Shaanxi province takes you along the Huanghe upstream to Tiemenzhen, where, in **Shifoxiang** ("Stone Buddha Village "), the **Hongqing Temple** (*hongqing si*, 6th c.) is decorated with bas-reliefs showing scenes from the life of Buddha. In **Yangshao**, north of Mianchi, lie China's most famous neolithic sites. There, in 1921, archaeologists discovered for the first time the fine black earthenware vessels of the *Yangshao* Culture. In the third millennium BC this culture extended over the whole of northern China and marks the beginning of Chinese civilization. Further west along the Huanghe, the **Gorges of the Three Gates** (*sanmen xia*) were one of the most feared places on the whole course of the Yellow River. For centuries they were an obstacle to shipping, and were one important reason why the capital, Luoyang, was built downstream from this dangerous stretch. In 1962 a dam was built here, the biggest in China at the time. North of Sanmenxia, on a hill near **Baishangling**, you can see excavations of the territorial state of Guo (8th – 5th c. BC), as well as the thirteen-storey **Echo Pagoda of the Baolun Temple.**

EAST: East of Luoyang, going towards Zhengzhou, **Mixian** has Buddhist caves from the Wei period as well as interesting **remains of iron-smelting works** of the Han epoch, and a Tang **pottery-kiln** on the banks of the Luohe. To the south, on the road to Songshan, near the village of Zhitianxian on the plain of the Luohe, you will find imperial tombs from the Song period. Following the example of

Right: Statues of Buddha in one of the caves of Longmen.

earlier tombs, stone statues guard the entrance to the tomb. Nearby, at the foot of Mt Dalishan, the **cave-temples of Gong Yi** contain nearly 8000 Buddha figures, as well as tombs dating from the Northern Song dynasty.

SOUTH: The short road from Luoyang south to Longmen passes near the Ming-period **Guandi Temple** (*guandi si*). Guandi, who was a military commander at the time of the Three Kingdoms (3rd c. AD) was subsequently worshipped as a god of war.

The caves of Longmen

Where the river **Yihe** flows into the valley of the Luohe, there are about 1350 caves and 750 niches in the steep west bank of the river. From the 5th century up to the Tang and Song periods, artists turned these into an enormous Buddhist shrine. In 494 AD, when the Northern Wei dynasty, under whom Buddhism was the state religion, transferred their capital from Datong in Shanxi, to Luoyang, the artistic work of Yungang (Datong) was continued near **Longmen**.

The finest remains of these artistically priceless sculptures and murals of the 5th and 6th centuries are found in the three-part **Cave which Greets the Sun** (*pingyang dong*) In the middle cave sit eleven great Buddhas with the subtle, ethereal smile of the Wei period, surrounded by Bodhisattvas and the most impressive reliefs in Longmen. The **Lotus-flower Cave** (*lianhua dong*) is dedicated to Guanyin and features a gigantic **lotus blossom**, symbol of purity and the sublime. One of the most valuable caves, **Guyangdong** (also known as the "Laotse Cave") contains the largest number of inscriptions from the Wei period. Scenes of adoration, executed with great style, have been preserved in the **Temple of the Caves** (*shiku si*). And in the **Cave of the Apothecary** (*yaofang dong*) there are 120 6th-century medical prescriptions.

The showpiece of Longmen is the incredibly large set of reliefs in the **Temple in Honor of the Lord** (*fengxian si*), from the Tang period. In the middle sits the humane and benignly smiling **Great Buddha**, 60 ft (18 m) high. At his side he is joined by his two favorite pupils, Ananda and Kacyapa, as well as celestial guardians and defenders of the faith.

Songshan – home of Kung Fu

The 4720 ft (1440 m) high **Songshan** is one of the five sacred mountains of China and represents the fifth point of the compass: the center. At the end of the 5th century AD, the **Shaolin Monastery** (*shaolin si*, or "Temple of the Lesser Forest") was built at the foot of the mountain, in what is now the Dengfeng district. Its fame was due to Damo (Bodhisharma), an Indian monk who came to Nanking in 520 AD, to visit the protector of Buddhism, the emperor Wu of the Liang empire. Unimpressed by the good deeds of the emperor, Damo retreated to the forests on Songshan, where he is said to have meditated for nine years. Thus the Shaolin Monastery became the fountainhead of *Chan* Buddhism (*Zen* in Japanese). Damo is known as the founder of the meditative school, and also introduced, as a physical discipline, the *shaolin quan* martial art, which was the earliest form of what is today called Kung Fu (*gongfu*).

In the **Stupa Forest** (*ta lin*), the most remarkable sight at the monastery, the old monks' cemetery, is marked by more than 220 stupas from the Tang to the Qing period. In the heyday of the monastery in the 8th and 9th centuries, many thousands of monks lived here. A steep path climbs up to the caves in which Damo is said to have meditated (*damo mianbi dong*). Not far away, the oldest wooden temple in Henan, the **Temple of the First Patriarch** (*chuzu an*), was built in 1125 in memory of Damo.

An unusual sight in the area is the **Observatory** (*guanxing tai*), 9 miles (15 km) south of Dengfeng, near Gaocheng-

zhen. The 33 ft (10 m) high brick tower faces north toward the summit of Songshan. Built at the beginning of Mongolian rule in the 13th century, it is the oldest surviving observatory in China.

Songshan is also known as *zhong yue,* "Mountain of the Middle." In 118 BC the great emperor and conqueror Han Wu Di paid a visit there and ordered the building of the Zhongyue Temple in honor of the sacred mountain. During the heyday of the Tang dynasty in the 8th century AD, it was replaced by what is now the **largest temple complex in Henan**, in which rulers of every dynasty made their offerings in gratitude to the mountain.

Kaifeng – the medieval capital

About 50 miles (80 km) east of Zhengzhou you reach the town of Kaifeng. It was the royal capital of various minor kingdoms, and during the North-

Above: Students of Kung Fu in the monastery of Shaolin.

ern Song period was the capital of the whole of China. At that time, a triple wall separated the imperial citadel in the center from an inner and an outer residential city. The prosperous city, surrounded by canals, was in those days the most important trading center in the Far East. However, in 1127 it was completely destroyed by the Jürchen who invaded from the north.

Only the slender **Iron Pagoda** (*tie ta*) has survived as a landmark. The 180 ft (55 m) 13-tiered wooden pagoda is covered with in iron-colored ceramic tiles and belonged to a monastery built in 1049. Once 230 ft (70 m) high, the tower of another pagoda from the Southern Song period, the stocky brick **Bota**, partially collapsed in the Ming period, losing two-thirds of its height. The 6th-century **Xiangguo Monastery temple** (*xiangguo si*) was swept away by floods in 1644, because the people of Kaifeng, in a desperate attempt to defend themselves against the Manchu, had breached their dykes. The present building dates from 1766.

SHANXI

Getting there

The provincial capital, **Taiyuan,** is on the railroad between Datong and Xi'an (Shaanxi) and can be reached from Beijing via Shijiazhuang. There are daily air services to/from Beijing.

Accommodation

TAIYUAN: *LUXURY:* **Shanxi Grand Hotel** (*shanxi dajiudian*), 5 Xinjian Nanlu, Tel. 404 3901. **Bingzhou Hotel** (*bingzhou fandian*), 32 Yingze Dajie, Tel. 404 2111. *MID-PRICE:* **Taiyuan Airport Hotel**, Wuxiu Airport, Tel. 707 5421. *BUDGET:* **Yingze Hotel** (*yingze binguan*), 51 Yingze Dajie, Tel. 443211. **DATONG:** *MID-PRICE:* **Yungang Hotel** (*yungang binguan*), 21 Yingbin Donglu, Tel. 521601. **Datong Hotel** (*datong binguan*), 8 Yingbin Xilu, Tel. 232476.

Tourist information

TAIYUAN: OTC, Pingyang Lu, Tel. 404 1155. **DATONG:** CITS, Yingbin Donglu (in the Yungang Hotel), Tel. 522265.

Excursions

From **Datong** you can make an excursion to the town of **Yingxian**, about 50 miles (80km) to the south. There, an unusual 230-ft (70m) **wooden pagoda** (*shijia ta*) has survived from the time of the Liao empire (11th century).

About half way from Datong to the nearby **Yungang Caves** you will find the **Guanyin Temple**. It was originally built in 1038 as a protective temple outside the shrine of the Yungang Caves, and contains interesting and well-crafted stone sculptures of the Liao era. There, on the Nine Dragon Wall of the Confucian temple you will also see a depiction of the **Dragon Wall** reminiscent of Datong, albeit on a smaller scale.

SHAANXI

Getting there

The provincial capital, **Xi'an**, in the valley of the Wei river, is situated on the main Peking–Lanzhou–Ürümqi railroad line. A motorway brings you to the international airport near Xianyang, fom which there are regular air connections to all the major cities in China.

Accommodation

XI'AN: *LUXURY:* **Golden Flower Hotel** (*jinhua fandian*), 8 Changle Xilu, Tel. 323 8921. **Holiday Inn** (*jiari jiudian*), 8 Huancheng Donglu Nanduan, Tel. 323 3888. **Hyatt Regency** (*kaiyue fandian*), 158 Dongdajie, Tel. 723 1234. **Sheraton,** 12 Fenhao Lu, Tel. 426 1888. **New World Dynasty** (*xi'an gudu dajiudian*), 48 Lianhu Lu, Tel. 721 6808. *MID-PRICE:* **People's Hotel** (*renmin daxia*), 319 Dongxinjie, Tel. 526 5111. **Bell Tower Hotel** (*zhonglou fandian*), Zhonglou, Tel. 727 9200. **Tangcheng Hotel** (*tangcheng binguan*), 7 Lingyuan Nanlu, Tel. 526 5711. *BUDGET:* **Jiefang Hotel** (*jiefang fandian*), Jiefang Lu (opposite the train station), Tel. 727 8946. **May First Hotel** (*wuyi fandian*), 351 Dongdajie, Tel. 721 0804. **YAN'AN:** *BUDGET:* **Yan'an Guesthouse** (*yan'an binguan*), 56 Dajie, Tel. 6333.

Tourist information

XI'AN: CITS, Chang'an Lu, Tel. 526 2066. Hotline: 725 1480.

HENAN

Getting there

The provincial capital, **Zhengzhou**, is an important railroad junction on the main Peking–Wuhan–Canton line and the Shandong–Shanxi line. There are regular air connections to the major cities of eastern China.

Accommodation

ZHENGZHOU: *LUXURY:* **Holiday Inn Crown**, Jinshui Dadao Dongduan, Tel. 595 0055. *MID-PRICE:* **Dukang** (*Dukang dafandian*), Tongbai Lu 178, Tel. 797 6888. **Henan International** (*henan guoji fandian*), 114 Jinshui Dadao Dongduan, Tel. 595 6600. **Zhongzhou Guesthouse** (*zhongzhou binguan*), 115 Jinshui Dadao Dongduan, Tel. 595 0055. *BUDGET:* **Zhongyuan Mansions** (*zhongyuan daxia*), near the train station. **KAIFENG:** *MID-PRICE:* **Dongjing Guesthouse** (*dongjing dajiudian*), 14 Yingbin Lu, Tel. 333115. *BUDGET:* **Kaifeng Guesthouse** (*kaifeng binguan*), 64 Ziyou Lu, Tel. 223901. **Songdu** (*songdu binguan*), Bianjing Lu, Tel. 223692. **LUOYANG:** *MID-PRICE:* **Friendship Hotel** (*youyi binguan*), 6 Xiyuan Lu, Tel. 491 2780. **Peony Hotel** (*mudan dajiudian*), 15 Zhongzhou Xilu, Tel. 491 3690. *BUDGET:* **Luoyang Hotel** (*luoyang lüshe*), opposite train and bus stations (very noisy at the front), Tel. 493 5181. **SANMENXIA:** *MID-PRICE:* **Friendship Hotel** (*youyi binguan*), Heping Lu, Tel. 22242.

Tourist information

ZHENGZHOU: CITS, 16 Jinshui Rd., Tel. 595 1134. **Henan CTS**, Jinshui Dadao Dongduan, Tel. 292 6637.

KAIFENG: CITS and CTS, in Dongjing Hotel. **LUOYANG:** CITS, Nanchang Lu, Tel. 491 1787.

THE SILK ROAD: WIND, SAND, DUST AND STARS

SINKIANG (XINJIANG)
GANSU
QINGHAI
NINGXIA

SINKIANG
China's Wild West

North America isn't the only area with a "Wild West;" China has one, too, but calls it the "Far West," (*yuan xi*). This term refers to today's Autonomous Uighurian Province of **Sinkiang** (*xinjiang uigur zizhiqu*). With 660,000 sq. miles (1.7 m sq. km) covering one-sixth of the area of China, Sinkiang is the largest of the country's provinces. With its scenery, ranging from desert to mountain glaciers, and its colorful mixture of Turkic Uighur people, Han Chinese and other races, Sinkiang is a profoundly fascinating place.

An east-west range of high mountains divides the province in two. These are the **Tianshan** ("Mountains of Heaven"), comparable to the Alps in extent, and reaching a height of 22,944 ft (6995 m) in the peak of **Hantengri Feng.** Above them, in the northern part of the province, lie the **Dzungarian Basin** and the **Gurbantünggggüt Desert**; in the south are the **Tarim Basin** and the **Taklamakan Desert.** The border with the republics of Kazakhstan and Kirghizistan runs diagonally across the Tianshan, and then fol-

Left: A Muslim Hui Chinese in the province of Gansu.

lows the line of the Pamir mountains down to the frontier with Afghanistan. The Pamirs are the mountainous heartland of Central Asia, a natural barrier separating two great cultures. The massif stretches in widening arcs as far south as the **Karakorum** range; on the southwestern side, the run-off from the range flows down through India and Pakistan to the Indian Ocean, but to the northwest it disappears into the soil of the landlocked Tarim Basin.

The **Kunlun** range, which runs into the Tibetan highlands, follows the southern rim of the basin; its rivers mainly run off to the north, into the Taklamakan Desert. A kind of counterpart to the Kunlun is provided by the mineral-rich **Altai** mountains in the northeast of Sinkiang, which form the border with Mongolia and Dzungaria.

For many centuries, the **Silk Road** represented the most important trade route between China and Central Asia, the Middle East and Europe. From its starting-point in the imperial capital of **Chang'an** (Xi'an), it ran first to Lanzhou, where the long caravans of Bactrian camels were assembled and loaded with costly silks and heavy brocade. The road followed the line of the Qilianshan range between the Tibetan border mountains and the Mongolian desert, a wall of

191

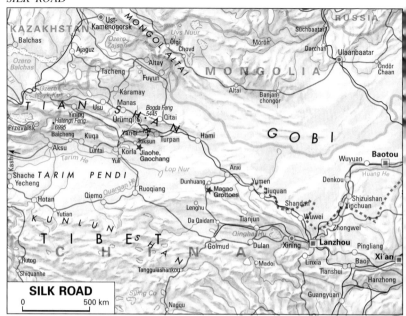

mountains and the Great Wall. Near **Anxi**, a road branched off to the northwest, through Hami to Ürümqi, Yining and on into Central Asia, the "Land of the Flying Horses." From Hami, there was a route to the **Oasis of Turpan** (Turfan), whence the principal route followed the southern edge of the Tianshan to **Kaxgar** (Kashgar). This northern branch of the Silk Road could also be reached from Dunhuang via the sunken city of **Loulan** (on the Lop Nor lake), joining the Silk Road at Korla. The Loulan oasis, which has today become a desert landscape used as a range for atomic weapons testing, marked the last outpost of the **Great Wall** in the Han period. It formed the horizon of the known Chinese world. From Dunhuang a branch of the Silk Road crossed the oft-described **Yangguan** ("Southern Pass") and followed the southern rim of the Tarim Basin, through the jade city of Khotan (Hotan) and

Right: A mosque in Ürümqi (Sinkiang / Xinjiang).

Shache (Yarkant) to Kaxgar. From Shache and Kaxgar, mountain passes traversed the Pamirs toward Central Asia and what is now Pakistan. These passes allowed the ingress into China, not only for foreign goods such as glass, grapes, peaches and gold coins, but also foreign ideas which enriched the country's culture.

The opening up of the Far West

The chronicles of the Western Han dynasty (206-225 BC) tell of 40 oases – little kingdoms which exchanged their horticultural produce for the meat, fleeces, leather and milk of the animals herded by the nomadic Xiongnu (Huns). However, these nomads were more of a curse than a blessing for the farmers of the oases and were even a threat to the whole Chinese empire. It was for this reason that the Han emperor Wu Di (140-86 BC) had the Great Wall, which had been begun by his predecessors, extended as far as Dunhuang and the lake of Lop Nor.

This "Wall 10,000 *li* long," (*wanli changcheng*) stretched for several thousand miles along the natural frontier between the steppe and the fertile lands – from the Bay of Bohai on the Yellow Sea to the Taklamakan Desert. The Conqueror-Emperor Han Wu Di extended the territory of China in every direction and, in several military expeditions against the Huns, made Chinese influence felt as far as the mountain barrier of the Pamirs. The oases at the foot of the mountains were built up into military outposts, which in turn became important trading centers on the route from China to India and Persia. It was along this route, in the 1st century AD, that Buddhism reached China, when the country was experiencing its first period of greatness under the Northern and Southern dynasties.

With the fall of the Tang dynasty in the 10th century, China once again lost its western territories. The vacuum was filled by Tibetans from the highlands, but chiefly by Uighurs, descendants of the eastern Turks.

At the beginning of the 20th century Sinkiang, under Uighur Muslim domination, was relatively independent and felt able to turn to Russia. Not until 1949 did China reassert its authority, which was given legal form in 1955 with the founding of the Autonomous Uighurian Province.

Ürümqi, land of fertile pastures

The capital of the Uighur state is Ürümqi (Chinese: Wulumuqi). Here, strangers are greeted not with the Chinese "ni hao" but with the Turkish words "yakshimshes" or "yakshi doslum" ("Good Friend"). In this city of over a million inhabitants you can still find pockets of down-home friendliness, where a baker offers delicious-smelling flat loaves or an innkeeper suggests a reviving glass of his tea.

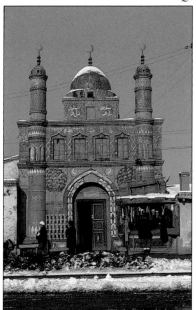

During the Tang dynasty Mongolian nomads came this way in search of new pastures. The region west of the **Bogdashan massif** (17,900 ft/5445 m) they named *Ürümqi* ("Fertile Pastures"). The town of **Ürümqi** only grew up in the 18th century, when a castle was built and people began to settle around it. Today it is a place where many races gather: Uighurs, Han Chinese, Hui (Muslim Chinese), Daur, Kazakhs, Kirghizi, Mongols, Russians, Tadzhiks, Uzbeks, Tatars and Xibo. As well as Mandarin Chinese, many people speak the Uighur (East Turkish) language, which is written both in Roman and, increasingly, in Arabic characters.

The pervasive presence of the Chinese, which local residents today regard more in the light of an occupation, is noticeable not only in the army and civil service, but also in the architecture and cultural colonization. Thus, many mosques are designed in the style of Chinese temples and pagodas, which clashes with the forms of Persian and Central Asian archi-

tecture. The construction of standardized Socialist apartment blocks and wide streets and avenues is gradually forcing out the mud-built houses which until recently gave the place its charm. The city's expansion has been directed to the north as a result of deliberate resettlement by Han Chinese. With their arrival, the city has developed into an industrial center, making use of its convenient proximity to the rich coal reserves along the north slopes of the Tianshan.

In the north of the Old City rises the **Kyzil dag** (*hong shan* or "Red Hill") with the **Treasure Pagoda** (*bao ta*) as its landmark. From there you get a view over the whole city, covering 27 sq. miles (70 sq. km), as far as the peak of Bogda Feng. Opposite, on the far bank of the Ürümqi river, lies the **People's Park**. Going north from there you come to the former Manchu city and the **Xinjiang**

Above: Caravan resting near Jiayuguan (Gansu). Right: Ruined city near the oasis of Turpan / Turfan (Sinkiang / Xinjiang).

194

Provincial Museum (*xinjiang bowuguan*). This contains an interesting exhibition about the Silk Road, which includes 124 replicas of Buddhist murals from the oases of **Kizil**, **Kumtura**, **Kizilhar**, **Simsim** and **Bexiklic**. Southeast of the People's Park, you'll find the Old City and the former imperial city, the east side of which is dominated by the Stalinist and pseudo-Islamic edifice of the **People's Theater**. Continuing south you reach the **zoo** and the former **headquarters** of the VIIIth Mobile Army, which in the 1930s and 1940s was the center of the Communist forces.

A day-trip from Ürümqi going east takes you along the north slopes of the eastern Tianshan to the massif of Bogda Feng. Half way on the 60 mile (100 km) journey to Bogda lie the summer pastures of **Baiyanggou**, where you will see the yurts of Kazakh herdsmen and their sheep, horses, camels and cattle. At the foot of the 17,860 ft (5445 m) Bogda Feng shimmers the crystal-clear, blue **Lake of Heaven** (*tian chi*). Nearly 350 ft

(105 m) deep, it nestles in an alpine land-scape with a green cloak of pines and firs, at an altitude of 6400 ft (1950 m). Legend has it that the "Noble Jade Lake" served as a mirror for Xi Wang Mu, who is con-sidered by the nomads of Tianshan to be their mother-goddess.

Turpan – the lowest point in China

From Ürümqi a mountain pass runs south to the oasis of **Turpan** (Turfan, 'Land of Fire"). From there you reach the lowest place in China, **Ayding Kol**, in the middle of the Turfan Basin, 500 ft (154 m) below sea level. Lack of rainfall (0.4 ins/16 mm per year) or water flowing off the dry southern slopes of the Tianshan, combined with high evaporation (3000 mm per year), have dried the lake down to a salt bog.

Turpan owes its flourishing oasis to a hydraulic system which came originally from Persia. The Chinese, being gifted engineers, introduced it more than 2000 years ago as a way of developing the per-imeter oases. A network of about 1300 crisscross ditches with a total length of some 1860 miles (3000 km) direct the clear run-off from the Tianshan into the center of the oasis. The well-shafts are as much as 100 ft (30 m) deep, and the water is brought by canals for about 25 miles (40 km) gently downhill from the foot of the mountain. The underground water-course, which prevents evaporation, can be recognized by the well-heads, which look like rows of molehills. In this way – in the midst of an inhospitable desert – a continuous supply of water keeps poplars and mulberry-trees green, and nourishes sweet seedless grapes, apricots, juicy melons and valuable cotton plants.

The encroaching desert has turned the outskirts of Turpan into ruins. About 6 miles (10 km) west of the present-day oasis, you come to the geometric street-pattern of the ancient city of **Yarchoto** ("cliff town"; or, in Chinese, Jiaohe, "town on the river crossing") on an island at the confluence of two rivers. It was built in the 2nd century BC by the troops

195

3rd to the 8th century, were found to contain valuable mummies, books and documents, as well as silk, linen, colored ceramics, murals and silk paintings.

Further to the north, a side road leads off from the main road into the Huoyanshan hills, to the Buddhist caves of **Beziklic**, the **Caves of a Thousand Buddhas** (*qianfo dong*). The priceless murals here have, however, been largely destroyed.

Between the 2nd and 14th centuries the oases along the Silk Road were lively centers of Buddhist faith, where artists created superb paintings and sculptures. After the 8th century, the influence of Islam grew stronger and began to loosen the bond of Buddhism which had thereto united many of the peoples of Central Asia and Buddhism, replacing it with a new one. It was not until the 19th and 20th centuries, however, that Buddhist monuments were systematically plundered – by Western scientific expeditions competing to enrich the collections of museums back home in London, Paris, Berlin and St Petersburg. On a cave wall in Beziklic, a crudely pencilled notice reads, "Bartus from Berlin cleared out this building on 16.10.1906." When Berlin was bombed in World War II, the most valuable finds from the Silk Road were destroyed.

Turpan itself presents the characteristic picture of an oriental town in Central Asia. Its central focus is the **Imim Mosque** with its enchanting **Tower of Uncle Su** (*sugong ta*). The simple 144 ft (44 m) minaret, whose monochrome brickwork is arranged in artistic patterns, was built in 1779 by Su (Suleiman) in honor of his father, Imam Goja, and of the Qing Dynasty.

of the conqueror-emperor Han Wu Di as a strategic base on the Silk Road. After its destruction by the Mongols in the 14th century it lay abandoned, and now the desert winds have blown a mantle of dust and sand over its palaces, temples, barracks and dwelling quarters.

About 28 miles (45 km) east of Turpan, the glowing colors of the **Fire Mountain** (*huoyan shan*) form a backdrop to the impressive ruins of **Ydyqutsahri** (in Chinese: Gaochang), whose mud-brick city walls, 3 miles (5 km) long and 36 ft (11 m) high, are reminiscent of a vast Hollywood film set. During the Tang period the capital of the Far West was transferred from Yarchoto to Ydyqutsahri, which was divided, like the imperial capital at Chang'an, into an Inner and Outer City and palace complex.

Not far away, the 500 or more tombs of **Astana** (*asitana gumqu*), dating from the

Going west along the old Silk Road, through the town of Toksun, you come to **Lake Bagrax** (formerly Xihai, "Western Sea"), the largest freshwater lake in Sinkiang, with an area of 386 sq. miles (1000 sq. km). The lake is set in a scenic para-

Above: Minaret of the Imim Sugonta mosque in the oasis of Turpan (Sinkiang / Xinjiang). Right: The yard of a house in Turpan.

dise; its clear waters reflect the snow-capped peaks of the Tianshan. Near **Yan-qui**, in the Autonomous Hui District, you can explore the Buddhist caves of **Chor-chuq**.

Beyond the historically important **Iron Gate Pass** (*yiemen guan*) at the western end of the lake, lies the **Korla oasis**, developed with Chinese assistance in the 1950s. There is a certain lack of planning in the irrigation and cultivation projects which were carried out by soldiers and prisoners in this newly opened up area. A rather silted-up canal system brings water from the **Konqi** river and the 1350 mile (2180 km) long desert river **Tarim** near Yüli. While the arable land between lake Bagrax and the river Tarim was briefly enlarged, the area round the **Lop Nur** was transformed into a dismal desert. Lop Nur (Mongolian: "The lake into which many waters flow") was a meeting-point for caravans on the Silk Road during the Han dynasty. When Sven Hedin went in search of the treasures of the lost city of Loulan, he described the "wandering lake," whose surface area had dwindled in the previous 50 years to a mere 3600 sq yds (3000 sq.m). Since 1975 the lake has become no more than a salt marsh, which is gradually drying out.

The former Silk Road continues westwards through **Bügür** (Luntai) to the **Kuqa oasis**. This was the site of the ancient Chinese military oasis of Kuizi, whose indigenous population were Tocharians, an Indo-European race. During the Tang dynasty, when musicians from Kuqa played at the imperial court at Chang'an, Kuqa was a Chinese protectorate, which was threatened by Tibet in the south and Turkic people in the north.

Barely 6 miles (10 km) west of Kuqa, a 50 ft (15 m) high watch-tower of the Han period is said to be the oldest and best-preserved of its kind on the northern Silk Road. Fourteen miles (23 km) east of Kuqa you will find the Buddhist temple city of **Subashi** (5th century), which is divided by the Kuqa river.

On the way to **Bay** (Baicheng) you come to the **Caves of a Thousand**

Buddhas (*qianfo dong*) at **Kizil**. This was once the most important Buddhist center in the Far West and consists of 236 caves, which were occupied from the end of the Han dynasty to the Tang dynasty. These caves are the largest on the southern slopes of the Tianshan and were bored into the sheer cliffs on the north bank of the **Muzat river**. This is fed by the glaciers of **Hantengri** (22,944 ft/6995 m). Below **Toksu** (Xinhe), its waters are diverted to newly laid out state farms, and no longer flow into the river Tarim. Only 74 of the caves are still decorated with the remains of superb murals. Most of the movable works of art were plundered by western expeditions in the first half of the 20th century.

Further upstream you come to the **Springs of a Thousand Tears** (*qianlei quan*), one of the most beautiful waterfalls in China. As these falls tumble down

Above: Clocktower and Id Kah Mosque in Kaxgar (Sinkiang / Xinjiang). Right: Muslim Uighurs in Kaxgar.

from the high cliffs, they illustrate in a very tangible way the huge contrast between the abundance of water from the Tianshan and the desert of Taklamakan. A 435 mile (700 km) stretch of road through the **Bay oasis** (Baicheng) and **Aksu** brings you from Kuqa to Kaxgar, where the two main branches of the Silk Road meet.

Kaxgar (Kashgar): Crossroads of Asia

The road from Pakistan to Sinkiang crosses the upper Indus valley and the perilous, debris-strewn gorges of the Gilgit and Hunza rivers. In the 1960s the Chinese built a new mountain road which crosses the 16,400 ft (5000 m) **Khunjerab Pass** between the Pamir and Karakorum. The road runs through Taxkorgan and passes the gigantic peaks of **Muztagata** (24,750 ft/7546 m) and **Kongur** (25,320 ft/7719 m); it then zigzags steeply downward into the valley of the Kaxgar river.

Long ago, the town of **Shule**, the "golden pearl of the Silk Road," stood here at a height of 4228 ft (1289 m). In the 2nd century BC, after a visit by the imperial emissary Zhang Qian, it fell under Chinese control, and later became an important administrative center for the Far West. This period is commemorated only by a few remaining ruins of mud-brick, next to the bed of the Kaxgar river, which is usually dry.

During the Song period (11th-12th centuries) **Kaxgar** was abandoned, but under the Manchu dynasty, in the 18th century, it became the center of government in southern Sinkiang and the rumor-mill for secret diplomacy between the rival world powers of Russia and Britain. In recent decades, this city has been rather cut off from the world, but there are signs that it may develop once again into a place of activity and meeting between Pakistan, Afghanistan, Tadjikistan and Kirghizstan.

Because Beijing Standard Time applies all over China, the day begins at night in Kaxgar. It is still dark when veiled women, bearded men, eager traders and street entertainers, and crowds of children make their way to the fountain, the market, the factories and schools, invariably "shadowed" by the ever-present Chinese militia.

In the central market, different produces from the oasis are enticingly laid out every morning.

North of the market and the workshops of the traditional craftsmen, which make Kaxgar so typical of Central Asia, the **Id Kah Mosque** is another popular meeting-place. The largest mosque in China, with its two soaring minarets, this mosque was built in the 15th century, but was redesigned more simply in the 19th. It holds more than 7000 worshippers.

The **Mausoleum of Abakh Hoja**, built in the Uighur style, is today of purely architectural interest. This leader of the struggle against the Qing dynasty is worshipped as a holy man and lies here with 72 other notables. However, the tomb of Yakub Beg, who led a revolt against

China in 1862 with British support, is said to be empty.

On the left bank of the river Tuman in Kaxgar there's a weekly Sunday Market. On other days, Uighur and Chinese meet in the center of the Old City at the oriental bazaar, with its traditional guilds of craftsmen and workshops making musical instruments and knives.

Nineteen miles (30 km) east of Kaxgar you come to the ruined mud-brick city of **Hanoi**, which was probably abandoned in the 11th century. To the northwest, high up in the cliffs beside the Qiamakh river, are the **Caves of the Three Immortals** (*sanxian dong*) with the remains of some frescoes.

A two-day tour by jeep along the Karakorum road takes you far up into the mountains. Here, beside the glacier lakes at the foot of the great **Kongur** and **Muz-**

Above: Cotton harvest in Dunhuang (Gansu province). Right: A pagoda-style structure protects the entrance of the Buddhist caves of Mogao in Dunhuang.

tagata peaks, you can escape the dust and heat of the desert among the Tadzhiks, who graze their herds of camel and yak in the summer pastures.

GANSU

Between Sinkiang and northern China, Mongolia and Qinghai, a corridor is formed by the province of Gansu (205,000 sq. miles/530,000 sq. km). It is inhabited by Han Chinese and minorities of Muslim Chinese (Hui), Tibetans, Mongols and Kazakhs. The old Silk Road is its transport artery, and leads to the main town of **Dunhuang** in the west, an oasis with cotton plantations.

Dunhuang gained its strategic importance from two military outposts at the end of the Great Wall. About 28 miles (45 km) to the south, near the town of **Nanhu** ("South Lake"), the **Yangguan** ("Southern Pass") was known as the last stop before the desert and the gateway to the far West. This fateful western frontier of Chinese civilization was celebrated, especially in the Tang period, in many songs and poems, such as these verses by Wang Wei: "Once more fill your glass and drink it dry / for west of the Southern Pass / no good things lie." About 50 miles (80 km) northwest of Dunhuang a great mud-brick building rises out of the plain. This is the second fortress guarding the **Yumenguan** ("Jade Gate Pass"), of which the poet Wang Zhimin wrote: "With the sound of thy flute/ do not bemoan the late coming of the pasture / for the wind of spring / never blows over Yumenguan."

Thus Dunhuang represented the final outpost of their homeland for Chinese conscripts, soldiers and exiles. But for travelers from the west, this caravanserai and military depot was the first friendly-looking place on Chinese territory.

With the advent of Buddhism, a cultural and religious community grew up in Dunhuang. In 366 AD, work began on

the **Mogao Caves** (*mogao ku*) on the steep west bank of the river Dang, and continued until the Mongol period in the 13th century. In 492 caves, with an area of 110 acres (45 ha), artists from all over Central Asia painted frescoes and modelled 2000 statues from clay. They built five great monasteries with pagoda-like structures in front of the cliff walls to protect the caves. During the Ming period the caves fell into oblivion, and were eventually buried under the sand. They were not rediscovered until 1900 when a refugee came in search of a hiding-place. In **cave 257** (4th-5th c.) one of the finest paintings in Mogao depicts the Buddha sitting in a grotto, while a monk has his head shaved. The finest statue dates from the Northern Wei period and stands in front of a pillar in **cave 248**: a Bodhisattva with characteristically beatific expression and marvelously modelled clothing. **No. 428** (6th c.) tells a story from the life of the Buddha. The artist chooses to link scenes from everyday life – images of hunting, farming, house-building, fishing, harvesting and milling corn – with Buddhist mysticism. In the Sui and Tang periods, when trading contacts with foreign countries were being developed, the predominant subjects were boats, carts, ploughs, spinning-wheels and looms. In **cave 323**, for example, you can see a typical Chinese boat landing in Canton with a Buddha made of sandalwood from India, a gift to a Chinese ruler of the 6th-century Liang empire. In **no. 258** a large horizontal mural shows soldiers gouging out the eyes of 500 robbers. A compassionate Buddha soothes the robbers' pain and persuades them to turn to the path of righteousness. **No. 194** contains a particularly well executed Bodhisattva from the Tang period. The elegant painted clay statue has an expression of worldly equanimity, reminiscent of the Baroque style in Europe. The people of the Tang epoch expressed their joy chiefly in music. But the same liveliness can be found in colorful abstract patterns, such as those of the ceiling painting in **cave 329**.

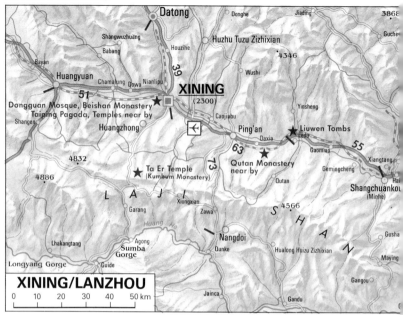

From Dunhuang, the road goes east to **Jiayuguan**. This massive fortress was built in the 14th century in a characteristically Chinese style. As the western outpost of the Ming empire, it also marked the end of the **Great Wall** during the Ming period.

Before the backdrop of the highest peak of the **Qilianshan** mountains (18,194 ft/5547 m), the town of **Jiuquan** lies 19 miles (30 km) to the east. It was founded in the 2nd century BC as a military camp, where the north-south road from Mongolia to Tibet crosses the Silk Road.

Nearby, amid the enchanting scenery of **Mt Wenshu** (*wenshu shan*) you will find the remains of Taoist and Buddhist temples. For a period after the 5th century, they were a hub of religious activity.

The Silk Road follows the edge of the Qilianshan range as far as **Wuwei**. But at the foot of **Mt Maomaoshan** (13,350 ft/4070 m) the road enters a pass through the Alp-like mountains and follows the valley of the **Zhuanglanghe river**, which flows into the **Yellow River** (*huanghe*) near **Hekou** ("River-mouth"). Upriver from Hekou is Yongjin, situated among steep hills of loess, beside a reservoir formed by a dam across the Huanghe. Nearby you will find the **Bingling cliff temple** (*bingling si*). Its caves were dug in the 6th century AD (North Wei dynasty) and its stone and clay sculptures mark the cultural transition between Dunhuang and Central China.

The capital of Gansu province, **Lanzhou,** has a population of over a million. About 25 miles (40 km) below Hekou, it stretches along both banks of the Huanghe at an altitude of 5,100 ft (1555 m). Historically an important trading city, it is now the location of sizeable plants in the petrochemical, engineering and textile industries, and its attraction lies in its scenic surroundings.

You get the best view of Lanzhou from the 5576 ft (1700 m) **Baitashan** hill, the city's landmark, which is crowned by the seven-tiered **White Pagoda** (*bai ta*), built in the 13th century. On the opposite

ated at the same time and in the same style as the caves of Longmen and Yungang. Testimony to the Buddhist center that grew up here during the Northern Wei dynasty (5th century) are some 200 or more caves with thousands of murals and stone or clay statues. Particularly fine is a gleaming white statue of the **Maitreya Buddha** (*Buddha of the Future*), 50 ft (15 m) high and dating from the Sui period. In the 6th century, a time of economic and social upheaval, he gave comfort and confidence to travelers on their long journey westward.

QINGHAI

Some 140 miles (230 km) west of Lanzhou lies **Xining**, the provincial capital of Qinghai. It is the only town of any size in the province and has been a Chinese military base and trading-post since the 16th century. From there you travel a further 12 miles (19 km) southward to the **Kumbum monastery** (also called Gunbum; in Chinese *ta'er si*), where the great reformer of Lamaism, Tsongkhapa, was born in 1577. The Tibetan-style monastery buildings cover an area of 35 acres (14.2 ha). At one time 4000 monks are thought to have lived here and there were 52 Buddhist prayer-halls.

At a height of 10,500 ft (3200 m), 120 miles (200 km) west of Xining, **Lake Koko Nor** (Lake Qinghai) lies among some of the most beautiful and characteristic scenery of the Tibetan highlands. This salt-water lake covers an area of 1,545 sq. miles (4000 sq. km) and is a unique habitat for birds. On its shores Tibetan herdsmen pasture their sheep, goats and yaks in a natural paradise.

bank of the Huanghe, the **Park of Five Springs** (*wuquan gongyuan*) contains a well-preserved temple (*chongqing si*), from the Ming period. In the **Gansu Provincial Museum** (*gansu sheng bowuguan*) there is an interesting display of articles found in tombs of the Han period, including a copy of the famous *Flying Horse*. It reminds one of the fact that China's military might was founded on the swift horses of the Han cavalry, which were introduced from the Fergana Basin.

South of the **Liujiaxia reservoir** in southwest Lanzhou, a mountain road takes you through the fascinating little town of **Linxia** to Labrang (Xiahe) on the border of Qinghai province. The **temple monastery of Labrang** was built in the 18th century, at a height of 9,500 ft (2900 m), and was one of the six most important Tibetan monasteries in China.

From the **Beidao/Tianshui** train station on the main line between Lanzhou and Xi'an (Shaanxi) a road runs southeast for 28 miles (45 km) to the Buddhist **caves on Mt Maijishan**. They were cre-

NINGXIA
North of the Silk Road

The Autonomous Hui Region of **Ningxia** lies north of the Silk Road, half encir-

cled by Gansu, and hitherto seldom visited by foreign travelers. It is an area full of contradictions: along the main artery of the Yellow River and its tributaries, the land is fertile, but the highlands are arid, hot in summer and bitterly cold in winter. Not surprisingly, most of the 4 million inhabitants live near the rivers. Although the official name of the province might lead one to think otherwise, the Hui (Chinese Muslims) only account for about one-third of the population. The colonization of peripheral regions by the Han Chinese shows itself clearly even here.

The capital, **Yinchuan**, in the northern tip of the province, also has two contrasting faces, one industrial, one traditional.

From the **Drum Tower** (*gu lou*), in the heart of the Old City, you can easily walk around the other sights. These include the **Northern Pagoda** (*bei ta*), the **Western Pagoda** (*xi ta*) and the 400-year-old

Above: Sutra drums in the Kumbum monastery (Qinghai province).

Yuhuang Pagoda (*yuhuang ge*). The **Southern Gate** (*nan men*) is a smaller copy of the Tiananmen Gate in Beijing, and nearby is the large **mosque** (*qingzhen si*).

About 19 miles (30 km) west of Yinchuan you will find the 72 **tombs** of the kings of the Western Xia kingdom (*xixia wangling*). This kingdom lasted for 190 years, until it was destroyed by Jinghis Khan in 1227.

Some 130 miles (208 km) southwest of Yinchuan, on the railroad that runs along the Huanghe, you come to the sleepy market town of **Zhongwei**. Its pretty, gabled **Gao Temple** (*gao miao*) is a place of meditation for Buddhists, Taoists and Confucians.

In the southern wedge of the province, 25 miles (40 km) northwest of Guyan are the Buddhist **caves of the Xumi Mountains** (*xumishan shiku*). Spread across five peaks are 132 caves, whose 300 statues tell of a past going back 1400 years. **Cave no. 5** contains a gigantic figure of Buddha, 62 ft (19 m) high.

SINKIANG / XINJIANG
Getting there

The capital, **Ürümqi**, lies on the Central Asian railroad (45 hours journey from Beijing). The airport has regular flight connections to Beijing.

Accommodation

ÜRÜMQI: *LUXURY:* **Holiday Inn**, 53 Xinhua Beilu, Tel. 281 8788. *MID-PRICE:* **Overseas Chinese Hotel** (*huaqiao binguan*), 51 Xinhua Nanlu, Tel. 286 7797. **Xinjiang Kunlun** (*xinjiang kunlun binguan*), Youhao Beilu, Tel. 484 0411. **Friendship Hotel** (*youyi binguan*), Yan'an Lu, Tel. 286 7495. *BUDGET:* **Hongshan** (*hongshan fandian*), Xinhua Nanlu 108, Tel. 282 4232. **Kunlun Guesthouse** (*kunlun binguan*), 51 Youhao Nanlu, Tel. 484 0411.

TURPAN: *MID-PRICE:* **Oasis Hotel** (*lüzhou binguan*), Qingnian Lu, Tel. 22365. **Turpan Guesthouse** (*tulufan binguan*), Qingnian Lu, Tel. 22301.

KAXGAR: *MID-PRICE:* **Kashgar Hotel** (*kashi g'er binguan*), Tawuguzi Lu, Tel. 222367.

Tourist information

ÜRÜMQI: **CITS**, in the Overseas Chinese Hotel, Tel. 282 1427. **Xinjiang Overseas Tourist Corp.**, Xinhua Nanlu 51, Tel. 282 5913. **CTS**, in the Overseas Chinese Hotel, Tel. 282 8885.

TURPAN: **CITS**, in the Oasis Hotel, Tel. 286 8885.

KAXGAR: **CITS**, 93 Seman Lu, Tel. 223156.

Excursions / sightseeing

TURPAN: In the old part of town, at the **bazaar** south of the bus-station, (Chinese: *nongmao shichang*, "peasant market") you can observe the unchanged lifestyle of the Uighurs.

From the **Fire Mountains** (*huoyan shan*) to the east you go southward through the desert to the almost completely dried out salt-lake of **Ayding Kol** (*aiding hu*). A contrasting landscape is provided by the Valley of Grapes (*putao gou*) north of Turpan, where the delicious, seedless Turfan grapes grow and where one can go for hikes in the desert.

On the way to the **ruins of Jiaohe** in the west, we suggest you stop to look at the entrances to the canals in some of the few surviving tunnel-streams of ancient times, which bring the fresh mountain water to the irrigation-channels of the Turpan oasis.

GANSU
Getting there

The capital, **Lanzhou**, lies on the main Beijing–Xi'an–Ürümqi rail route, and is the terminus of the Beijing–Datong–Hohhot–Yinchuan line. There are regular flights to / from Xi'an and Peking.

Accommodation

LANZHOU: *LUXURY:* **Ningwozhuang Guesthouse** (*ningwozhuang fandian*), 238 Tianshui Lu, Tel. 841 6221. *MID-PRICE:* **Friendship Hotel** (*youyi fandian*), 14 Xijin Xilu, Tel. 843 3051. **Jincheng Hotel** (*jincheng binguan*), 363 Tianshui Lu, Tel. 841 5254. **Lanzhou Hotel** (*lanzhou fandian*), 204 Donggang Xilu, Tel. 841 0861. *BUDGET:* **Victory Hotel** (*shengli binguan*), 127 Zhongshan Lu, Tel. 841 0221.

DUNHUANG: *MID-PRICE:* **Dunhuang Hotel** (*dunhuang binguan*, also has a dormitory), 1 Dong Dajie, Tel. 222415. **Liyuan**, Dongmen, Tel. 222047. *BUDGET:* **Feitian Guesthouse** (*feitian binguan*), Dingzi Lu, Tel. 222337. **Silk Road Hotel** (*silu binguan*), 2 Dong Dajie, Tel. 222371.

JIAYUGUAN: *MID-PRICE:* **Great Wall**, 6 Jianshe Xilu, Tel. 25233. *BUDGET:* **Jiayuguan Hotel** (*jiayuguan binguan*), 1 Xinhua Beilu, Tel. 26981.

JIUQUAN: **Jiuquan Hotel** (*jiuquan binguan*), 2 Cangmenjie, Tel. 22544.

Tourist information

LANZHOU: **CITS**, Tianshui Lu (in the Jincheng Hotel), Tel. 882 1966.

DUNHUANG: **CITS**, Dong Dajie, Tel. 222492.

JIAYUGUAN: **CITS**, in the Great Wall Hotel, Tel. 25233.

QINGHAI
Getting there

By rail from Lanzhou (Gansu province) the journey to **Xining**, the capital of Qinghai province, is about 143 miles (230 km).

Accommodation

XINING: *MID-PRICE:* **Qinghai Guesthouse** (*qinghai binguan*), 20 Huanghe Lu, Tel. 444365. *BUDGET:* **Xining Guesthouse** (*xining daxia*), 93 Jianguo Lu, Tel. 777991. **Xining Hotel** (*xining binguan*), 215 Qiyi Lu, Tel. 445901.

Tourist information

XINING: **CITS**, in the Xining Hotel, Tel. 445901.

NINGXIA
Getting there

By rail, the Peking–Hohhot–Baotou–Lanzhou line runs (down the Huanghe valley) through **Ningxia** province and its capital, **Yinchuan**.

Accommodation

YINCHUAN: *MID-PRICE:* **Ningxia Hotel** (*ningxia binguan*, best hotel), 3 Gongyuanjie, Tel. 222131. **Yinchuan Hotel** (*lüzhou fandian*), Jiefang Xijie, Tel. 222615.

Tourist information

YINCHUAN: **CITS**, 150 Jiefang Xijie, Tel. 445555.

STEPPE, SHEEP
AND
MARE'S MILK

INNER MONGOLIA

Beyond the Great Wall

As a counterpart to "Outer Mongolia," which is China's name for the Mongolian People's Republic, China founded the autonomous province of Inner Mongolia in 1947. It was created out of the district (*aimak* or *meng*) of **Hulunbuir**, the most northerly and the largest of the districts, which extends west of the **Great Hinggan Mountains** (*dahinggan shan*) over an area of 97,000 sq. miles (250,000 sq. km), and which, until the end of the Second World War, lay within the Japanese puppet state of Manchukuo. After the war Inner Mongolia was steadily expanded until, by 1969, it embraced eight districts stretching across the dry steppe plateau between Outer Mongolia and the Great Wall and covering an area of over 460,000 sq. miles (1.2 million sq. km), from Amur in the east to Sinkiang in the west.

During the Cultural Revolution, China's tense relations with the Soviet Union and her vassal-state, (Outer) Mongolia, the territory of Inner Mongolia was reduced by about one-third; at the same time most of Mongolian nomads were resettled away from the border zones.

Left: A much-decorated Mongol gives a celebratory address at the festival of Nadom.

Today, Inner Mongolia once extends over the area it occupied before 1969. Mongols represent the majority of its population of 13 million, but there is a large minority of Han Chinese who have been resettled there, as well as several small ethnic communities. The Mongols themselves are divided into the Xilingol, Zachar and Ordos Mongols. Their nomadic way of life has been replaced by a settled existence. The overlaying of Chinese culture and the integration of the Mongols into a Communist social system has wiped out the traditional structure based on Arats (nomads) and Tayiji or noblemen. The privileges of the monasteries and their senior Lamaist monks are also a thing of the past.

Nevertheless, traces of the Mongolian tradition can still be found. Its folklore, preserved with the support of official Chinese propaganda, can be seen in traditional folk costumes and such long-established sports as horse-racing, archery and wrestling. But in everyday life as well, tradition is very much alive. Away from permanent settlements, yurts, the circular tents that the Mongols call *gir*, are signs that the nomadic herdsman's way of life has to some extent survived. Their cuisine, too, remains entirely different from that of the Chinese. It consists almost exclusively of meat and dairy pro-

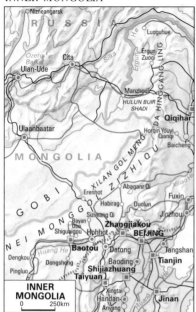

ducts, including *kumyss,* an alcoholic drink made of soured mare's or camel's milk. However, the most pronounced difference between the Inner Mongolians and their kinsmen to the north, on whom the Russians imposed their Cyrillic alphabet, is that the former have retained the Mongolian script which originated in the Middle East and was the model for the Manchurian script.

In the 17th century, as tsarist Russia pushed eastwards to the Pacific and across the Bering Sea, the Manchu dynasty took power in Peking. China put up the barriers against Russia. With military force, especially during the reign of the emperor Kangxi (1662-1722) all the outer regions – Manchuria, Mongolia, Sinkiang, Tibet – were incorporated into the Qing empire. It was not merely the ethnic affinity between the Manchus and Mongols which seemed to justify the an-

nexation of Mongolia. Their common history carried even more weight: after all it was the Mongols who, in the 13th century, had founded the greatest empire in the world, with its capital in Peking.

Previously, in the struggle for supremacy over the Mongolian tribes, it was Temüjin, the chieftain from the Borjighin clan who emerged victorious. In 1206 the great *chural*, the assembly of nobles, met at the Spring of Oron and elected him *Kha-Khan* ("Khan of all the Khans") of the Mongols, with the title of *Chengis Khan* (Jinghis Khan, "Emperor of the Seas"). Their code of honor, strict laws and military discipline (*yassa*) enabled the Mongols to storm the very gates of Europe.

In 1260 the fourth successor of Jinghis Khan came to power: he was Khubilei Khan (Khublai Khan, 1260-1294) who elevated Peking to capital of China and of his whole empire (*khan balik / da du*). The Yuan dynasty which he founded remained in power until 1368. It introduced many impressive innovations to China,

Above: Wooden Russian house in Manzhouli. Right: The Five Pagoda Temple – emblem of Hohhot (Inner Mongolia).

uch as post offices, state granaries, paper money, libraries and academies; but they also brought exploitation and racial discrimination. The riches gained from trading along the Silk Road did not trickle down to the Chinese people who were in fact impoverished under the Yuan rulers. The Mongols took over the Chinese administrative system, but their philosophy of life was shaped by Tibetan Buddhism.

The successor to the Mongol empire was the Central Asian, Islamic nation led by the Turkish-Mongolian tyrant, Timur Leng (Tamerlane, 1336-1405), who created his magnificent capital at Samarkand. But after his death the vast empire fell apart. China in the Ming period, isolating itself from the rest of the world, built a Great Wall for the second time.

Hohhot

The capital of Inner Mongolia, Hohhot ("Green City"), lies at the foot of the **Daqing Mountains** (*daqing shan*) in the upper valley of the **Dahei river** (*dahei he*) at an altitude of 3280 ft (1000 m). It is situated at the geographical center of the province and enjoys good transportation links with China. But the outer reaches of the province in the west and east are a great distance from here. From **Manzhouli**, the frontier town at the common border of Mongolia, Russia and China, the train journey to Hohhot, via Beijing, takes about 50 hours.

Dominating the south of the city, the **Temple of the Five Pagodas** (*wuta si*) is all that is left of a monastery in the former Old City. Its five seven-tiered pagodas with green glazed tiles and impressive reliefs rise from a rectangular base which is itself divided horizontally into nine sections. It was built in 1740 in a blend of Chinese and Tibetan styles. To the west stands the **Great Temple Monastery** (*da zhao*) dating from 1580. Facing it, a little to the north, stands the 14th-century **Xiletuzhao**, also designed in the Sino-Tibetan manner. It has a large library and an attractively decorated roof.

Further north, the **Great Mosque** (*qingzhen dasi*) was built in the Chinese style in the 18th century, during the flowering of the Qing dynasty. The majority of its large congregation were Muslim immigrants from Sinkiang.

It is worth paying a visit to the **White Pagoda** (*bai ta*), 11 miles (18 km) east of the city in the village of Baitacun. The octagonal, 8-tiered tower is 140 ft (43 m) high and built of wood and brick. Dating from the Liao empire of the 10th and 11th centuries, it is typical of the sturdy, fortress-like buildings of the Kitan. About 6 miles (9 km) south of Hohhot, on the bank of the Daheihe, you will find the **tomb** of Wang Zhaojun Mu, a Chinese princess of the Han period. She was sent as a diplomatic "bridal gift" to appease the Mongols and ended her life here.

During the Cultural Revolution a 4.3 mile (7 km) long system of **defensive tunnels** was dug to the north of Hohhot.

Above: Minus 30° Centigrade in Hailar (Inner Mongolia).

Excursions from Hohhot

A high point of any stay in Inner Mongolia is a visit to a state commune on the **Mongolian grassland**, where you can observe the traditional life of the herdsmen. Bookings can be made in Hohhot for these excursions, which include an overnight stay in a yurt (*gir/menggu bao*). Fifty-four miles (87 km) to the north you reach the village of **Xilamuren**, at an altitude of 5576 ft (1700 m). A further 75 miles away in the "banner" of Siziwang are the villages of **Huitengxile** and **Gegentala** ("Gleaming Grassland"). Ninety miles (145 km) north, travelers find a tented camp with a new *Nadom* market. The tourist program in the grassland is enlivened by displays of traditional Mongolian sports like horse- and camel-racing, wrestling and archery, as well as folk-dancing and singing. And around the camp fire in the evening you can sample the Mongolian specialities of roast mutton, mare's milk milky tea and fermented *kumyss*.

Baotou

In complete contrast to Hohhot, the largest town in the province is **Baotou**, an industrial center on the north bank of the Yellow River. Founded in the Tang period as a fortified oasis, Baotou's urban development did not begin until 871 with the building of a city wall. After being linked to the railway network in 1921, Baotou grew in economic importance. Rich coal deposits (at Shiguaigou in the Daqing Mountains), iron ore at Bayan Obo in the Ulanqab district), and the exploitation of thermal energy for aluminium-smelting have turned Baotou into a hub of heavy industry.

About 43 miles (70 km) northeast, in a valley near Wudanggou, lies the Lamaist monastery of **Wudangzhao** (Tibetan: *Badaga'r*, or "White Lotus-flower"). This fortified monastery was built in the Tibetan style in the 17th century, under the Qing emperor Kangxi, and enlarged in the 18th, in the reign of Qianlong. With its wonderfully painted prayer-rooms, it is the only completely preserved Lama temple in Inner Mongolia. The complex comprises 2500 rooms and demonstrates the close links between Mongolian and Tibetan culture.

Excursions from Baotou

At 3600 ft (1100 m), up in the banner of Dalad, you breathe the pristine air of the Gobi Desert. You can climb over the **Singing Sand-dunes of Kubiqi** and spend the night in a forest. Near Dongsheng in the Gandeli steppe, 77 miles (124 km) south of Baotou is the **tomb of Jinghis Khan**. Today you see a reconstruction of three yurt-shaped burial-halls and a palace in the Sino-Mongolian style.

Xilinhot

In July the annual festival of *Nadom* takes place in **Xilinhot**, the chief town of

INNER MONGOLIA

Getting there
The provincial capital **Hohhot** lies on the main Peking–Datong–Baotou–Lanzhou rail route. There are also regular flights from Beijing and Lanzhou.

Accommodation
HOHHOT: *MID-PRICE:* **Zhaojun Hotel** (*zhaojun dajiudian*), 11 Xinhua Dajie, Tel. 662211. **Inner Mongolia Hotel** (*neimenggu fandian*), Hulun Nanlu, Tel. 666241. *BUDGET:* **Hohhot Guesthouse** (*huhehaote binguan*), 7 Yingbin Lu, Tel. 662838. **Xincheng Guesthouse** (*xincheng binguan*), 23 Hulun Nanlu, Tel. 665754.
BAOTOU: *MID-PRICE:* **Qingshan**, Tel. 334091. **Baotou Guesthouse** (*baotou binguan*), 19 Ganglie Dajie, Tel. 226612. *BUDGET:* **A'erding Hotel** (*a'erding fandian*), near train station.

Tourist information
HOHHOT: **CITS**, in the Inner Mongolia Hotel, Tel. 664494. **Overseas Tourist Corp.**, in the Inner Mongolia Hotel, Tel. 666774.
BAOTOU: **CITS**, Xifulou (Baotou Guesthouse), Tel. 224115.

the **Xilingol Meng** district, situated about 300 miles north of Peking.

Just as at the *Nadom* festival in Ulaan Baatar, the capital of Outer Mongolia, people from all over Inner Mongolia come streaming into the town dressed in traditional costume. They gather to celebrate the festival with a colorful fair and contests in the time-honored Mongolian sports.

In front of a vast encampment of yurts, games are played on horseback, accompanied by theatrical performances and various other entertainments.

Excursions from Xilinhot

Halfway between Xilinhot and Zhangjikou a road branches off eastward near Habirag, to the village of **Dolonnur** (Chinese: Duolun), 59 miles (95 km) away. There you can marvel at the ruins of the **Palace of Kublai Khan**, which Marco Polo, who came here in the 13th century, described as the "marble palace of Xanadu."

THE GOLDEN GOOSE

HONG KONG ISLAND
KOWLOON
NEW TERRITORIES
LANTAU
CHEUNG CHAU
LAMMA

July 1st, 1997, a date both coveted and feared, marks the return of the British Crown Colony of Hong Kong to China. Seen from the Chinese perspective, it means the end of the colonial occupation of China (or at least a part thereof). Until the massacre on Tianamen Square in 1989, the people of Hong Kong looked upon the change of government and overlordship with a mixture of joy and serenity. After all, it was Chinese people living on both sides of the border. But ever since the tanks rolled over China's democracy movement, fears have arisen as to how the rigid government in Beijing might react to the entrepreneurial spirit of the Hong Kongers. Many of the more wealthy inhabitants of the colony moved their business headquarters and bank accounts abroad, or packed up tools and baggage and moved away.

The colonial history of Hong Kong began with the two Opium Wars of 1842 and 1856 respectively. The net result for the British Empire was first of all the island of Hong Kong, which was then named after Queen Victoria, followed by Kowloon, the southern tip of the main-

Previous pages: Time travel through "Victoria" with a 1904 tramway. Left: Open pocketknife crowned by two chopsticks – the Bank of China in Central.

land. This "war booty" was granted to the British "forever." In 1898, they acquired a 99-year lease on the so-called New Territories and 235 islands.

The British were only required to return the leased areas on July 1st, 1997, but the government decided to give back the entire Crown Colony. An agreement to this effect was signed by Queen Elizabeth and Deng Xiaoping in 1984. It establishes Hong Kong's status as a special administrative zone of China for 50 years. Left-hand traffic, the currency and the educational system will thereby remain unaffected by the new situation.

During the 50-year interim period, the border will remain in place, and Chinese citizens will still need a special permit to visit Hong Kong. Whether the Beijing government intends in the long run to follow the conditions of the agreement to the letter remains to be seen. Since July 1, 1997, eventual international protest could be dismissed as mere meddling in China's internal affairs. On the other hand, Beijing would be ill-advised to slaughter its newly-acquired golden goose, since the bulk of all investments in China flows through Hong Kong (the city has the world's largest concentration of banks). The Taiwan issue is also open to debate: China would like to show Taipei that the "one state, two systems" formula can ac-

tually work. Hong Kong could be seen as a test case for unification with its "renegade province," as Red China tends to call Taiwan. The Taiwanese are on the skeptical side, needless to say.

For many short-term vacationers, a trip to Hong Kong consists mainly of shopping and night life. The city does, however, have more to offer than just consumerism and a spot checking of the local scene. Visitors with a little time and sensitivity will learn to feel the energy arising from the tension between high-tech and Big Business on the one hand, and profound religiosity, ancestor worship and superstition on the other, for a lot of old China has survived the city's drive into the 20th century. Colorful Chinese

markets and temples and shrines smelling of incense nestle between the shiny cliffs of modern sky scrapers, and just beyond the heart of the city are solitary hiking paths, peaceful sand beaches, ancient Chinese culture and pristine nature.

HONG KONG ISLAND

Central District

The British gave the name *Victoria City* to this part of the island. They set up their capital here after being forced away from Happy Valley because of malaria. The district known as **Central** is nowadays the seat of local government and the banking quarter. The way leading from

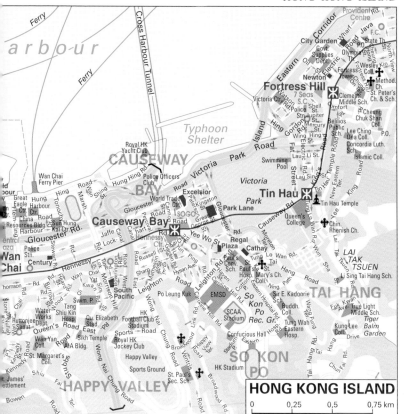

HONG KONG ISLAND

| 0 | 0,25 | 0,5 | 0,75 km |

he Star Ferry pier is lined to the right by a sky-scraping tower, the **Exchange Square** housing the Hong Kong stock exchange, and next to it **Jardine House**, a building with round windows, where the information and souvenir center of the Hong Kong Tourist Association is located. The patch of green straight ahead is called **Statue Square** and features the effigy of a bank director who lived in the crown colony in the 19th century. The skyline, as seen from this vantage point, is an overwhelming mixture of different styles. The **Bank of Hong Kong and Shanghai**, located on the other side of Des Voeux Road, was designed by the British star architect Norman Foster and is considered one of the world's most modern buildings. It consists of glass and steel units that can be completely dismantled. To its south is a sun "shovel," which, thanks to a computerized system, reflects sunlight into the bank's atrium, thereby saving electrical energy for lighting. To the east of Statue Square stands a domed Victorian construction. The **Legislative Council**, where the Parliament meets, is like a relic from another world altogether.

Farther off to the southeast, the silvery, shimmering, angular silhouette of the **Bank of China** skyscraper pierces into the heavens. Until 1992, this creation by architect You Ming Pei was Asia's tallest. It resembles a large, open pocket knife, and the two antennas poking off

217

the roof are like two chopsticks. Unlike Norman Foster, Pei failed to stick to the geomantic guidelines (*feng shui*) that rule Hong Kong's architectural design, so for years the Bank of China actually had difficulty renting out office space and finding customers.

25-acre **Hong Kong Park**, which was laid out in 1991, is the green lung of Central. Its main attraction is a huge walk-in volary done up as a tropical rain forest with over 150 bird species. **Flagstaff House**, standing in the northern corner of the park, was erected in 1846 as the residence of the military commander. Nowadays it houses the **Museum of Teaware**, which documents the history of tea-drinking. **St. John's Cathedral**, a neo-Gothic building on Garden Road, was consecrated in 1849 and is the oldest Anglican church in eastern Asia.

Above: A rare sight – junks in Victoria Harbour. Right: Repulse Bay, a place for daytrips.

Also on Garden Road is the **Peak Tram** stop. The tramway shimmies its way up to the **Peak**, a 1264-ft-high (395 m) outlook from which the entire city can be seen. This funicular was set up in 1888. Before then, the more wealthy people used to let themselves be carried up the hill. The way up through the **Peak Galleria** shopping arcade passes by pretty fountains and ends at a lookout terrace with a superb view of Kowloon and Central. The sight is particularly attractive in the evenings: The windows and the reflecting façades of the high-rises glitter like a million diamonds, colorful neon advertising with Chinese lettering pulsates in the distance, jet boats, freight barges, the odd junk and the dignified green and white Star Ferry plough their way through the waters of the bay, creating abstract stripes of white on the greenish waters. The whole city seems softer in the gentle, dusky light.

Even more beautiful is the approximately one-hour walk along the **Peak Trail**, which rounds the hilltop. From here, you can steal a glance at the odd billionaire's mansion rising in isolated splendor out of the greenery. A fitting conclusion to this little excursion is a refreshing drink at the colonial **Peak Café**.

Back in Central, meanwhile, the nighthawks are on the prowl in **Lan Kwai Fong** and the surrounding streets (D'Aguilar Street, Ice House Street and Lower Albert Road). The area is peppered with restaurants, little galleries, discothèques and pubs. These establishments are usually filled to the brim; the customer barely has time to pick up a drink at the bar before being virtually pressed out the door, so the streets generally look like one big party.

Western District

In the early days of the English occupation, the Chinese workers used to live in this part of town. When you step out of

the MTR Sheung Wan station, you will still see some relics from those distant days. The **Western Market** at the juncture of Connaught Road and Morrison Street, for example, was built in 1906 as a covered market for fish and meat. It was restored in 1991 and placed under monument protection order. Chinese handicraft artists and textile shops have settled in the old market since. A good *dim sum* restaurant opened on the first floor.

Morrison Street continues on to the area of **Hollywood Road** and its myriad side streets, home of hundreds of small antique dealers all patiently waiting for customers. A special sight is **Man Mo Temple** at Hollywood Road and Ladder Street. Two gods are honored in this typically Taoist temple: The civilized god of officials and intellectuals Man Cheong, holding his characteristic writing brush, and the god of war Kwan Kung, who carries a sword. A motley crew of intellectuals, policemen and small-time criminals light incense sticks here and seek help from their protective gods.

Hollywood Road on the way toward Central soon runs into **The Lanes**, a set of four streets, where a lively market forms a sharp contrast to the uniform high-rises of the surrounding area. Anything is available here, from shoes, tote bags and clothing, to carved Chinese signets (Pottinger St., Li Yuen St., East and West, and Ma Wan Lane, daily from 10:00 a.m. to 6:00 p.m.).

The **Hillside Escalator**, the world's longest escalator (2560 ft/ 800 m), begins at the junction of Queens Road and Stanley Street and leads up to Conduit Road (down from 6:00 am to 10:00 am, up from 10:00 am to 10:00 p.m.). This means of public transportation has been shuttling about 30,000 people daily since it was completed in 1993. The ride offers a chance to observe the daily rituals of Hong Kongers and a view of the 1915 **Jamia Mosque**. The Caine Road exit is a short way from the **Zoological and Botanical Gardens** on Upper Albert Road, a veritable oasis of tranquillity after the tumult of the city.

Wan Chai, Causeway Bay and Happy Valley

Wan Chai is the former entertainment section of the city. Many nightclubs are still operating to this day, especially between Luard Road and Fenwick Street, but life is just as exciting in the streets during the day. The keys of the city were given over to the Chinese on July 1, 1997, in the mellifluous **Convention and Exchange Centre**, which rises near the Star Ferry pier.

The **Causeway Bay** district has been given the nickname *Little Japan* because of its many Japanese department stores. The **Sogo** and **Seibu** stores (both in Hennessy Road) are well worth seeing even if you are not buying anything. Clothing and food can be had in the market alley **Jardine's Bazaar**, which exudes a very Chinese atmosphere (daily from 11:00 a.m. to 10:00 p.m.). The **Noon-Day Gun**, resting on a platform in front of the Excelsior Hotel, has been fired every day at noon since the mid-19th century.

After the British fled their **Happy Valley** community in 1846, they used the area for a racetrack. Unbelievable sums are wagered here every Wednesday and Saturday. A very popular spot with Hong Kongers is the colorful sculpture park **Tiger Balm Garden** (Aw Boon Haw Gardens), which was opened in 1935. Chinese mythology is exhibited in extravagant grottos in wonderful, corny, dramatic, or amusing manner. (Tai Hang Road, east of Happy Valley, bus No. 11 from the MTR Admiralty station).

The Island's south

The south side of the island is accessible via the Aberdeen Tunnel. The **Ocean Park** amusement park lies on a spit of land. Its main attraction is the **Middle Kingdom Museum**, with a presentation of Chinese history, the **Dinosaur Discovery Trail**, a shark aquarium, the **Ocean Theatre**, and **Kid's World**, with games and shows for children. The park is good family fun especially weekdays, when the crowds are not so heavy (shuttle bus from Admiralty station and from the Star Ferry pier in Central). Neighboring **Water World** has giant water slides and pools (open April to October only).

One of the most beautiful beaches of the island is located in **Deepwater Bay**. For golf players, the road leads to the **Royal Hong Kong Golf Club**. An idyllic path runs along the coast to **Repulse Bay**, where an attractive beach and numerous restaurants and bars await the visitor. This is where you'll find the "apartment house with the hole," which serves as an absolutely necessary "approach lane" for dragons. *Feng shui* experts know full well that a dragon lives in the slope behind the house and goes to bathe in the sea every morning. He would destroy any house standing in his way. There is another, more profane explanation for the architecturally delightful open space: Repulse Bay is not protected from typhoons, and without a passageway, the wind could do damage to the house.

There is a small temple to the **patron goddess Tin Hau** on the beach of Repulse Bay. Opposite a large statue of the goddess sits a fat Buddha with a money bag on his knees. Anyone successfully throwing a coin into it will become rich, so the superstition. Out at sea are a row of buoys marking the spot where shark nets have been placed – a few years ago there were shark incidents here.

The old fishing village of **Stanley** has grown into a large discount market with innumerable shops offering factory and handicraft surplus goods. Genuine old Hong Kong life can be found beyond the busy commercial streets. Stanley used to be a hideaway for pirates, and if you're not careful while bargaining, you'll find out that their descendants still live here... There is yet another **temple to the pa-**

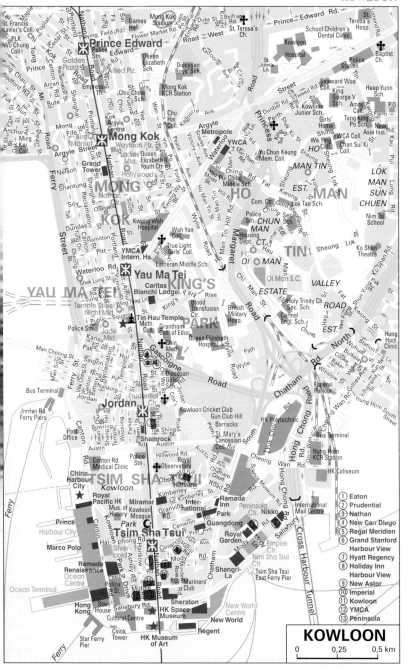

KOWLOON

1. Eaton
2. Prudential
3. Nathan
4. New Can Diego
5. Regal Meridien
6. Grand Stanford Harbour View
7. Hyatt Regency
8. Holiday Inn Harbour View
9. New Astor
10. Imperial
11. Kowloon
12. YMCA
13. Peninsula

0   0,25   0,5 km

tron goddess Tin Hau, built in 1767, which is worth visiting. (No. 6 or 260 bus from Exchange Square).

Once upon a time, the Chinese built ships out of aromatic camphor wood in the old and protected harbor of **Aberdeen**, hence the name *Hong Kong*, which means "aromatic harbor." Junks and cutters that are home to entire families lay at anchor in the typhoon-proof port. The multi-story restaurant ships known as **floating restaurants** are very picturesque public attractions, but the service is often third-rate and the Chinese food is overpriced and sloppily prepared. A trip through the floating junk community in sampans will soon be a thing of the past: The yacht harbor is planning to expand into these waters of this bay. Take No. 73 bus from Exchange Square or No. 7 from the Peak ride down to the sampan embarkation point.

Above: Traditional Chinese fastfood (Night Market on Temple Street). Right: The Bird Market on Hong Lok Street.

KOWLOON

The name Kowloon means "nine dragons" and refers to the eight mountains that delimit the peninsula to the north. One of the Sung emperors, who asked about the ninth dragon, was told that he himself was the creature, and the other eight had been waiting for him.

The main attraction in Kowloon is the southern tip called **Tsim Sha Tsui**, which real Hong Kong insiders simply call *TST*. It consists of thousands of shops where one can indulge in unadulterated consumerism. In the midst of this hubbub is the odd special spot worth seeing for its own sake. The **Waterfront Promenade**, for example, provides a wonderful view of Victoria Harbour and the skyline of Hong Kong Island.

The old train station used to stand on the Star Ferry pier. It was torn down in 1975, and all that remains is the 140-ft (44 m) **Clock Tower** built in 1916. Some sarcastic tongues have named the **Cultural Centre** standing behind it a "baby

pink ski jump." This windowless construction was built in 1989 as a venue for concerts, theatrical performances and exhibitions. The promenade along the cultural centre is a favorite meeting place for Hong Kongers off duty, and making acquaintances is easy. The adjacent **Hong Kong Museum of Art** shows classic Chinese masterpieces and contemporary artists from Hong Kong; opposite stands **the Hong Kong Space Museum** and the **Planetarium**, which explore the worlds of astronomy and space travel.

The **Peninsula Hotel**, built in 1928, is located to the north on Salisbury Road. If planning to take coffee or tea here in the afternoon, please keep the dress code in mind: A necktie is not obligatory, but socks are! The international jet set usually meets at **Felix**, a restaurant-cum-night-club on the 29th floor designed in futuristic style by star decorator Philippe Starck. Even if the crowd leaves you cold, the view of the city is superb.

Shopping hounds will salivate more heavily when reaching **Nathan Road**, and their wallets are bound to become lighter at lightning speed. Everything the world can offer is available in the area. The further northward you go, the lower the prices. A right-hand turn behind the Sheraton Hotel takes you to a park with the **Signal Tower**, built in 1884. Every day, a copper ball was dropped to communicate the time to the captains in the harbor. An electronic system replaced the old one in 1933. Continuing to the north on Nathan Road, you come across a **mosque** (left side of the street), which was erected in 1984.

Neighboring **Kowloon Park** is a place to relax, with a Chinese garden, a sculpture park and a swimming pool. The history of the former colony is documented in the **Hong Kong Museum of History**.

Markets in Yau Ma Tei and Mong Kok

Two lively districts stretch to the north of Tsim Sha Tsui: Yau Ma Tei and Mong Kok, with numerous specialty stores and

traditional markets. The **Jade Market** is the place to find the coveted gemstone in all shades from milky white to bottle green (corner of Kansu Street and Reclamation Street under a highway overpass, daily from 10:00 am to 3:00 p.m.). A popular meeting spot is the four-temple complex of the **Tin Hau Temple** a little to the north. **Temple Street**, with its **Night Market**, is just a stone's throw away. From 7:00 p.m. onwards the crowds are so dense, one can hardly get through: Peddlers of clothing, watches, electronics, fast foods, omens and street art share the narrow space on the street. Traditional shops offering herbs, incense and household utensils are lined up along **Shanghai Street**. The **Ladies' Market** is located along Tung Choi Street to the east of Nathan Road in Mong Kok (daily 4:00-10:00 p.m.): The wide range of wares on display is not only for women!

Above: Ober 3 million believers bring sacrifies to the Daoist Wong Tai Sin Temple each Year.

The **Bird Market** is held on Hong Lok Street (during the day until 6:00 p.m.), the **Flower Market**, featuring flowers from all over the world, takes place on Flower Market Road, and the **Goldfish Market** (early mornings) is on Boundary Street all the way to the north of Mong Kok. Have your future revealed by a fortune teller in the large, popular **Wong Tai Sin Temple** (North East Kowloon, MTR Wong Tai Sin).

NEW TERRITORIES

Most of the New Territories consists of open country dotted by little oases of ancient culture, little villages and fishing ports. The *Countryside Series* hikers maps for the New Territories are available at Swindons (Lock Road, Tsim Sha Tsui), or at the Government Publication Centre (Star Ferry pier, Central). The longest and most beautiful hike is on **MacLehose Trail**, 60 miles (100 km) long and interspersed with 10 stops. The first and second segments, which boast the most ttractive landscape, skirt the Sai Kung eninsula. **Wilson Trail** (45 miles/75 km) raverses the New Territories from north o south, crossing the 3062-ft (957 m) Tai Mo mountain range, Hong Kong's ighest elevation. Significantly shorter nd easier is the **Ping Shan Heritage Trail**. It lies to the northwest near Yuen Long, and connects ten sights, which can e easily reached within two hours – for xample, former private schools of the different clans, or walled villages.

To visit the **Monastery of the 10,000 Buddhas**, take the train to **Sha Tin** KRT tation, walk a short distance (in the same direction as the train) and turn left into Pai Tau Street. From there, follow the igns. The monastery was founded in the 950s by a Buddhist abbot, whose mortal emains did not decompose. His body vas embalmed, covered in gold leaf and et up in a glass case. An estimated 13,000 figures of Buddha are collected in he monastery. The **Bo Fook Ancestral Worship Hall** is situated below the monastery. Believers can purchase or rent a niche in the wall for their future urn. Farher down is a Thai-inspired shrine housng the **Four-faced Buddha**, who sees he misery of the world at all four cardihal points. The **Sha-Tin Horse Track**, northeast in **Fo Tan**, is worth seeing even outside the racing season for the Chinese garden in its middle.

The **Tai Po Kau Nature Reserve**, beween Sha Tin and Tai Po owes its existnce to a reforestation program, but it is hevertheless a must for lovers of nature. A 2200-ft (700 m) nature trail with educational displays introduces the visitor to he tropical vegetation. The information gathered here can be tested on paths ranging from 2 to 6 miles (3-10 km). You might also spot butterflies and birds, or, with a little luck, one of the rare muntjak deer (University KCR station or No. 72 bus from Prince Edward MTR station).

The best-kept secret of the New Territories is **Tai Long Bay**, located amidst a beautiful landscape in the east of **Sai Kung Country Park**. Getting there is something of an odyssey: The Tolo Harbour Ferry connects the University KCR station with Chek Keng. This is followed by a 2-mile (3 km) hike south on a difficult trail.

The Tang clan settled in the New Territories in the 10th century and multiplied to such an extent, that four centuries later they occupied six neighboring villages. They built high walls to defend against pirates and tigers, creating the village complex known as **Kam Tin Walled Village**. Tourist throngs invade the largest of these walled villages, **Kat Hing**, the locals sell tickets and souvenirs. Taking snapshots costs an obolus as well! None of this detracts from the essential beauty of the powerful walls, the graves and towers, which give a sense of what life must have been like in this formerly rich community. **Shui Tau**, next door, is somewhat quieter. The settlement can be reached using the No. 51 bus leaving from Tsuen Wan MTR station.

LANTAU

Lantau is the largest island of the former Crown Colony and at least until now a thinly settled one at that. The building of the new airport on the northern coast will mean significant change. Once the project has been completed, Lantau is to be populated through a settlement program. At this point, however, an excursion to the island still means peace and tranquillity. Buses leave from the disembarkation point Mui Wo in Silvermine Bay to all noteworthy sights. Their schedules are synchronized with the ferries.

The **Po Lin Monastery** built in 1921 on the Ngong Ping plateau is the most popular place to visit on the island. The one-hour drive to the monastery crosses a landscape of gently rolling hills. The world's largest sitting bronze Buddha, inaugurated in 1993, has been placed on a

hill outside the monastery and can be seen from afar. The socle of the statue contains an exhibition detailing the life of Buddha. In the main hall of the monastery are three other Buddhas, which are supposed to represent the temporal existence of Buddha in the past, present and future. At the foot of the entrance stairway is a replica of the Heavenly Altar in Beijing. An interesting acoustical phenomenon can be observed here: If you stand on the middle platform and speak loudly (don't scream), your voice will be considerably amplified.

Visitors to the monastery can enjoy vegetarian meals and sleep in a rather Spartan dormitory.

Tai O is a fishing community of the Tanka ethnic group. The tenements at the entrance of the village are empty, because the inhabitants preferred to stay in their stilt houses. Until two years ago, a ferry connected the two sections of the

Above: Old stilt houses and sampans are still the rule in the village of Tai O.

village. This service stopped after the bridge was built. **Tung Chung Fort** was used by the last emperor of the Sung Dynasty as a layover place while traveling A fortress village was erected here during the Qing Dynasty at the beginning of the 19th century as protection against pirates and foreigners. A school and the land administration of the island have established themselves in the restored village. Some old cannon can still be spotted here and there. From the village you can glance across one of the world's largest construction sites: In order to build the new airport **Chek Lap Kok**, two islands were completely dynamited. In addition, two suspension bridges for a highway and train service will be built to connect with Hong Kong Island.

The 42-mile-long (70 km) **Lantau Trail** cuts across two nature parks. Most of its twelve sections are well suited for plain walking, the sections that cross **Lantau Peak** and **Sunset Peak** are for more experienced hikers. Added together, the sections form a path circuiting

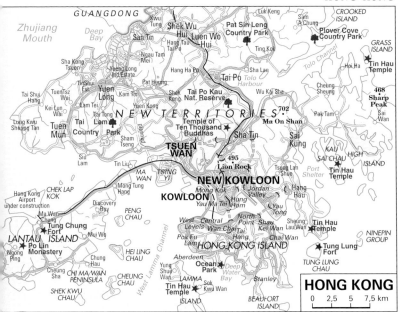

HONG KONG

0   2,5   5   7,5 km

the island. It begins and ends at the ferry harbor **Mui Wo**. Hiking maps are available at the offices of the Hong Kong Tourist Association. If you have a little time before your ferry takes off in the evening, you should not miss the opportunity of a stroll along the beach to the north of the pier.

CHEUNG CHAU AND LAMMA

The name Cheung Chau means *long island* when translated. To be precise, it looks rather like a weight lifter's barbell. The beautiful village, with its narrow streets, is nested on the narrow middle segment of the island. Ships only drop anchor in the western bay, which offers protection from typhoons. Good fish restaurants line the harbor promenade called **Praya**. Traditional Chinese life can still be observed in the narrow streets of the village. Toward the north, you'll find the Taoist **Pak Tai Temple** built in 1783 in honor of the highest Taoist deity, the "highest ruler of the dark heavens." The

building was renovated in 1989. The week-long **Bun Festival**, a feast to pacify the spirits of the victims of pirate attacks, begins at the temple every spring and soon takes over the whole town, ending with a huge street procession. The Taoist **Kwan Kung Pavilion** on Peak Road was erected in honor of the god of war. In the south of the island, in front of the Warwick Hotel, are several incongruous **rock sculptures** dating from the Bronze Age. A little farther to the south, the infamous cave of the **pirate Cheung Po Tsai** is open to the public.

On **Lamma**, there are two very attractive beaches: **Lo So Shing** on the western coast and **Hung Shing Ye** a little bit to the north. A day can easily be spent lazing about in the sun and water, and then moving to one of the restaurants on the **Sok Kwu Wan** harbor for the evening. They are built on stilts and offer delicious sea food under the star-spangled sky. Taking the ferry back to Aberdeen you slowly glide past the glittering skyline – an unforgettable experience.

HONG KONG
Immigration

A passport still valid for a year is necessary for traveling to Hong Kong. Visas are seldom required for short stays. After 3 months, citizens of Great Britain and the Commonwealth countries will have to apply for a visa. For citizens of the USA, Canada and South Africa, a visa is needed after 1 month. Immigration Department, Immigration Tower, Wan Chai, Tel: 28246111, Fax: 28777711.

Airplanes land at the old **Kai Tak Airport** after a breathtaking approach. On leaving the arrivals building turn left and walk about 60 ft to the airport bus station. It departs every 15 minutes, and the hotels at the different stations are announced. Airbus line No. 1 goes to Kowloon, A2 to Central, and A3 to Causeway Bay.

If you come in from China by ferry or train, you will arrive in the middle of Kowloon. Taxis await.

Accommodations

LUXURY: **The Peninsula**, Salisbury Rd., Tsim Sha Tsui, Tel: 23666251, Fax: 27224170; the most exclusive address, best location. **Hyatt Regency**, 67 Nathan Rd., Tsim Sha Tsui, Tel: 23111234, Fax: 27398701; this is Kowloon's second top address. **Holiday Inn Golden Mile**, 50 Nathan Rd., Tsim Sha Tsui, Tel: 23693111, Fax: 23691788; newly renovated. **Grand Stanford Harbour View**, 70 Mody Rd., Tsim Sha Tsui East, Tel: 2721516, Fax: 27322233; located at the quiet end of the Harbour Promenade. **Furama Kempinski**, 1 Connaught Rd., Central, Tel: 25255111, Fax: 28459339, good for businesspeople. **Grand Hyatt**, 1 Harbour Rd., Wan Chai, Tel: 25881234, Fax: 28020677; exclusive. **Luk Kwok Hotel**, 72 Gloucester Rd., Wan Chai, Tel: 28662166, Fax: 28662622. **Excelsior Hotel**, 281 Gloucester Rd., Causeway Bay, Tel: 28948888, Fax: 28956459; with a nice view across the yacht harbor.

MODERATE: **Imperial Hotel**, 30-40 Nathan Rd., Tsim Sha Tsui, Tel: 23662201, Fax: 23112360. **International Hotel**, 33 Cameron Rd., Tsim Sha Tsui, Tel: 23663381. **The Salisbury YMCA**, Salisbury Rd., Tsim Sha Tsui, Tel: 23692211, Fax: 27399315; not only for young men as the name suggests, but rather a chic hotel right next to the Peninsula; not exactly cheap, but has dormitories. If there are four of you, rent a four-bed room: it is cheapest and most comfortable. **Caritas Bianchi Lodge**, 4 Cliff Rd., Yau Ma Tei, Tel: 23881111, Fax: 27706669; off the beaten path, clean, inexpensive. **New Harbour Hostel**, 41-49 Hennessy Rd., Wan Chai, Tel: 28611166, Fax: 28656111. **Emerald Hotel**, 152 Connaught Rd., Western District, Tel: 25468111, Fax: 25590255. **Garden View International House**, 1 McDonnell Rd., Central, Tel:

28773737, Fax: 28456263, from second Peak Tram stop, *the* tip on the island.

BUDGET: The **Chunking Mansions** at 36 Nathan Rd. are unique: A centrally located block of houses with many small B&Bs accessible via very slow elevators. If staying here you should have ascetic tendencies and not be claustrophobic. To find the individual B&Bs, stroll about Nathan Rd. with a rucksack or a suitcase, you will be addressed. Some of the establishments are nice and clean, most are terrible. Be sure to check the room first before saying yes. The great advantage of these B&Bs is their information value. Most China backpackers stay here and share tips and infos.

Victoria Hotel, 33 Hankow Rd., Tsim Sha Tsui, Tel: 23760621, Fax: 23692609, entrance is in the watch store, clean, good place for China information. **Ocean Guest House**, 11/F Jordan Rd., Yau Ma Tei, Tel: 23850125, Fax: 27826441.

Restaurants

Restaurants are clean and ingredients are fresh. One can even eat well in the canteens of Mong Kok, Causeway Bay and Temple Street. Restaurants are by and large located on the first floors above the shops, since the rents are cheaper there. It is customary to wait for someone to show you to your table.

CANTONESE: **Bodhi**, 32-34 Lock Rd., Tsim Sha Tsui, Tel: 23668283; fresh food, inexpensive, and in some branches good Dim-Sum buffets from 7:30 a.m. to 10:30 a.m. *Dim-Sum* is boiled or fried dough with various fillings. **House of Canton**, 101 Caroline Centre, 2 Yun Ping Rd., Causeway Bay, Tel: 28821383; modern furnishings, traditional food, affordable. **Yung Kee**, 38-40 Wellington St., Central, Tel: 25221624; simple, fine food. **Zen**, LG1 Pacific Place Mall, Queensway, Central, Tel: 28454555, tops, expensive. *CHINESE*: **Peking Garden**, with branches. The main restaurant is in the Alexandra House, Chater Rd., Central, Tel: 25266456, every evening public demonstration of noodlemaking. **Andy's Kitchen**, 25 Tung Lo Wan Rd., Causeway Bay, Tel: 28908137; Shanghai cuisine, looking into thew pots is allowed, inexpensive, good. **Red Pepper**, 7 Lan Fong Rd., Causeway Bay, Tel: 25773811; spicy Sichuan cuisine. **Sichuan Garden**, Shop 4, Pacific Place, Queensway, Central, Tel: 28458433, Sichuan, not as hot as Red Pepper. **Yü**, Regent Hotel, Salisbury Rd., Tsim Sha Tsui, Tel: 23132340, harbor view on one side, giant aquarium on the other, exclusive dishes and prices. *ASIAN*: **Spices**, Repulse Bay Rd., Repulse Bay, Tel: 28122711, Indian, Thai, Vietnamese, Arabic specialties. **Bananaleaf Restaurant**, 70 Nathan Rd., Tsim Sha Tsui, Tel: 27213513, with branches; Indian dishes served on banana leaves, McD's type atmosphere, but excellent food. **Beirut**, D'Aguilar

St., Central, Tel: 28046611; Central Asian and Lebanese delicacies in 1001 Nights setting. **Singapore Restaurant**, 130-131 Connaught Rd., Central, Tel: 28151566; inexpensive restaurant in mid-range, large selection of meat and fish from Chinese to European. *EUROPEAN*: **M at the Fringe**, 2 Lower Albert Rd., Central, Tel: 28774000; Mediterranean cooking, distinguished atmosphere. **Gaddhis**, Peninsula Hotel, Apt. No. 3989, Salisbury Rd., Tsim Sha Tsui, Tel: 23666251; the French restaurant in this luxury hotel is considered the best in all Asia. **Margaux**, Shangri-La Kowloon, 64 Mody Rd., Tsim Sha Tsui, Tel: 27212111, light French gourmet cuisine, Hong Kong's largest wine selection.

A good tip for a bite in between: Excellent sandwiches, pastries, coffee and freshly-pressed orange juice is available in the branches of **Oliver's Super Sandwich** and **Deli France**.

Nightlife / Culture

If looking for Suzie Wong's daughters, you'll have to go to **Wan Chai**. But beware: A night on town around Luard Rd. and Fenwick St. can mean no more money for shopping the day after. The best address by far for every evening –weekends in particular – is the alley **Lan Kwai Fong** in **Central**. Restaurants, galleries, discothèques and pubs are located here and in neighboring D'Aguilar St., Ice House Rd. and Lower Albert Rd. More refined and quiet is **Felix**, 28/29th floor of the Peninsula Hotel, futuristically decorated by star designer Philippe Stark. **The Jump** has good American cuisine, superb cocktails and more locals than tourists: 7/F Causeway Bay Plaza II, 463 Lockhard Rd., Causeway Bay. Jazz concerts are held in **Dickens' Bar** in the Excelsior Hotel every Sunday; otherwise its a quiet place for a nice chat. Lively and cheery British atmosphere in the **White Stag**, 72 Canton Rd., Tsim Sha Tsui. **Ned Kelly's Last Stand** is at 11A Ashley Rd., live Dixie music every evening.

For a wide range of concerts or theatrical performances, there is always **City Hall**, Edinburg Place, Central, Tel: 29212840. The **Cultural Centre** at the southern tip of Kowloon, Salisbury Rd., Tsim Sha Tsui, Tel: 27342009, presents a broad spectrum of Hong Kong and international artists. Its calendar of events can be found there, in hotels and at the Hong Kong Tourist Association.

Shopping

You must be well-informed, otherwise the city will be more expensive than your home country! Haggling is a must, basically. It is realistic to assume that half the named price is the actual value of the wares you would like to buy, especially with regards to silk and jewelry. The shops of some clothing chains do have fixed prices. Hong Kong is duty-free, so the *name Duty Free Shoppers* is in fact a trademark, and the signs proclaiming *Sale, last three days*, have usually been hanging there for years...

MALLS: **Harbour City**, Canton Rd., the largest single complex of the city, offers international top brands at corresponding prices on three stories. **Pacific Place**, Queen's Rd., Central, services customers with expensive taste in its splendid surroundings. The third place to find fine wares is **Times Square**, Causeway Bay. The **Japanese department stores** display a wide range of international fashions: **Sogo**, 555 Hennessy Rd., Causeway Bay, right near the MTR station. **Seibu** in the Pacific Place, 88 Hennessy Rd., Central.

CLOTHING: The shops in Tsim Sha Tsui and Causeway Bay have a huge selection of inexpensive clothing on offer. Numerous chains, such as **Giordano**, **U2**, **Theme Plus**, **G2000**, **Ballino** and **Crocodile** have a large supply of jeans and other confectionery goods. In addition, there are the international firms, who manufacture their products cheaply in the city. Browsing about **Granville Road** is a good idea, an outlet for surplus wares and cut-outs of the major brands (recognizable from the cut labels). Hunters and gatherers will also find satisfaction at **Stanley Market**. *BEWARE*! No tailor can cut a complete suit in nine hours. Ask your hotel for advice when having a suit made.

LEATHER GOODS, SUITCASES AND HANDBAGS: The shops in Tsim Sha Tsui and Causeway Bay offer an unbelievable array of shoes and handbags or suitcases. The **Mandarin Duck** chain offers two bags for the price of one. The shops of Mong Kok are better priced, because they are somewhat off the beaten path. **Temple Street** also has a large, inexpensive selection. You will frequently find the **Mimeo** brand: bags, suitcases, rucksacks made of artificial materials, but top-quality. The Chinese department stores of the **Yue Hwa chain** also have top-notch suitcases for a bargain – at the Park Galleries in Tsim Sha Tsui, for example.

WATCHES AND JEWELRY: The world price for gold is the same all over, but working the metal is cheaper in Hong Kong. Dropping by a jeweler's is worth it (Tsim Sha Tsui and Causeway Bay). Even the top watch brands are cheaper here, although they still cost quite a lot. Lower prices can be found in the shops of the **City Chain**, which has designer names. Temple Street offers an unfathomable selection of imitations and fashion watches.

MUSIC: The largest selection (classical and jazz as well) is at **HMV**, Peking Rd., Tsim Sha Tsui. **Tower Records**, Shops 701 & 731, Times Square, 1 Matheson St., Causeway Bay, has South Chinese pop music. Large selection of musical instruments: **Tom Lee's Music** in the first side street to the left of Cameron Rd., looking from Nathan Rd.

PHOTOGRAPHY AND ELECTRONICS: If you don't know the local prices for cameras, computers and CD players, be very careful. Besides, when buying, you have to make sure you have a certified world guarantee. No Hong Konger would dream of buying a camera in Tsim Sha Tsui. The best place to shop is on the 7th floor of the **Times Square**, Causeway Bay, and **in Sai Yeung Choi** Street in Mong Kok. On the 3rd floor of the **Ocean Centre**, Canton Rd., Tsim Sha Tsui, you'll find top-notch photo and audio material. **Kimberley Rd**. and **Hankow Rd**. are good sources of used photo material of all brands, both in Tsim Sha Tsui.

SPECS AND CONTACT LENSES: Chains such as **Optical 88** and **Comfort Optical** in Tsim Sha Tsui and Causeway Bay attract customers with their huge array of top-quality material. Be sure to avoid computer analyses of your eyes, the old-fashioned method is still the most precise one. The glasses are usually finished within 20 hours, sometimes even faster. Unusual frames: **Professional**, UG 141-143, China Hong Kong City, 33 Canton Rd., Tsim Sha Tsui. Good consulting: **Colors in Optics**, 8K Humphreys Avenue, Tsim Sha Tsui.

Museums

Flagstaff House Museum of Teaware and **K.S.Lo Gallery**, Hong Kong Park, MTR station Admiralty, daily exc. Wed and holidays 10:00 a.m.-5:00 p.m. **Hong Kong Museum of Art**, at the Cultural Centre, Salisbury Rd., Tsim Sha Tsui, Mon-Wed, Fri-Sat 10:00 a.m.-6:00 p.m., Sun and holidays 1:00-6:00 p.m. **Hong Kong Science Museum**, 2, Science Museum Rd., Tsim Sha Tsui East, Tue-Fri 1:00-9:00 p.m., Sat-Sun 10:00 a.m.-9:00 p.m., hands-on science and technology. **Hong Kong Space Museum**, Salisbury Rd., Tsim Sha Tsui, Mon, Wed-Fri 1:00-9:00 p.m.. **Hong Kong Railway Museum**, On Fu Rd., KCR Tai Po Market station, daily exc. Tue 9:00 a.m.-4:00 p.m., in the old train station, railway history. **Fung Ping Shan Museum**, University of Hong Kong, Bonham Rd., Mon-Sat 9:30 a.m.-6:00 p.m., ceramics, Buddhist sculptures. **Law Uk Folk Museum**, near MTR Chai Wan station, Tue-Sat 10:00 a.m.-6:00 p.m., Sun 10:00 a.m.-2:00 p.m., 200-year-old Hakka house. **Sam Tung Uk Museum**, signposted from MTR Tsuen Wan station, restored village with exhibition of peasant life. **Tsui Museum of Art**, Bank of China Bldg., 11/F 2A Des Voeux Rd., Central, Mon-Fri 10:00 a.m.-6:00 p.m., Sat 10:00 a.m.-2:00 p.m., changing exhibitions, Chinese handicrafts. **Hong Kong Museum of History**, Kowloon Park, Mon-Thu, Sat 10:00 a.m.-6:00 p.m., Sun 1:00-6:00 p.m. **Police Museum**, 27 Coombe Rd., Tue 2:00-5:00 p.m., Wed-Sun 9:00 a.m.-5:00 p.m., history of crime.

Parks

Tiger Balm Garden, Tai Hang Rd., Tai Hang, 9:30 a.m.-4:00 p.m. **Hong Kong Park**, Cotton Tree Dr., Central, 7:00 a.m.-11:00 p.m. **Zoological and Botanical Gardens**, Upper Albert Rd., Central, 6:00 a.m.-6:00 p.m. **Kowloon Park**, Nathan Rd., Central, 6:00 a.m.-midnight. **Ocean Park** and **Middle Kingdom**, Ocean Park Rd., Aberdeen, 10:00 a.m.-6:00 p.m. **Sung Dynasty Village**, Mei Lai Rd., Laichikok, 10:00 a.m.-8:30 p.m., go to MTR Mei Foo station, from there it is signposted; excursion into the days of the Sung Dynasty, information on Chinese handicrafts, music and acrobatics. **Tai Po Kau Nature Reserve**, No. 72 bus from MTR Prince Edward station.

Transportation

The public transportation network is safe, clean and efficient. It generally operates from 6:00 a.m. to midnight, after that rely on taxis. Beware when crossing the street, they drive on the left in Hong Kong.

KOWLOON CANTON RAILWAY KCR: This 21-mile-long (34 km) train track ends near Lo Wu on the Chinese border. There are transfers to China from that point on. The air-conditioned trains leave the main station Hung Hom in Kowloon every 10 minutes.

SUBWAY MTR: MTR stands for Mass Transit Railway, one of the fastest, safest and cleanest systems in the world. Schedules and pricing are easy to read at the ticket machines. The tickets are the size of a credit card. You insert them into a slot at the turnstile, and they come out the other end. Signs lead easily through the tunnels. It's important to make note of the letter combination of the entrance nearest your hotel. It is usually posted at the entrance.

TRAMWAY: An 8-mile (13 km) stretch in the north of Hong Kong Island connects Kennedy Town to Shau Kei Wan. These colorful, double-deckers have been rumbling through the city for 90 years. You get in at the back, and throw your exact fare in a glass box near the driver in the front before getting out. Video filmers should take a seat on the second floor.

PEAK TRAM: A bus shuttles from Central to the ground station in Garden Rd. free of charge. The tram crawls up the mountain in eight minutes. The view from the top is spectacular. The Peak Tram was inaugurated about a century ago, but it has been modernized since.

BUSES: The Star Ferry piers have large bus stations. The individual lines are clearly posted, the proper fare is paid on entering.

TAXIS: Taxis can be flagged down where the street has no double yellow line along its edge. Most cabbies speak English, but it is advisable to let your hotel write your destination in Chinese. The meter is turned on right away, but tolls for the tunnels between the mainland and the island do not appear. The 20 HK$ must be paid extra. If you tell your driver to use the Cross Harbour tunnel as a throughway, you will save yourself a tour of the town; otherwise the (more expensive) ride will go through the Eastern Harbour Cross Tunnel.

STAR FERRY: These green-and-white ships have been shuttling between Kowloon, Central and Wan Chai since 1898. The 2-HK$ first-class fare is dropped into a glass box at the turnstile on boarding.

FERRIES: Ferries to the islands depart at the Star Ferry pier in Central. If taking the cheap ferry to Lantau or Cheung Chau, you won't need the official tour of the harbor. Departures are hourly. The ferry to Lamma leaves from Aberdeen, the one to Macao from Shun Tak Centre (MTR Sheung Wan station). The current ferry schedule is available at hotels and from the Hong Kong Tourist Association.

CITY AND HARBOR TOURS: The Hong Kong Tourist Association at the Star Ferry offers day-long, half-day and evening tours.

GENERAL TRAVEL INFORMATION
Embassies

AUSTRALIA: 23-24/F Harbour Centre, 25 Harbour Rd., Wan Chai, Tel: 28278881. Open Mon-Fri 9:00 a.m.-Noon, 2:00 p.m.-4:00 p.m. *CANADA*: 11/F-14/F, Tower 1, Exchange Square, 8 Connaught Place, Central, Tel: 28104321. Open daily exc. Sun: 8:30 a.m.-12:30 p.m., 1:30-4:00 p.m., closed Wed and Sat afternoons. *NEW ZEALAND*: 27/F, 2705 Jardine House, Central, Tel: 28774488. Open Mon, Wed, Fri 9:00 a.m.-12:45 p.m., 1:45-4:30 p.m., Tue 10:00 a.m.-12:45 p.m., 1:45-4:30 p.m. *USA*: 26 Garden Rd., Central, Tel: 25301190. Open Mon-Fri 8:30 a.m.-12:30 p.m., 1:30-5:30 p.m.

Festivals

Chinese festivals are celebrated according to the lunar calendar, which is why the exact dates can't be determined according to the western solar calendar. The Hong Kong Tourist Association earmarks the following dates: *Beginning of February:* Chinese New Year, 15 days later: Lantern Festival. *Beginning of April:* Birthday of the protective goddess Tin Hau. *May 8th:* Birthday of the weather god Tam Kung and of Buddha. *June 5th:* Dragon Boat Festival in honor of the poet Qu Yuan. *August 15th:* Yue Lan Festival. *September 15th:* The most important date of the year is the Moon Festival. According to tradition, the September moon is supposed to be the only round one. Celebrated with moon cakes and a lantern procession through Wun Sha Street (MTR Tin Hau station). *October 9th:* Ancestor Festival.

Currency Exchange

It's easiest at your hotel. The exchange rate is not so good, but the bank fees usually eat up the profit from the better rate. There are moneychangers at just about every street corner, but their rates are usually very bad. Most shops and restaurants accept the well-known credit cards.

Police / Fines

All policemen have a number on their epaulettes. If the number is underlined in red, the officer speaks English. Emergency police number: 25277177. Smoking, drinking, eating and spitting in the subway can bring a 5000 HK$ fine. All smaller sins and their fines are posted throughout the city.

Emergencies / Doctors / Hospitals

Fire, ambulance, muggings: 999 (toll-free). **Free emergency doctor**: Kowloon: 27135555; Hong Kong Island: 2576655; New Territories: 26392555. **Emergency hospitalization**: *Kowloon*: **Queen Elizabeth Hospital**, 30 Gascoigne Rd., Tel: 27102111; *Hong Kong Island*: **Queen Mary Hospital**, Pokfulam Rd., Tel: 28554111. The most important medication is stocked at the branches of the **Watson** chain, on Nathan Rd., for example.

Telephoning / Post Offices

Prefixes: **USA** and **Canada**. 0011; **Great Britain**: 00144; **Australia** 00161; **New Zealand**: 0064. Phone calls can be made from hotels, the 24-hour 7-11 stores and from the IDD-Centre of Hong Kong Telecom on Middle Rd., Kowloon (near the Sheraton)). It's a bit hidden in a cellar.

Stamps can be purchased at all hotel receptions. **Main Post Office Kowloon**: 405 Nathan Rd., Mon-Fri 9:30 a.m.-6:00 p.m., Sat 9:30 a.m.-1:00 p.m. Main **Post Office Central**: Star Ferry Concourse, Mon-Fri 8:00 a.m.-6:00 p.m., Sat 8:00 a.m.-2:00 p.m.

Tourist Information

Hong Kong Tourist Association Offices abroad: *AUSTRALIA*: Level 4, 80 Druitt St., Sydney, NSW 2000, Australia, Tel: (02) 92833083, Fax: 92833383. *CANADA*: 3rd Floor, Hong Kong Trade Center, 9 Temperance St., Toronto, Ontario M5H 1Y6, Tel: (416) 366-2389, Fax: 366-1098. *NEW ZEALAND*: PO Box 2120, Auckland, New Zealand, Tel: (09) 575 2797, Fax: 575 2620. *UK*: 4th/5th Floors, 125 Pall Mall, London SW1Y 5EA, Tel: (0171) 9304775, Fax: 9304777. *USA*: 5th Floor, 590 Fifth Avenue, New York, NY 10036-4706, Tel: (212) 869-5008, Fax.730-2605. Suite 1220, 10940 Wiltshire Blvd., Los Angeles, CA 90024-3915, Tel: (310) 208-4582, Fax: 208-1869.
Internet address: http://www.hkta.org.
In Hong Kong: **Hong Kong Tourist Association**, 11/F Citicorp Center, 18 Whitfield Rd. Northpoint, Tel: (00852)28076543, Fax: 28060303. **HKTA Information Centre** and souvenir shop in Jardine House, Connaught Place, Central, Mon-Fri 9:00 a.m.-6:00 p.m., Sat 9:00 a.m.-1:00 p.m. Information offices are located at the Star Ferry piers.

PHILOSOPHY AND TABLE ETIQUETTE

When you return from your stay in China and start cooking in your own *wok*, you can happily do this without all the intellectual baggage of Chinese gastronomic philosophy. For "cooking in harmony with the elements" – a concept born of religious convictions, medical experience and "thinking with the stomach" – has created a highly complex hierarchy of bodily organs, seasons, elements and a harmonizing of tastes and energies. This fabric is all the harder for outsiders to understand because cooking ingredients are also organized according to color, taste, consistency, shape and even the depth at which they grow in the ground.

What would a Chinese *maître de cuisine* recommend on an ice-cold winter's night in Harbin to a shivering citizen suffering from a spleen complaint? Obviously: a hot dish of dog-meat with steamed carrots, some ginger and honey.

The majority of Chinese have subconsciously inherited a basic knowledge of this method of combining different energies. For the most part, however, they allow their cookery to be guided by the harmony of contrasting flavors: mild and spicy, sweet and sour, bitter and salty. Courses also have to alternate between vegetables, meat and fish.

Is China really a Land of Plenty? Emphatically not, if one thinks of the hardship brought about, throughout its history, by rebellions, mass emigration and the Communist revolution of 1949. These wretched conditions still prevail today in many parts of China, which, admittedly, are unlikely to be seen by tourists. Yet China *is* a Land of Plenty, for Chinese cuisine is the "art of making wealth out of poverty." The lack of arable land, the density of population and short-

Right: Noodles are the secret of long life – a cook at the summer palace in Chengde.

age of energy resources have combined to produce a culture which makes a virtue out of necessity: it is energy-efficient because it is based on cooking things quickly. Baking-ovens, which are so wasteful of energy, are hardly known in China, and so bread that can be stored is not known either. This means that Chinese cooking is very healthy. The food does not have all the nutrients cooked out of it; and the fresh colors are also preserved to delight the eye and arouse the appetite. What is more, poverty has imposed a frugal approach to food, with a a predominantly plant-based diet of rice, wheat and vegetables.

Eating, and developing the palate, are the most fundamental sensual gratifications of the human species, a phenomenon which has led to the pithy traditional saying: "The way to a man's heart is through his stomach." For the peoples of Asia, eating is a celebration of sensual delight and togetherness.

Eating is not a solitary activity: In a restaurant, the Chinese prefer to eat at round tables. This obliges people to communicate, while everyone can easily help himself from the dishes on the rotating "lazy Susan" in the middle of the table. Communal eating is not only more fun, it increases the number of dishes which all the diners can sample. Locals smile pityingly at the groups of western visitors, each of them sitting in front of her "own" separate meal. A lavish dinner can consist of more than a dozen courses served one after the other; for more meager meals, the dishes are all brought to the table at once. The number of courses is normally calculated as the number of diners plus one. Rice is the last thing to be served, so as to avoid giving the impression that you are supposed to fill yourself up with it.

Culinary etiquette: If you should be invited to a meal as an honored guest, sit beside your host – the principal guest on his right and facing the door, for reasons

of "security." If you are placed opposite your host (with your back to the door), this unfortunately means that you have not been shown the proper esteem.

The host's invitation, "Qing!" ("please!") is meant to convey the conuite admission that this pitiful meal is certainly an insult to your palate. Since the table will be groaning under the weight of mouth-watering delicacies, you are naturally expected to protest enthusiastically to the contrary. The rituals continue as follows: the host encourages the guest of honor to help himself. When the latter holds back modestly, the host presents him with a generous plateful. With equal politeness you should then place a small portion of food on the plate of the dinner-guest sitting next to you, before you help yourself – always remembering to make the mental calculation of how much to take (amount of food divided by number of diners).

The table will be laid with rice-bowls, plates, porcelain soup-spoons and chopsticks. Next time you are in a Chinese restaurant at home, take a look at how awkwardly supposedly cosmopolitan diners handle their chopsticks. In fact, eating with these is really quite simple. All you have to do is remember that one stick is *fixed* and the other *moves*.

With the cutlery provided (or failing that, with your chopsticks) you fill your plate from the various dishes or else put small pieces of meat or vegetables directly on top of the rice in the deep bowl. If you help yourself from the dishes with your chopsticks, you must remember to make the polite gesture of placing the portion of food briefly on your own plate before putting it into your mouth. If you are right-handed, you should lift the rice-bowl with your left hand and shovel the rice into your mouth with your chopsticks. It is not at all elegant – a fact often misunderstood in the west – to perform the awkward balancing act of carrying the food the furthest possible distance from plate to mouth.

Unpleasant experiences: Many table habits of the Chinese strike their western

fellow-diners as rather distasteful. But is simply the fact that the Chinese behave in rigorously practical manner – rather like Columbus and the egg. They see no point in daintily peeling prawns or extracting crab-meat from its shell. With one hearty crunch, they separate the edible from the inedible with gusto and then spit the shells out on to their plate. The same separation process is performed with fish-bones. And you will not infrequently see Chinese using toothpicks and then spitting out the remains of food on to the floor.

A consequence of the Cultural Revolution, and one which some foreign visitors to China may well second enthusiastically, was a contempt for the table manners of the so-called "upper crust." Except for blowing your nose loudly – which should definitely be avoided at table – you can basically do anything you feel like doing. However, you should surreptitiously model your behavior on that

Above: It's not but difficult to eat with chopsticks (Shaghai).

of your neighbor at table. One thing which is not merely allowed but actually recommended is noisily slurping your soup, tea and noodles. This custom pays audible tribute to the sensual experience of eating and drinking and introduces an atmosphere of well-being.

Rounding off the meal: If you should try to show your Chinese host, by cleaning your plate, how delicious you found the meal, your intended compliment will be taken as an insult: nothing is more shameful to a host than the impression that his lack of generosity has left you less than fully satisfied. Courtesy demands that you should always leave a little on your plate, "for Mr Manners," as we used to say in the old days.

Saying goodbye to your host after a private invitation also follows a prescribed formula. Your host will accompany you not just to the door, but into the street, to the car-park, the next corner or bus stop, unless you dissuade him by repeating the words "Bu yao song!" ("You don't have to come with me!"). The polte host will finally exhort your to take care as you go home: "Man man zou!" "Go slowly!").

And after a restaurant meal, who picks up the tab? If no one has specifically offered to treat the others, then a violent but contrived fight breaks out after a meal as to who should have the privilege of paying the bill. However, the person who really intends to pay will already have quietly slipped away to settle up at the desk. But he is usually caught and a friendly war of words begins again. The victor is not the most gifted orator, but the one whose turn it proves to be according to some unspoken system of reckoning. So you should not try to exploit this charming ritual in your favor. Next time you must insist on your "right to pay." When the western members of a dinner party try to split the check and pay their own share, Chinese faces look glum.

GAINING FACE AND FRIENDS

Since tourism has become an important source of foreign currency for many developing countries, the populations of these "afflicted" countries have often developed a sullen toleration of foreigners, whom they regard as "useful idiots" or "hard currency barbarians." Hence, things that start out as minor misunderstandings in custom can often lead to mutual culture shock. Our little "ABC of good behavior" is intended to help you develop an understanding of Chinese manners and mores, to avoid committing crass social blunders, and so to gain both "face" and sympathy. If you come away from China with the knowledge that a straight line is not always the quickest way of joining two points, then you will give some satisfaction to our friend and mentor Kuan Yu-Chien from Shanghai, who lives in Europe and has provided valuable suggestions for this chapter.

Arrogance: Lu Xun, the most celebrated Chinese poet of the 20th century, gives, in his story *Ah Q*, a sharply ironic account of the traditional combination of ignorance and arrogance in which the Chinese are still trapped. What makes the Chinese so self-satisfied is their pride in their cultural heritage. In the *Kingdom of the Middle*, they believe, lies the cradle of human culture and civilization. Chinese who visit India, Egypt, Greece and Italy often react with baffled amazement at the discovery of other cultures as sophisticated as their own. The almost arrogant pride in their past – as well as in what has been preserved to the present day – compensates for the feeling of inferiority experienced by the people of a developing country when faced with the enormous technological lead which the west and Japan have gained over them. So, when you visit China, you should be aware of this gulf and not be tempted into the slightest condescension, however well-intentioned it might be. If difficulties arise, you must show patience and understanding and concentrate on areas of agreement and common interest.

Beards: In former times, men who had become grandfathers were proud to grow some hair on their chins. It earned them the respect accorded to the old. So if any bearded foreigners with fair hair (which looks white to a Chinese) travel through China, they must expect to have "Grandpa" shouted after them by children. At the very least, Chinese will have difficulty in judging your age and therefore the correct behavior to adopt towards you.

Business contacts: The great difference between the Chinese and western economic systems, and thus between our respective concepts of responsibility and management structure, make any negotiations between Chinese and western parties difficult from the start. Added to this are conflicting social values: whereas western expressions like "getting down to business" and "talking turkey" are meant to appear dynamic and purposeful, they simply throw the Chinese into a state of shock. For them the preliminaries are just as important as the main event (i.e. the signing of a contract). The preliminaries include a mutual "warm-up" such as having a meal together and discussing personal matters, enquiring about the family of your Chinese colleague or the opportunities for his daughter to study abroad. The guiding principle is not: "Let's get business over with and then enjoy ourselves," but rather: "Let us create harmony, and the rest will follow naturally." A most important motto for business survival in China is not the Cartesian *cogito ergo sum*, but rather *cartulam habeo ergo sum* ("I have a card, therefore I am"). As a business executive in China, you are nobody unless you can hand out plenty of business cards, preferably printed in Chinese on one side, which indicate your status in your company or profession.

Cleanliness: It is likely that you will find both the toilets and the spittoons in China pretty disgusting. Though the Chinese are careful about personal hygiene, they still leave their toilets in a mess. Frequent complaints by tourists have led to public discussions, though not to any improvement. The only advice we can give is that you take toilet-paper with you, and in remote country districts seek out some secluded spot when nature calls. Spitting is something else. If the person opposite you drives you crazy with his noisy throat-clearing and spitting on the floor or into a spittoon, you can get rid of him by blowing your nose loudly in a handkerchief.

Compliments, exaggeration and understatement: There is some truth to the Western stereotype that orientals love flowery hyperbole. While the Chinese may be given to understatement when referring to themselves, they are unstinting in their praise of others. Should you attempt to put our mini-language guide (see p. 250) into practice, your linguistic gifts will be praised to the heavens. The more you demur, the more insistent will be the compliments.

Criticism: Being critical can cause bad feeling in China. The political campaigns of *Criticism and Self-criticism* have, since 1949, left behind deep social and psychological traumas. Even though a Chinese may be content to hide his light under a bushel and jokingly belittle himself, he will not accept criticism of any kind except from members of his immediate family. To be criticized – especially in front of others – means to lose face. If you really must criticize someone, then do it discreetly and disguise it as praise. Positive criticism means focussing on people's good points, showing sympathy if someone is under pressure and endeavoring to find mutually acceptable solutions to practical problems. When talking to friends and acquaintances, keep your criticism of conditions in China to yourself – even if you're talking about the bureaucracy, which is universally despised by all Chinese.

Curiosity: As the sight of foreign travelers becomes more familiar to the Chinese, they are less likely to gather in curious groups around every "long-nose." Nevertheless, you should accept with good grace the fact that – in remote districts especially – you possess a high entertainment value, particularly if you are fair-haired, bearded and have a long, aristocratic nose. In conversation, Chinese often demonstrate a friendly curiosity, which is not surprising, as the country has been cut off from the world for decades. You should not be offended, even as a woman, to be asked your age: for to be old is to be honored. Nor should you be inhibited in admitting what you earn. If you are a dentist, for instance, you can explain your income in relation

Right: The Chinese are passionate gamesmen (Chongqing, Sichuan).

:o the long years of training and heavy expenses. If you are a single person traveling alone and are asked about your children, do not try to extol the virtues of your independence. It is better to invent a few offspring, otherwise you will be subjected to Chinese efforts to convert you.

Dress: Many people still have a vision of China teeming with blue-overalled workers and grey-tunic'd functionaries. But for a long time now it has not just been the children who are colorfully turned out. In Shanghai, designers are producing fashions which not many years ago would have been reviled as "bourgeois decadence." Today, conservatives merely describe the racy Shanghai style as "foolish." However, practical necessity, shortage of energy and extremes of climate have meant the preservation of the traditional Chinese "onion-skin" system, which is adapted to changing seasons. As it gets colder, handknitted long-johns are put on over the long cotton underwear, two layers of long-sleeved undershirts are augmented by a pullover, over which a shirt and jacket are buttoned. As summer approaches, layer after layer of the "onion" is peeled off – with a remarkable lack of inhibition. Men often roll their trousers up to the knee and their undervest up to the armpits, while the women have no compunction about hitching up their skirts to keep cool. A peculiarly Chinese fashion for little children is the "bare-bottom decollté," since disposable diapers are still unknown on the Chinese market.

Eroticism and prudery (see also Physical Contact): On the one hand, there's stern Confucianism with its paternalistic repression of women, symbolized by the binding of feet. On the other, there's the liberal folk-culture of the "barefoot" country women, as well as ribald *bride-books* and unashamedly erotic literature. These contradictions persist to this day. The ideal of chastity contrasts with the lively demand for "yellow," under-the-counter literature – mostly hard and soft pornography from Hong Kong. Foreigners who are caught bring-

ing in dubious (or pornographic) material will incur official wrath.

Friendship: Having friends in a foreign country can open doors to the life and culture of its people. But striking up friendship with Chinese in China is not without its dangers, particularly if your are traveling on a journalistic or diplomatic assignment, and more so if the friendship is with the opposite sex. Therefore you should allow your Chinese acquaintance to decide if and to what extent the friendship should develop and deepen. You should also remember that Chinese may have an ulterior motive in making contact with a foreigner, such as arranging a stay in a western country.

Gesture and mime: When your knowledge of the spoken language fails, you have to resort to sign-language. But here, too, problems of comprehension can arise: the Chinese, for example, have

a different way of counting on their fingers. For 10, they simply cross their index fingers. Shrugging tshoulders or spreading out arms means nothing to a Chinese. On the other hand, do not feel insulted if he sticks his tongue out at you – it is merely an expression of embarrassment. If you want to beckon to friends, children or waiters, do it with the palm of the hand facing down and fingers folded inwards. Pointing at someone is not insulting in China (as it is in Southeast Asia, for example); however, it is more polite to use the whole outstretched hand.

Hassle and patience: One of the elements of the Chinese philosophy of harmony is patience. But it is necessary for more mundane reasons: the sheer density of population, economic shortages, bureaucratic inefficiency and rigidity. When you return from China you will notice, hopefully, that your internal clock is running more slowly, and your biorhythm has a steadier rate. Yet every virtue has its negative side. Admittedly the Chinese, unlike many southeast Asian races, do

Above: Family life provides security (Picnic in the imperial palace, Peking).

ot go berserk when their patience is overtaxed. Nevertheless, their behavior when they try to crowd on to buses or trains may well give the impression of something like mass hysteria.

Modesty: In the west, modesty is regarded as an outmoded virtue. This is not the case in China. Even today the Confucian and Taoist virtue of self-effacement is still valued, even though it may have been terrifyingly perverted by Communist propaganda campaigns. The host disparages the meal before you sit down to eat; the highly-qualified scientist derides his own incompetence before starting a lecture; the successful novelist invites criticism in his foreword. Needless to say, courtesy requires you to contradict such Chinese modesty. It is true that, when asked how you like China, you should certainly not reply: "Worthless as I am, I defile the ground which gave birth to the greatest culture of mankind!" Nevertheless, modesty will increase your standing, rather than cause a loss of face.

Noise: The violinist Yehudi Menuhin once claimed that we all have a "right to silence." Maybe the idea came to him on a visit to China. The Chinese, on the other hand, often find central and northern Europe uncomfortably quiet. The sounds which go to make up the Chinese cacophony include the hooting of car-horns, the tinkling of bicycle-bells, the clatter of pieces in a *Mah-Jong* game, people shouting down telephones, women scolding their neighbors, radios blaring... Only the children seem quiet.

Physical contact: Whereas homosexuality is completely tabu in China it is perfectly natural for familiarity and even tenderness to be displayed openly between people of the same sex. Young women and men go strolling hand in hand, or with their arms around each other, patting, nudging and punching each other playfully. Even older people show affection when talking to someone of the same sex, for example by plucking a hair from the other person's shoulder, constantly touching them or twisting a button on their jacket – all of which would be forbidden between people of different sexes, but... In the big cities the younger generation does show heterosexual affection, even in public. The gestures of tenderness which the rebellious young, in their teens and twenties, exchange in the parks of Shanghai are already well up to western "standards." But probably the most beautiful thing to see is the physical bond between mothers and their babies, wrapped up and firmly tied to their backs. Many western parents would give anything for their children to demonstrate such relaxed contentment.

Politeness: The Communist revolutionaries were right to challenge many traditional rules of behavior, manners and customs. Yet in the end these were replaced by a "cult of the proletariat," which crudely dismissed as "bourgeois decadence" all the civilized conventions of behavior that oil the wheels of social contact and make life more pleasant for everyone. The more rough-and-ready you were, the more it proved your proletarian and revolutionary credentials. After the Cultural Revolution it was necessary, for practical reasons, to mount a campaign to rehabilitate courtesy. Many members of the Red Guard had forgotten how to say "thank you." In the Chinese bureaucracy and in state-owned business the campaigns seem to have had no effect whatever. Their idea of service makes life just as difficult for the Chinese as for foreigners. The words "Mei you" ("we don't have any") will soon become part of every foreigner's vocabulary.

Smiling and laughing: The oriental smile is said to be mysterious and inscrutable, even erotic in a woman. This impression may be correct in some Asiatic countries (the Thais, for instance, laugh to conceal mental anguish). But Chinese today use the same facial expressions as we do to convey their feelings.

GUIDELINES

A word of warning

As the Greeks used to say:*Panta rhei* ("everything flows on") – and nowhere more so than in China. Modern technology is being introduced, and a dazzling range of long absent services and facilities are being brought back on stream. Telephone networks are being renewed. Travel timetables are being revised, hotels built, road networks expanded... Under these circumstances it is obviously difficult to provide the traveler with reliable information. Official Chinese sources of "the most up-to-date information" are, as you are told with a disarming smile, certainly not to be taken literally. So it has been left to our authors to use their tracker instincts, bush-telegraph and extensive fax enquiries to collect whatever is avaible by way of concrete information, even though its accuracy cannot be guaranteed.

PREPARATIONS

Climate / travel seasons

Most western travelers, used to the relatively temperate climes of Europe or North America, must remember that China covers an area of continental magnitude and has corresponding extremes of climate. You must expect astonishing differences and some surprising similarities. While the average January temperature in Harbin is -19°C., in Canton it climbs to +13°C. On the other hand, in July the temperature both in Canton and Harbin is around 35°C – but in the south it is humid, and in the north the air is dry.

The optimum season for traveling is in October and November, before the Siberian cold has arrived in the north, but after the tropical monsoon storms have calmed down. Failing this, you must limit your tour to a region which has the best weather at the time of year when you plan to be in China.

What to wear

In China the old proverb "clothes make the man" simply does not apply. It is true that the once politically correct "blue ant" uniform of the Cultural Revolution has given way to a colorful variety of fashions, which in Shanghai can border on the extravagant; but in general dress style is tailored to comfort and practicality. People do not even "dress up" to go to a concert or theater. The only chance for a woman to wear her chic "little black number" let alone a full evening outfit, is in the luxury hotels. You are better advised to pack lots of comfortable, easy-care clothes. Loose-fitting garments in natural fibers help you to tolerate the summer heat – but come armed with a pullover to combat the overly effective air-conditioning. The very cold winters in northern China make warm clothing essential, and even in the south the cool, damp winter air (though seldom below 10° C) is uncomfortable if you are not wearing a jacket or pullover. The "Longnoses" with their open-necked shirts and revealing cleavages attract a great deal of interest among the Chinese.

Health precautions

Unless you are entering China from countries with endemic diseases, you are not required to have **innoculations** against yellow fever, typhus, cholera or smallpox. Nevertheless, anyone traveling to South China during the summer, should have these injections – and also take anti-malaria medication – after consulting your doctor. In any event it is advisable to have anti-tetanus injections, in case you injure yourself, and take gammaglobulin to strengthen your resistance to liver infections. Your luggage should include a small traveling pharmacy: with medication for chills, colds and gastroenteritis, analgesics, disinfectant ointment, plasters, bandages, sun-protection cream and perhaps a general-purpose antibiotic.

Entry requirements / Visa

To travel to the People's Republic of China you need a visa, which you obtain either from the **consular section of the Chinese embassy** in your home country. Some international airports (Haikou/Hainan, for example) offer a "visa upon landing." Beijing provides such a visa only if you have an invitation from a Chinese business partner. If you are traveling in a group, the tour operator will take care of all the formalities. Your passport must have six months validity beyond the expiry-date of your visa. The visa itself is normally valid for 90 days. However, you may renew it twice, for a further 30 days each time, at the **Office of Public Security** (*gongan ju*) which can be found in every city in China.

Currency and exchange

The national currency in China is the *Renminbi (RMB)*, also known as the *Yuan* or, in popular parlance, the *Kuai*. The *Yuan* is divided into 10 *Jiao* or 100 *Fen*. You may bring foreign currency into China, either in cash or as travelers-checks.

Meanwhile, most large hotels and Friendship Shops accept credit-cards, as do most branches of the Bank of China, which you will find in all towns and cities, and in many large hotels and Friendship Shops. When you leave China, you can convert your *FECs* back into any chosen hard currency (on presentation of your original receipt).

GETTING THERE

By air

Now that China's tourism is so far developed, it is served by many foreign airlines. A number of these offer flights not only to Peking, but also to Shanghai, Canton, Guilin, Dalian, Hainan, Kunming, Lhasa and Ürümqi. Hong Kong has long been the favorite jumping-off point for visitors to mainland China, especially if you are including it in a tour of Southeast Asia.

By train

FROM HONG KONG: The Hong-Kong – Canton Express leaves Hong Kong's Hunghom terminus (in Kowloon) at roughly 2-hourly intervals. You can buy tickets at the station on the day of your departure.

ON THE TRANS-SIBERIAN VIA MANCHURIA: Like the Orient Express, the Trans-Siberian Railroad from Moscow to Vladivostok (with branches to China) is wreathed in a nostalgic aura of luxury, far-away places and a sense that something amazing will happen to you. It is probably for this very reason that the luxury class is usually booked up months ahead. Specific equipment for the Trans-Siberian trip includes a track-suit, aspirin (for vodka hangovers), toilet-paper and (for photographers) an ice-scraper, window-cleaning liquid and a cloth. Specialized tour-operators will, for a fee, arrange reservations and visas for independent travelers. The Russian route runs north and east of Mongolia and down through Manchuria. The trains are considered to be less clean and comfortable than the Chinese ones. The journey lasts nearly a week.

...AND VIA MONGOLIA: The Chinese Trans-Siberian trains run through Mongolia, where it is well worth breaking your journey for some excursions. The issue of visas has recently been made considerably easier thanks to the efforts of various tour-operators. You should apply in the first instance to the embassy of the Mongolian People's Republic in your home country.

By ship

FROM HONG KONG: Every day at 9pm a comfortable night ferry leaves Hongkong (China Ferry Terminal, Kowloon) for **Canton** (arriving 7am the next morning). A hydrofoil also leaves from

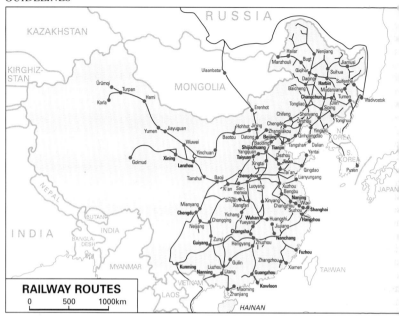

RAILWAY ROUTES

0   500   1000km

the same pier (journey-time: 3 hours). There are other connections by ship to **Shanghai**, **Shantou**, **Xiamen**, **Wuzhou** and **Hainan**.

FROM MACAO: The overnight ferry to Canton sails from Pier 14 in Macao's Inner Harbor and docks at the Zhoutou-zui Pier in Canton. The trip along the light-spangled coast of Macao and into the Pearl River – like the voyage from Hongkong – is an altogether delightful experience.

Via the Karakorum Highway

The **Karakorum Highway**, completed in 1986, takes you through mountain scenery of astounding beauty, up the historic Indus Valley and over the Khunjerab Pass (15,400 ft/4700m) into China – then on to the Silk Road. The pass is closed during the winter months and in periods of political unrest, as occurred in 1990 in Kaxgar (Kashgar). The Chinese Embassy in Pakistan (Islamabad, Ramna 4) issues visas within 24 hours. Overland buses depart from Rawalpindi.

TRAVELING WITHIN CHINA

By air

Air China is the official international and internal airline of China. Smaller regional airlines, which have ostensibly been created to generate competition, are in reality very much under the wing of the big bird. (Previously Air China was called *CAAC* – which, people said, stood for "Chinese Airline Always Cancels" – and it had a very bad reputation among tourists for overcrowding and delays as well as cancellations). However, its safety standards are reckoned to be adequate. Since the airline has become a commercial corporation, foreign passengers have to allow for a doubling of fares.

By train

Socialist China makes no distinction between **carriage classes**, but some modes of ing are – as George Orwell might have said – more equal than others. There is the following choice of caegories: hard seats (*ying zuo*) and soft seats (*ruan zuo*), hard bunks (*ying wo*) and soft beds (*ruan wo*). The *Ruanzuo* carriage class is usuall*/* only provided on short journeys. The *Ruanwo* category consists of separate 4-bed compartments, while the harder bunks are found in open compartments for six people. The Chinese **railroad network** (see map) covers more than 37,500 miles (60,000 km), of which admittedly only about one-tenth is electrified. The **state of the toilets** often gives cause for complaint; so be sure to bring toilet-paper and anti-septic wipes with you. **Restaurant-cars** are provided on long journeys. In order to avoid the frustration of standing in a long line at ticket-booths and a life-and-death struggle for the non-reservable hard seats, you should **buy your ticket and make your seat-reservation** at your hotel, at the CITS or at the foreigners' ticket counter in large stations.

By bus

Places which are not served by rail can usually be reached by bus. The bus-stations for overland routes (*changtu qichezhan*) are usually to be found on the main roads leading out of town in the relevant directions. The seats are numbered and therefore must be booked well in advance. Sometimes the buses stop at restaurants where you can get out to eat and (on long journeys) they make night stops at modest hotels. The driving technique of these Chinese "Kings of the Road" is little short of homicidal: the bus-drivers fling their creaking vehicles around the countryside with complete abandon, accompanied by a horn concerto in every idiom, from Heavy Metal to Mozart's *Eine Kleine Nachtmusik*. This is augmented by the din of voices inside the bus.

Local transport

Local buses: If you appreciate the British discipline of forming an orderly line, you are in for a rude awakenening in China. The Chinese will stop at nothing to get aboard one of the chronically over-crowded city buses. Whereas, a few years ago, foreigners were still treated with respect, today they are swept along by the thundering herd. Should you disdain to join the vulgar fray, you will be standing at the bus-stop all day. If you are not familiar with the (very low) fares, just hold out your hand to the bus-conductor with a few coins in it. If you have been able to make clear to him your desired destination, he will usually tell you when you have reached the correct stop. Maps of the city and its bus-routes can be bought everywhere, even from street-traders.

Cycling: Cynics describe the lungs of Chinese cyclists as catalytic converters for the exhaust-fumes of the cars. In spite of the polluted air and and lowly status in traffic, where might is right, cycling does give one a high degree of flexibility, though parking can be a real problem even for bikers. Random parking is not permitted; and even if it were, for security reasons it is advisable to tether your metal steed in a supervised stall. When you rent a bicycle (often possible at your hotel) you will be required to leave a deposit either in the form of your passport or cash.

Taxis: Taxis (*chuzuche*) will pick up passengers who hail them on the street. If the car is not fitted with a taximeter, negotiate a fare before you start, to avoid unpleasant surprises. Your hotel reception can tell you approximately what a journey should cost. Officially registered taxis display the kilometer price on a sticker on the rear doors. Taxis can also be hired by the hour or day.

Many tourists feel uncomfortable about being carried in a pedal-rickshaw, and this form of human-powered taxi was, until recently, banned in the People's Republic. However, commercial necessity has overcome any sensitivity about former colonial oppression.

PRACTICAL TIPS

Accommodation

We have tried, in the Guidepost features at the end of each chapter, to list hotels by classification. The luxury-class hotels are usually joint ventures with an international hotel chain – but some are old-fashioned establishments whose service is still excellent. The borderline between the "mid-price" and "budget" hotels is often rather fluid, since the sleeping accommodation can range from a suite to a dormitory.

In rural areas – especially near religious monuments or beauty-spots – simple inns, temples or monasteries take foreign guests. But they do not always provide bed-linen, which means that independent travelers should always bring a sleeping-bag.

Alcohol

In China the partaking of alcohol is not limited to furtive drinks in the bars of privileged international hotels. Only in Muslim regions is there a restriction on the sale of alcohol. Classsical Chinese literature is peopled with convivial philosophers whose motto is *in vino veritas*. However, you should be aware that the most popular Chinese wines are not made from grapes but from rice, and are drunk warm from little porcelain cups. Also: the alcoholic strength of rice wine is higher than ordinary wine. Cheep Chinese wine made from grapes is sweet and comparable with port or a liqueur; many of these wines are also fortified with herbs and have "medicinal" (OK, aphrodisiac) properties. Meanwhile, the Chinese produce dry wines of acceptable quality. The Qingdao (Tsingtao) beer is known as "German" beer, and was first produced by a German master-brewer in the colony in 1903. It is made with spark-ling spring water and is exceptionally refreshing. *Maotai* is a firewater distilled from wheat and sorghum, and foreign greenhorns are exhorted by the Chinese to gulp it dow; ("gan bei!") – which invariably bring tears to their eyes!

Business hours

Banks, CITS offices, governmental es tablishments, public facilities (museums zoos, parks, cultural monuments), shop and restaurants, all keep such differen business hours, often further varyin; from season to season and city to city that here we can do no more than refe; your to the Guidepost sections and tc **core times**, when you will hopefully no be frustrated by the notorious *xiuxi* (midday break) or *xiabanle* (evening closing time). This core time begins betweer 8am and 9am, stops between 11.30am and 12.30am for a 2-hour break (which may only be one hour in winter, or as much as 3 hours in high summer), and finishes between 5pm and 6pm.

If only it were that simple: Sunday is normally a day off, but some shops and businesses, including the Friendship Shops and the CITS offices open in the morning, and close on Wednesday afternoons instead. Parks, zoos and other public facilities are also open on Sundays and well into the evening on most weekdays... State-owned restaurants usually close at 8pm or 9pm, though private establishments show greater flexibility.

Customs duty

When you enter China you must fill in **Health** and **Customs Declarations**. You keep a copy of the customs declaration, to be presented when you leave the country. It lists the valuables (jewelry, cameras etc) that you are bringing in with you. If you are checked, especially as an independent traveler, when you leave China, the items you carry must match those on the list. *If* you are examined, and *if* some of your valuables are missing and *if* you are suspected of having sold them for profit – then it *may* happen that you are obliged to pay duty on them. There is

ban on the import of pornography, weapons, drugs and any material harmful to
state interests. Antiques may only be ex-
ported with a certificate, and the same is
true for rare plants and animals.

Electricity

Electrical equipment such as hairdriers
or shavers, that you bring with you, can
be used in China. The current in hotels is
220 V/50 Hertz. Sometimes the variation
in socket-types makes it necessary to use
adapters, which the hotel reception
usually keeps available.

Festivals and holidays

The opening up of minority regions to
tourism has brought their colorful festivals to the attention of travelers. The
overseas tourist offices of the People's
Republic will send you three free bro-
chures about festivals and other events:
China –The Major Festivals (in color);
Major Events (listing); *Chinese Folk Festivals* (in color). Here we only list the
Han-Chinese festivals and holidays
which are held throughout the country:

New Year's Day (in the solar calendar)
1st January, a day off work.

Spring Festival (in the lunar calendar,
the date varies from year to year). In
1994, 10th February, 3 days off work.

Lantern Festival (*yuanxiao jie*), 1994:
24th February, end of the New Year celebrations.

Labor Day (*laodong jie*), 1st May.

Qinming Festival, 1994: 15th May, festival in memory of the dead.

Birthday of Buddha, 1994 25th May.

Dragon-boat Festival (*duanwu jie*),
1994: 13th June.

Moon Festival (*zhongqiu jie*), 1993 1st
September.

National Holiday (*guoqing jie*) 1st October.

Birthday of Confucius, 1993: End of
September.

Song Hanyi Festival (*song hanyi jie*),
1993: 14th November, ancestor festival.

Independent travelers

The most comfortable way to discover
China is with a tour group. You travel as
if on a magic carpet and at nights you
sleep on an oriental divan. But even if
you go independently, your trip can be
easy and stress-free, if you take one of
the full packages or mini-packages offered by various travel companies. In this
way, either the complete arrangemnts or
the basic elements of your tour are prepared and booked for you. If, however,
you decide to go entirely under your own
steam, you must prepared to "sit around
drinking tea" a lot, and also learn to stam-
mer a few fragmentary phrases of
Chinese. Be prepared for the fact that organizing transport and accommodation
will present difficulties and require flexibility on your part – but most of all it will
take a lot of time.

If the attraction of a journey to China
consists for you in escaping just once
from the trip-hammer routine of your
working life, then this improvised style
of ing may well give you a lot of fun; you
will share more directly the pain and
pleasure of everyday life in China and be
able more easily to establish contact with
the people. Apart from this, the local offices of **CITS** (China International
Travel Service, in Chinese: *lüxingshe*) or
OTC (Overseas Tourist Corporation) are
at the disposal even of "unbooked" independent travelers – though they make a
charge for bookings.

Pharmacies (chemists) and medical emergencies

Most large hotels provide their own
emergency medical service, or will arrange for a doctor to see you. In the big
cities medical standards are high. Beijing, Shanghai and Canton even have hospital departments for foreigners. Because
of an overanxiety to give foreigners the
best treatment, you may find that the doc-
tors will indiscriminately prescribe anti-
biotics for every little ache or pain.

Pharmacies in China are, thanks to the long pharmaceutical tradition of the country, real funds of eastern and western medical knowledge. If you speak no Chinese, however, this rich store will generally remain inaccessible to you. This throws you back on the resources of your travel-kit of medication and/or an English-speaking doctor.

Photography and filming

The Chinese are pleased if their well-scrubbed children arouse the interest of a tourist with a still- or movie-camera. But the parents themselves like to be asked before being immortalised on film. One reason for this reticence is that, for them, photos are not just happy snaps, but are meant to represent an "ideal portrait."

Photgraphing military installations is forbidden. At religious sites the limits of what is permitted depend either on formal notices or your own sensitivity.

Post and telephones

Sending mail from China presents no problems since, in addition to the local post-offices, most tourist hotels have postal counters, where helpful advice is available. Your dispatch will be speeded on its way if you can write the destination country on it in Chinese script – see the names of countries in the mini language course at the end of this section. The international post-offices in the big cities have *poste-restante* counters. All larger hotels have recently installed fax machines. Many also provide international direct-dialling facilities via satellite. Getting long-distance connections within China is very time-consuming. Even when making calls within a city, the voice at the other end often sounds so distant that the speaker feels obliged to bellow into the mouthpiece to be heard. This peculiar form of communication always starts with the gruff and abrupt word "Wei!" ("Hallo!") with which calls are answered.

Restaurants

When Chinese have a meal they need no candle-light and whispered intimacies to create a mood. For them the act of eating – preferably in company – is an experience in itself. For this reason Chinese restaurants, especially the state-owned eating establishments, display all the charm of a neon-lit gymnasium. Yet everyone is enjoying themselves. The smaller private restaurants usually look more comfortable, the service is faster and more friendly and the food usually better, but when the bill arrives, they quite often take foreign customers for mugs. If you think that the figure exceeds any tacitly agreed allowance for your superior purchasing-power, you should calmly ask for a detailed listing and a comparison with the menu. In really hair-raising cases, where there is no common ground, you should threaten to call the Office of Public Order (*gongan ju*).

Security

The new "discreet charm of the bourgeoisie" is making itself felt in China, not least through its much less agreeable side-effect – namely, crime. The days are, alas, long gone when the more zealous socialist citizens would go to great lengths to reunite the foreign tourist with his dropped handkerchief. But harsh punishments – especially for offences against foreigners – seem to be effective in China. The country is known for being comparatively safe. Nevertheless, pick-pockets are active, particularly in Friendship Shops. Any woman who has ever ridden on the subway in Mexico City will feel as safe in China as on her mother's lap. In Muslim regions, however, women should always dress in way that is appropriate to the moral conventions of Islam.

Shopping

SHOPPING OPPORTUNITIES: The small shops in hotels are limited to kiosk-type stocks (cigarettes, drinks, postcards, toiletries, camera film etc). The **Friendship Shops** (*youyi shandian*), which are also designed for tourists, offer a mixture of imported goods and "typically" Chinese souvenirs such as silk, jade, printing-blocks and porcelain. The shop staff will, for a considerable fee, handle the packing, customs clearance and dispatch. The attraction of the state-owned **department-stores** is that they often have a wider range – and are cheaper – than the Friendship Shops. In the open-air street markets there are no fixed prices. Here you can put your bazaar technique to the test by haggling. As well as imported goods from Hong Kong, you will find everyday articles, often made of bamboo, which are not only useful but make attractive souvenirs.

What can you fill your shopping basket with? A wider range of typical Chinese souvenirs, and of a better quality, can be found in Hong Kong. But in fact the humblest articles – kites, polished stones, hats made of natural fibers, musical instruments, traditional medicines – are often the most treasured mementoes. Among the bargains to be picked up are local handcrafts, which can be bought in the markets of minority districts.

Time

Beijing Time applies right across China. When the clocks strike midday in the capital, they also strike midday in Kashgar even though it is in fact far earlier there. (Midday in China is 4am in London and 11pm – the previous night – in New York).

Tipping

After the Communists came to power in 1949 it was considered a disgrace to offer someone a tip. But with the opening up of the country to mass-tourism this attitude has changed. Both in tourism and in business tipping or the greasing of palms is normal. The staff of big hotels and expensive restaurants accept tips –

but these must be handed over discreetly. For small acts of attentiveness, western cigarettes are appreciated as "payment in kind." Needless to say, it is only your own sensitivity which will tell you when, where, in what form and amount a tip will seem appropriate.

Weights and measures

The metric system has become more or less universal throughout China. However you will sometimes find traditional denominations still in use. Therefore you should be prepared to encounter the following: 3 chi = 1 meter (3 ft), 2 li = 1 km (0.6 mile), 15 mu = 1 hectare (2.5 acres), 1 gongsheng = 1 liter (2 pints), 2 jin = 1 kg (2 LBs).

ADDRESSES

Tourist offices

The China International Travel Service (CITS) has offices in London, Paris, New York, Los Angeles, Frankfurt, Sydney and Tokyo.

Embassies of the P.R. of China

AUSTRALIA: 15 Coronation Drive, Yarralumla ACT 2600, Tel. (06) 286 4780. CANADA: 515 St Patrick St, Ottawa ON K1N 5H3, Tel. (613) 234 2706. IRELAND: 40 Ailesbury Rd, Dublin 4, Tel. (01) 2691707. NEW ZEALAND: 2-6 Glenmore St, Wellington, Tel. (04) 472 1382. UNITED KINGDOM: 49-51 Portland Place, London W1N 3AH, Tel. (071) 636 9375, Consular Section, 31 Portland Place W1N 3AG, Tel. (071) 636 5637. USA: 2300 Connecticut Avenue NW, Washington DC 20008, Tel. (202) 328 2500.

Foreign embassies in Beijing

AUSTRALIA: 21 Dong Zhi Men Wai Dajie, Beijing 100600, Tel. (01) 532-2331. CANADA: 19 Dong Zhi Men Wai Dajie, Beijing 100600, Tel. (01) 532-3536. IRELAND: 3 Ri Tan Dong Lu,

Beijing 100600, Tel. (01) 5322691.
NEW ZEALAND: 1 Ri Tan Dong Er Jie,
Chaoyang Qu, Beijing 100600. Tel. (01)
532 27 31. UNITED KINGDOM: 11
Guang Hua Lu, Jian Guo Men Wai, Beij-
ing. Tel (01) 532 1961. USA: 3 Xiu Shui
Bei Jie, Beijing 100600, Tel. (01) 532
3831.

Airlines

British Airways: Room 210, Scite
Tower, 22 Jianguomenwai Dajie, Beijing, Tel. (01)512 40700.

THE LANGUAGE

Pronunciation and transliteration

Even *Pinyin*, the international spelling
of Chinese, presents some pronunciation
problems for westerners. You only have
to hear how trained newscasters stumble
over the name Deng Xiaoping (pron.:
derng hsiaoping). We cannot turn you
into brilliant linguists here, but we can at
least give you a few tasters to get your
tongue around. The following hints are
intended to help English-speaking ers
achieve the correct pronunciation of of
words in the *Pinyin* transliteration:
ai = *i* in *wine* /e = *er* in *her* (or German
ö) / ei = *ay* in *say* / ian = *i-en* / o = *o* in *hot*
but before -ng = *oong* / ao = *ou* in *out* / ou
= *o* in *hope* / x = *hs* / q = *ty* in *not yet* / zh
= *j* in French *Jean* / ch = as in *chin* / s = as
in *so* / z = *dz* in *adze* / c = *ts*. As a practical
example, the Chinese word for "bus-sta-
tion" is *qichezhan*, pronounced: "tyee-
cher-jan". You will find plenty of words
to practise on in this guide-book.

Mini-vocabulary

Even if the pronunciation doesn't
come easy you should try to master these
few words, expressions and emergency
signals:

Hallo, Good morning etc.	*ni hao*
Goodbye	*zaijian*
Thank you	*xiexie*
Excuse me	*duibuqi*
I am lost	*wo mi lu*

No; that is not right	*bu shi*	
No; I do not have any	*mei you*	
Never mind, that's OK	*mei shi*	
No thank you	*bu yao*	
Do you understand	*dong ma?*	
I do not understand . .	*wo ting budong*	
Toilet	*cesuo*	
Too expensive	*tai guile*	
Money-changing	*huan qian*	
America	*meiguo*	美国
Australia	*aodaliya*	澳大利亚
Britain, England	*yingguo*	英国

Numbers

0	*ling*	零
1	*yi*	一
2	*er, liang*	二, 两
3	*san*	三
4	*si*	四
5	*wu*	五
6	*liu*	六
7	*qi*	七
8	*ba*	八
9	*jiu*	九
10	*shi*	十
11	*shiyi*	十一
12	*shi'er*	十二
13	*shisan*	十三
20	*ershi*	二十
21	*ershiyi*	二十一
30	*sanshi*	三十
31	*sanshiyi*	三十一
100	*yibai*	一百
101	*yibaiyi*	一百一
200	*liangbai*	两百
1000	*yiqian*	一千
2000	*liangqian*	两千
10.000	*yiwan*	一万
100.000	*shiwan*	十万

Finger dictionary

I need a doctor urgently!
我急需一个医生！

I am looking for a pharmacy (chemist).
我想找一个药房。

I am looking for a bank to change money.
我想找个能挽钱的银行。

Where is the post-office?
请问邮政在哪儿？

Where is my luggage?
我的行李在哪儿？

I need a taxi.
我想要一部出租汽车。

I would like to make a phone-call.
我想打电话。

Where is the train station?
火车站在哪儿？

From which platform does the train leave for...?
到...去的火车在第几站台？

I want to go to the airport.
我想到飞机场去。

I am looking for a hotel.
我想找一个旅馆。

Please write down the address for me in Chinese. 请用中文把这个地址写下来。

AUTHORS

Dr. Engelbert Altenburger: Sinologist and geographer, is married to Dr. Li-Chao Altenburger, and lives in Nördlingen, southern Germany. ("The Fulcrum of Chinese History," "From the Red Basin, down the Yangtze," "The Heart of the Middle Kingdom," "The Silk Road" and "Steppe, Sheep and Mare's Milk.")

Dr. Ulrich Menzel: Professor of International Politics at the universities of Frankfurt and Duisburg. ("Where China's Pulse Beats")

Peter Hinze: Travel journalist, editor of the magazine *Focus* in Munich. ("The Sensuous South" and "Landscape in Watercolors.")

Claudia Ille: Travel journalist and photographer based in Berlin. ("Yin and Yang of Sea and Mountains")

Angelika Lange-Gao: Sinologist and chief executive of a China consultancy firm with offices in Munich and Beijing; has lived in Beijing for ten years. ("Heavenly Peace – Earthly Power")

Kai-Ulrich Müller: Travel journalist and photographer based in Berlin. ("Cradle of the Red Revolution")

Gerd Simon: Editor and journalist, Simon & Magiera Publishing Co. ("History and Culture," "From the Red Basin, Down the Yangtze" and the Features)

Volker Kienast, geographer and guide for cultural tours, PhD on traffic planning in China. ("The Golden Goose")

Dr. Klaus Dietsch, Sinologist and China travel guide, did the revisions for this edition.

PHOTOGRAPHERS

Explore the World

AVAILABLE TITLES

Australia
Bali / Lombok
Berlin and Potsdam
Brittany
California
Las Vegas, Reno,
Baja California
Cambodia / Laos
Canada
Ontario, Québec,
Atlantic Provinces
Caribbean
The Greater Antilles,
Bermuda, Bahamas
Caribbean
The Lesser Antilles
China – Hong Kong
Corsica
Crete
Cyprus
Egypt
Florida
Greece - *The Mainland*
Hawaii
Hungary
India
Northern, Northeastern
and Central India

India - *Southern India*
Indonesia
Sumatra, Java, Bali,
Lombok, Sulawesi
Ireland
Israel - *with Excursions*
to Jordan
Kenya
London, England and
Wales
Malaysia
Mexico
Morocco
Moscow / St Petersburg
Munich
Excursions to Castels,
Lakes & Mountains
Nepal
New York - *City and State*
New Zealand
Paris
Philippines
Portugal
Prague / Czech Republic
Provence
Rome
Scotland
South Africa

Spain - *Pyrenees, Atlantic*
Coast, Central Spain
Spain
Mediterranean Coast,
Southern Spain,
Balearic Islands
Sri Lanka
Thailand
Turkey
Tuscany
U.S.A.
The East, Midwest and
South
U.S.A.
The West, Rockies and
Texas
Vietnam

Nelles Guides – authorative, informed and informative.
Always up-to-date, extensivley illustrated, and with first-rate relief maps.
256 pages, appr. 150 color photos, appr. 25 maps

Explore the World

AVAILABLE TITLES

Afghanistan 1 : 1 500 000
Australia 1 : 4 000 000
Bangkok - *Greater Bangkok,*
Bangkok City 1 : 75 000 / 1 : 15 000
Burma → *Myanmar*
Caribbean Islands 1 *Bermuda,*
Bahamas, Greater Antilles
1 : 2 500 000
Caribbean Islands 2 *Lesser Antilles*
1 : 2 500 000
Central America 1 : 1 750 000
Crete - *Kreta* 1 : 200 000
China 1 - *Northeastern*
1 : 1 500 000
China 2 - *Northern* 1 : 1 500 000
China 3 - *Central* 1 : 1 500 000
China 4 - *Southern* 1 : 1 500 000
Egypt 1 : 2 500 000 / 1 : 750 000
Hawaiian Islands
1 : 330 000 / 1 : 125 000
Hawaiian Islands 1 *Kauai*
1 : 125 000
Hawaiian Islands 2 *Honolulu*
- *Oahu* 1 : 125 000
Hawaiian Islands 3 *Maui - Molokai*
- *Lanai* 1 : 125 000
Hawaiian Islands 4 *Hawaii, The*
Big Island 1 : 330 000 / 1 : 125 000
Himalaya 1 : 1 500 000

Hong Kong 1 : 22 500
Indian Subcontinent 1 : 4 000 000
India 1 - *Northern* 1 : 1 500 000
India 2 - *Western* 1 : 1 500 000
India 3 - *Eastern* 1 : 1 500 000
India 4 - *Southern* 1 : 1 500 000
India 5 - *Northeastern - Bangladesh*
1 : 1 500 000
Indonesia 1 1 : 4 000 000
Indonesia 1 *Sumatra* 1 : 1 500 000
Indonesia 2 *Java + Nusa Tenggara*
1 : 1 500 000
Indonesia 3 *Bali* 1 : 180 000
Indonesia 4 *Kalimantan*
1 : 1 500 000
Indonesia 5 *Java + Bali* 1 : 650 000
Indonesia 6 *Sulawesi* 1 : 1 500 000
Indonesia 7 *Irian Jaya + Maluku*
1 : 1 500 000
Jakarta 1 : 22 500
Japan 1 : 1 500 000
Kenya 1 : 1 100 000
Korea 1 : 1 500 000
Malaysia 1 : 1 500 000
West Malaysia 1 : 650 000
Manila 1 : 17 500
Mexico 1 : 2 500 000
Myanmar (Burma) 1 : 1 500 000
Nepal 1 : 500 000 / 1 : 1 500 000

Trekking Map *Khumbu Himal /*
Solu Khumbu 1 : 75 000
New Zealand 1 : 1 250 000
Pakistan 1 : 1 500 000
Philippines 1 : 1 500 000
Singapore 1 : 22 500
Southeast Asia 1 : 4 000 000
Sri Lanka 1 : 450 000
Tanzania - *Rwanda, Burundi*
1 : 1 500 000
Thailand 1 : 1 500 000
Taiwan 1 : 400 000
Uganda 1 : 700 000
Venezuela - *Guyana, Suriname,*
French Guiana 1 : 2 500 000
Vietnam, Laos, Cambodia
1 : 1 500 000

FORTHCOMING

Colombia - Ecuador 1 : 2 500 000
Peru - Ecuador 1 : 2 500 000
Trekking Map *Kathmandu Valley /*
Helambu, Langtang 1 : 75 000

Nelles Maps in european top quality!
Relief mapping, kilometer charts and tourist attractions.
Always up-to-date!